Values Sexual

Opposing Viewpoints®

Other Books of Related Interest in the Opposing
Viewpoints Series:

Sexual **Values**

Opposing Viewpoints®

David Bender & Bruno Leone, *Series Editors*

Charles P. Cozic, *Book Editor*

OPPOSING
VIEWPOINTS
SERIES®

Greenhaven Press, Inc., San Diego, CA

Greenhaven Press, Inc.
PO Box 289009
San Diego, CA 92198-9009

Cover photo: Rocky Thies

Library of Congress Cataloging-in-Publication Data

Sexual values : opposing viewpoints / Charles P. Cozic, book editor.
    p.   cm. — (Opposing viewpoints series)
  Includes bibliographical references (p.   ) and index.
   ISBN 1-56510-211-8 (lib. : acid-free paper) — ISBN 1-56510-210-X (pbk. : acid-free paper)
   1. Sexual ethics. I. Cozic, Charles P., 1957–   . II. Series: Opposing viewpoints series (Unnumbered).
HQ34.S48   1995
306.7—dc20   94-4978
                                      CIP
                                      AC

"Congress shall make no law . . . abridging the freedom of speech, or of the press."

First Amendment to the U.S. Constitution

The basic foundation of our democracy is the first amendment guarantee of freedom of expression. The Opposing Viewpoints Series is dedicated to the concept of this basic freedom and the idea that it is more important to practice it than to enshrine it.

Contents

Why Consider Opposing Viewpoints?

"The only way in which a human being can make some approach to knowing the whole of a subject is by hearing what can be said about it by persons of every variety of opinion and studying all modes in which it can be looked at by every character of mind. No wise man ever acquired his wisdom in any mode but this."

John Stuart Mill

In our media-intensive culture it is not difficult to find differing opinions. Thousands of newspapers and magazines and dozens of radio and television talk shows resound with differing points of view. The difficulty lies in deciding which opinion to agree with and which "experts" seem the most credible. The more inundated we become with differing opinions and claims, the more essential it is to hone critical reading and thinking skills to evaluate these ideas. Opposing Viewpoints books address this problem directly by presenting stimulating debates that can be used to enhance and teach these skills. The varied opinions contained in each book examine many different aspects of a single issue. While examining these conveniently edited opposing views, readers can develop critical thinking skills such as the ability to compare and contrast authors' credibility, facts, argumentation styles, use of persuasive techniques, and other stylistic tools. In short, the Opposing Viewpoints Series is an ideal way to attain the higher-level thinking and reading skills so essential in a culture of diverse and contradictory opinions.

In addition to providing a tool for critical thinking, Opposing Viewpoints books challenge readers to question their own strongly held opinions and assumptions. Most people form their opinions on the basis of upbringing, peer pressure, and personal, cultural, or professional bias. By reading carefully balanced opposing views, readers must directly confront new ideas as well as the opinions of those with whom they disagree. This is not to simplistically argue that everyone who reads opposing views will—or should—change his or her opinion. Instead, the series enhances readers' depth of understanding of their own views by encouraging confrontation with opposing ideas. Careful examination of others' views can lead to the readers' understanding of the logical inconsistencies in their own opinions, perspective on why they hold an opinion, and the consideration of the possibility that their opinion requires further evaluation.

Evaluating Other Opinions

To ensure that this type of examination occurs, Opposing Viewpoints books present all types of opinions. Prominent spokespeople on different sides of each issue as well as well-known professionals from many disciplines challenge the reader. An additional goal of the series is to provide a forum for other, less known, or even unpopular viewpoints. The opinion of an ordinary person who has had to make the decision to cut off life support from a terminally ill relative, for example, may be just as valuable and provide just as much insight as a medical ethicist's professional opinion. The editors have two additional purposes in including these less known views. One, the editors encourage readers to respect others' opinions—even when not enhanced by professional credibility. It is only by reading or listening to and objectively evaluating others' ideas that one can determine whether they are worthy of consideration. Two, the inclusion of such viewpoints encourages the important critical thinking skill of objectively evaluating an author's credentials and bias. This evaluation will illuminate an author's reasons for taking a particular stance on an issue and will aid in readers' evaluation of the author's ideas.

As series editors of the Opposing Viewpoints Series, it is our hope that these books will give readers a deeper understanding of the issues debated and an appreciation of the complexity of even seemingly simple issues when good and honest people disagree. This awareness is particularly important in a democratic society such as ours in which people enter into public debate to determine the common good. Those with whom one disagrees should not be regarded as enemies but rather as people whose views deserve careful examination and may shed light on one's own.

Thomas Jefferson once said that "difference of opinion leads to inquiry, and inquiry to truth." Jefferson, a broadly educated man, argued that "if a nation expects to be ignorant and free . . . it expects what never was and never will be." As individuals and as a nation, it is imperative that we consider the opinions of others and examine them with skill and discernment. The Opposing Viewpoints Series is intended to help readers achieve this goal.

David L. Bender & Bruno Leone,
Series Editors

Introduction

"[Sex] is still in a mess. If hushing up had been the cause of the trouble, ventilation would have set it right. But it has not."

C.S. Lewis, Mere Christianity, 1952

"Eroticism can be expressed in many diverse ways without causing problems of any kind."

Marty Klein, The Erotic Impulse, 1992

At several leading hotel chains, guests switching television channels may come across one that offers adult movies. On this channel, even children can anonymously select any of a dozen X-rated movies from an on-screen menu, preview a selection for five minutes at no charge and, if desired, watch an entire movie.

While this may shock many people, others see it merely as part of America's ongoing sexual liberation. Consider also these examples: the willingness of network censors to allow nudity on ABC's police drama *NYPD Blue*, the availability of pornography on computer bulletin boards and disks, and condom ads and distribution programs targeted to young people.

For better or worse, open attitudes toward sex and sexual imagery are pervasive. Sexual permissiveness has become the norm in the minds of most Americans and is accepted, indeed almost expected, by many. But despite this apparent victory of liberal sexual ideals, they are in fact engaged in an ongoing battle with more restrictive views. Debate is still fierce over whether sexual liberation or restraint serves society best.

Much of this debate focuses on the Sexual Revolution—the radical transformation of sexual attitudes and mores that began in the 1960s—and its effect on women. As its defenders point out, the Sexual Revolution expanded women's options regarding sex. For example, women had better access to birth control, and societal censure of nonmarital sex and cohabitation dramatically decreased. Young women faced with pregnancy could either have an abortion or opt for single motherhood, with less stigma attached to both, and felt less obligated to enter into an unwanted marriage. As author Lillian B. Rubin writes, "Women, reveling in their newfound liberation, sought the sexual freedom that had been for so long 'for men only.' "

But many believe that the Sexual Revolution has come at too high a cost for women. According to columnist Marilyn Gardner of the *Christian Science Monitor*, "Instead of the freedom and equality they thought they had achieved, too many find themselves shackled by unplanned pregnancies, abortions, single motherhood, infections, or infertility." Adding to the criticism are those feminists who argue that by readily assenting to sex, too many single women have relinquished the power they traditionally wielded in relationships with men.

Echoing these sentiments, the most organized response against sexual liberation has come from the so-called Religious Right. Whether Christian fundamentalist, Catholic, or other denomination, many staunch conservatives have condemned what they view as sexual licentiousness. They argue, for example, that casual sex, homosexual behavior, and pornography threaten a decent society and violate God's will. Norman F. McFarland, Roman Catholic bishop of Orange, California, writes: "It was Pope Paul's warning that the isolation of sex from its designed unitive and procreative roles, and sought for its own pleasurable sake, can only lead to the savaging of our culture and undermine the stability of society itself."

Conservatives such as McFarland blame sexual liberation for compounding social ills in America, among which they include high rates of abortion, divorce, and sexually transmitted disease. They stress the importance of abstinence among singles and heterosexual monogamy among married couples, proclaiming these the only acceptable forms of sexual conduct.

However, opponents charge that such thinking is closedminded and ignores the realities of modern sexual behavior. A more realistic and progressive approach, they argue, celebrates sexuality rather than cloaks it and can be achieved by emulating more liberally inclined European nations. In Scandinavia and the Netherlands, for example, attitudes are much more tolerant of homosexuality, pornography, and comprehensive sex education than in America. According to Dutch health minister Hedy d'Ancona, "In the Netherlands, prevailing attitudes allow people to speak very frankly about sexuality in the broadest sense. Sex has come to be seen as a part of life like any other." This openness is credited for the fact that approximately 90 percent of sexually active Dutch teenagers use contraceptives and their pregnancy rate is the world's lowest—one-seventh that of American teens.

Whether America will evolve into a similarly open society and thrive from it is uncertain. For now, the forces of both sexual

13

liberation and restraint continue to mold sexual ideals. The authors in *Sexual Values: Opposing Viewpoints* debate some of the most contentious issues of sex in the following chapters: How Is Sexual Behavior Changing in America? Is Sex Eroding Moral Values? How Should Society Regard Homosexuality? Is Pornography Harmful? What Sexual Values Should Children Learn? Sexual attitudes and behavior in America have changed dramatically in recent decades. How these values continue to change will play an important role in shaping society.

Is Sex Eroding
Moral Values?

Chapter Preface

Sex has been a matter of religious concern throughout history. In the Book of Genesis, for example, sex for the sake of procreation was extolled as fulfilling God's will. But Genesis also condemned the sexual acts of adultery and incest as attacks on the very foundation of the family. Thus, religious teaching considered sex at the proper time and in the proper context to be essentially good, solidifying the bonds between husbands and wives.

With the advent of Christianity, however, sex took on a more negative image, according to author and rabbi Michael Gold. As Gold writes in *Does God Belong in the Bedroom?*:

> Although Christians disagreed on the nature of Adam's [original] sin in the Bible, it was generally believed to be tied up with sexuality. This identification of sex with sin was further developed by the early fathers of the church, particularly Augustine, and has remained influential in Christianity to this day.

Indeed, according to many Christians—from the pope to Protestant fundamentalists—all sex outside of marriage is immoral. Other religions, though, hold more liberal attitudes toward birth control, homosexuality, and other sexual matters. For example, Gold writes that "Judaism teaches that sex has a purpose above and beyond procreation, leaving room for a more liberal view."

Of course, sex is an important part of people's moral codes regardless of their faith. But whether sex is immoral depends on one's beliefs and values. Such individual beliefs are expressed by the authors in this chapter as they question whether sex is eroding moral values.

"The Bible treats lust as deadly serious. Our Lord says that lust is tantamount to adultery."

Lust Is Immoral

Tim Stafford

Tim Stafford is a senior writer for *Christianity Today* and the author of several books, including *Love, Sex, and the Whole Person* and *Sexual Chaos: Charting a Course Through Turbulent Times*. In the following viewpoint, Stafford asserts that lust, or covetousness, is a basic component of sin. Lust for sex, Stafford contends, shows ungratefulness toward God and makes sexual fulfillment an object of worship that dominates individuals. Stafford proposes that people overcome lust for sex by seeking salvation and self-control through prayer, worship, and service to God.

As you read, consider the following questions:

1. How does the "psychology of lust" develop, according to Stafford?
2. According to the author, what makes lust a powerful urge?
3. How can the spirit of Jesus provide freedom from lust, in Stafford's opinion?

Tim Stafford, "Getting Serious About Lust," *Christianity Today*, January 10, 1994. Used by permission, *Christianity Today*, 1994.

Lust is hard to speak about seriously in our era. When Jimmy Carter, running for President, told an interviewer that he had often committed adultery in his heart, the reaction in the press was what John Updike described as "nervous hilarity." "How strangely on modern ears," continues Updike, "falls the notion that lust—sexual desire that wells up in us as involuntarily as saliva—in itself is wicked!"

Our modern way of handling lust is to pretend that it has no hold on us—to see it as inevitable and healthy, even fun. Is it really so? We don't have to look hard to see that lust is not nearly as frivolous as our society would like to believe.

In the first place, we don't experience it as frivolous. Let even the most mature adults get tangled in the foolishness of lust— channel-surfing for TV sex in a motel room or plotting the next meeting with someone they want to devour mentally—and they find themselves in a helpless, robotic daze. They may try to joke about it, but the light-heartedness is an act. Lust may be thrilling—like an encounter with a shark is thrilling—but it is not a laugh.

Our society is not finding lust such a laugh, either. While it is hard to trace a direct connection between *Playboy* and modern social disintegration, our infatuation with lust surely has something to do with the spread of AIDS, teenage pregnancy, and divorce.

The Bible treats lust as deadly serious. Our Lord says that lust is tantamount to adultery. For Christians, that should settle it. But it is not only because of Scripture that we take lust seriously. Scripture is underlined by experience.

What Lust Is

I have spent much of the past 20 years talking and writing about sex, and I know from experience that a contingent of Christian parents and pastors would rather never mention it. When they speak of battling lust, they really mean eliminating all thoughts of sex. Essentially, they would rather teenagers never enter puberty.

The Bible, however, is frank and unsqueamish about sex. Sex is not really that big a topic in Scripture, and the Bible's concern with lust is only partly about sexual lust. In English, the word *lust* generally connotes lurid sexual fantasies. It is closely associated with the mental pictures of naked bodies to which males are so typically drawn.

This English meaning of *lust*, however, has no equivalent word in New Testament Greek. The word translated *lust* in Matthew 5:28 (*epithumia*) means simply *desire*. On occasion, the word, in fact, has a positive meaning, as when Jesus tells his disciples that he has "desired with desire" (as the King James puts it) to eat the Passover meal with them (Luke 22:15). Clearly, Jesus

18

does not mean that he has fantasized about the Passover meal, mentally drooling over the menu. *Epithumia* is not a sensual fantasy. Jesus means that he has deeply longed for the occasion.

The same Greek word is used to render the Hebrew word translated *covet*, as in, "You shall not covet your neighbor's wife, or his manservant or maidservant, his ox or donkey, or anything that belongs to your neighbor" (Exod. 20:17, NIV [New International Version]). Here we strike at the heart of the problem of lust, as the Bible conceives it: We want things that don't belong to us. Leave sex out of it entirely, for the moment. We are not content with what we have. We want something more—and that desire drives us.

Sexual Thoughts

When sexual thoughts come into your mind, it's quite possible to thank God for beautiful girls and for sexuality and just to feel good about being alive as a male in a world full of sexual beauty. You can imagine how wonderful it will be to be married someday. That's good and healthy, I believe. There's nothing evil about those desires.

What's not good is to take those thoughts and build on them, manipulate them, obsess yourself with the thought of how much joy you'd get from going to bed with one of those girls. Whether you act on your desires or not, you've made sex into something dirty. Jesus doesn't want you to turn off your sexuality (as though you could). He wants you to turn it in the proper direction. And, always, he wants you to turn toward him.

Tim Stafford, *Love, Sex, and the Whole Person*, 1991.

Lust, or covetousness, is a basic component of what the Bible calls sin. All two-year-olds, and all truthful forty-year-olds, confess it: I want what I want because I want it. Nobody and nothing else figures. Jesus' comments on sexual lust fit into that. Lust shows that, in your heart of hearts, you want somebody else's sexual life. When a man lusts for a woman, he is not grateful for what God has given him. He is making himself sick thinking about what he *wishes* God would give him.

The psychology of lust is a simple process: It begins with attraction; it turns quickly to dissatisfaction; it results in fixation. It leaves us ungrateful, discontented, and obsessive. When you are filled with lust—for it does indeed seem to fill you—you can have nothing in your mind but that appetite for what you lack. This is true not just of sex.

The "flesh"—that is, our lives without God—urgently desires

many things. It wants power. It wants pleasure. It wants wealth. It wants status and admiration. None of these is wrong in itself. And nothing would be wrong with liking these things. But desire, or lust, is more than liking. It is the will to possess. Lust turns good things into objects of worship.

And that is why lust, or covetousness, is so closely linked to another biblical word: *idolatry*. What we lust for, we worship. We may joke about our lusts, but our behavior shows a more fundamental allegiance. We look to our idols to give us what we need—to make our lives rich and purposeful. In our culture, an idol many people look to is the god of sexual fulfillment.

The Right to Desire

Look at the magazine covers in the grocery-store check-out line, and you will be reminded of how crazy the biblical view sounds to modern people. The ordinary North American takes it as a given that people want things that are not theirs. Naturally a man envies his neighbor's new car. Of course a woman looks at Paul Newman and thinks how good he would be in bed. What is wrong with wanting it—so long as you don't commit a crime to get it?

In fact, we have come perilously close to embracing lust as a fundamental human characteristic—if not a right. Most discussion of homosexuality assumes this: people have a deep, helpless sexual desire for a certain kind of partner, they argue; therefore, it would be cruel and inhuman to deny them the freedom to fulfill that desire.

And deep, helpless desires are not confined to homosexuality. Nearly all desire seems deep and uncontrollable. I am not aware of choosing to desire what I desire. The Bible may tell me not to covet my neighbor's wife or house, but I don't seem to have a choice about it. I see it; I want it. I can take a cold shower, avert my eyes, avoid a second glance, even undergo psychotherapy— but in a world full of beautiful things, my desires cannot be done away with easily. They keep welling up.

Still, the Bible tells me, "You shall not covet." Jesus says, in the context of sexual lust, that if my eye causes me to sin, I should pluck it out (Matt. 5:29). Just because I can't help lust does not make it acceptable. Jesus is dedicated to bringing in another kingdom. To be his disciple, I must put lust to death. I must learn to want what he wants for me and to put away everything else.

Replacing Desire with Desire

As a boy raised in church, I learned that lust is serious. With some encouragement from other Christians, I tried to stamp out lust in the most obvious way: through techniques of self-control.

20

One strategy was systematically to comb my environment to remove all stimuli to lust (movies, magazines, bathing suits). Another technique was to comb my mind to root out every lustful thought (sexual images).

Anyone who has taken lust seriously can add to the list of self-control techniques. Cold showers, exercise, staying busy, scriptural mantras: all these have been tried to push lust down. Broadly speaking, they don't work. They may keep lust at bay for a time, but they certainly do not eliminate it. The human mind is so strong it can use any raw material for lusting. (Think of conservative Islam, compelled to cover even women's faces.) And trying to root out lustful thoughts can be as futile as trying not to think of pink elephants.

Interestingly enough, I found none of these techniques in the Bible. Clearly, in the New Testament, they come in second to an utterly different form of salvation.

"Since, then, you have been raised with Christ," the apostle Paul wrote the Colossians, "set your hearts on things above. . . . Set your minds on things above." Only then does he continue, "Put to death, therefore, whatever belongs to your earthly nature: sexual immorality, impurity, lust, evil desires and greed, which is idolatry" (Col. 3:1-5, NIV).

The Spirit of Jesus

First things first: think on things above. Salvation is offered in Jesus—in his life, death, and resurrection. He forgives us for our lusts; he justifies us from our lusts; and he sends his Spirit to sanctify us from our lusts. Life in the Spirit transforms us. Self-control is a fruit of the Spirit, a result of the Spirit-filled life. Paul's promise to the Galatians is clear and optimistic, if maddeningly general: "Live by the Spirit, and you will not gratify the desires of the sinful nature" (Gal. 5:16, NIV).

Walk by the Spirit? Our society is dedicated to exciting lust for commercial purposes. We are bathed daily in imaginary, electronic sexual stimulation. Against this, the Sunday-school advice to think pure thoughts seems feeble, almost naïve.

Yet I believe Paul is thinking less of the moment of temptation than of the lifetime of spiritual warfare. Desires do not go away simply because we want them to. They do not generally disappear like a soap bubble when we pray. They do fade into the background, however, when a greater desire replaces them. Jesus taught us to pray for that desire: "Our Father in heaven, holy be your name. Your kingdom come. Your will be done."

So the Spirit operates, planting a desire for holiness in our heart, a righteous lust that grows up and puts all other desires in the shade. A "just-say-no" strategy alone is never sufficient for the long haul. Scripture encourages us to say yes—yes to the way of the Spirit.

Having been "buried" with Christ in our baptism, we are now "made alive" with him by the Spirit. We therefore make our choices accordingly—to the point of becoming "slaves to one another" out of love (Gal. 5:13), rather than serving the self and its lusts.

When we walk by the Spirit—that is, live a full-hearted Christian life in prayer, worship, and service—we get on to better things. We apply self-control *because we desire what God desires for us*. We want something better, something given by God himself. We desire life in Christ and all that he gives within that life.

Greater Desires

This is the good kind of lust. A man and woman who desire the sexual life that *has* been given—sex with a marriage partner—shows God's work in their lives. Desiring your spouse is good. This is part of life in the Spirit—desiring what God gives.

Life in the Spirit is a difficult walk on a narrow path. The finest, most Spirit-filled and devoted Christians struggle with misdirected desire. They may even be tempted far more powerfully than others, for an evil power is always at work. They may make progress only in the sense that evil uses stronger and subtler means to tempt them. They may "graduate" from a lust for *Playboy* to a lust for power. We do not have the techniques to eliminate sin, let alone temptation, from our lives. We will struggle with it until we see Jesus.

Yet we will see Jesus. And he is with us now—giving us greater desires.

*"How strangely on modern ears falls the notion
that lust . . . in itself is wicked!"*

Lust Is Not Immoral

John Updike

John Updike is an esteemed essayist, novelist, and poet and the
Pulitzer Prize-winning author of the *Rabbit* quartet of novels. In
the following viewpoint, Updike protests Christianity's condemnation of lust as sinful. Updike argues that lust is a fulfilling, inherent part of human nature that should not be repressed.

As you read, consider the following questions:

1. How did early Christian saints regard lust, according to
   Updike?
2. In Updike's opinion, what was the goal of religious
   prohibitions against sex?
3. How is lust rewarding, according to the author?

John Updike, "The Deadly Sins/Lust: Even the Bible Is Soft on Sex," *The New York Times
Book Review*, June 20, 1993. Copyright ©1993 by The New York Times Company. Reprinted
by permission.

Originally the word [lust] simply meant pleasure and then was modulated to signify desire and, specifically, sexual desire. How can sexual desire be a sin? Did not God instruct Adam and Eve to be fruitful and to multiply? Did He not say, having created woman from Adam's rib, that "therefore shall a man leave his father and his mother, and shall cleave unto his wife: and they shall be one flesh"? The singleness of flesh is itself a vivid metaphor for copulation. The organic world is soaked in sex; Lucretius, in his epic "On the Nature of Things," begins by saluting Venus: "Yea, through seas and mountains and tearing rivers and the leafy haunts of birds and verdant plains thou dost strike fond love into the hearts of all, and makest them in hot desire to renew the stock of their races, each after his own kind."

Venus alone, in the rousing translation by Cyril Bailey, is "pilot to the nature of things"—without her aid nothing "comes forth into the bright coasts of light, nor waxes glad nor lovely." Two millenniums after Lucretius and his fellow Latin celebrants of all-powerful love, Sigmund Freud and his followers have reconfirmed the helplessly sexual nature of humankind and have announced the harmfulness, not to say the futility, of sexual repression. How strangely on modern ears falls the notion that lust—sexual desire that wells up in us as involuntarily as saliva—in itself is wicked! With what nervous hilarity did we greet Jimmy Carter's famous confession: "I've looked on a lot of women with lust. I've committed adultery in my heart many times." Mr. Carter was running for President at the time; his opponent, the incumbent Gerald Ford, was a more typical post-Freudian man. Asked how often he made love, he healthily responded, "Every chance I get." Impotence, frigidity, unattractiveness—these are the sins of which we are truly ashamed.

Early Christian Moralists

But to the early Christian moralists, of whom St. Paul and St. Augustine are the greatest, the body was a beast to be tamed, not a master to be served. In that decadent, brutal first-century Roman world, sex possibly did not seem to Paul a very big deal; the world was about to be dissolved in the second coming of Christ, and procreation, of such concern to the Old Testament God, was practically irrelevant. The seventh chapter of Paul's first letter to the Corinthians treats lust tersely: "It is good for a man not to touch a woman. . . . I say therefore to the unmarried and widows, It is good for them if they abide even as I. But if they cannot contain, let them marry: for it is better to marry than to burn."

Augustine had had more experience of burning than Paul. In Carthage's "caldron of dissolute loves," his "Confessions" tell us, he fell "in love with loving." Some chapters after sketching his

24

youthful life and his concubine, he confides to God, "I had prayed to you for chastity and said 'Give me chastity and continence, but not yet.' For I was afraid that you would answer my prayer at once and cure me too soon of the disease of lust, which I wanted satisfied, not quelled."

Abelard on Pleasure and Sin

Early Scholastic theologians invented a new form of marriage, modeled on the purely spiritual bond of the virginal Joseph and Mary. . . . William of Auvergne (d. 1249), the bishop of Paris, advised married couples to "flee all physical pleasure." It was wonderful, he remarked, that "sometimes young men remain cold with their wives, even when they are beautiful."

Peter Abelard, a leading medieval theologian and the famous lover of Heloise, was one of the few to oppose this anti-sexual value system. "No natural pleasure of the flesh may be declared a sin," he declared, "nor may one impute guilt when someone is delighted by pleasure where he must necessarily feel it. . . . From the first day of our creation, when man lived without sin in Paradise, sexual intercourse and good-tasting foods were naturally bound up with pleasure. God himself has established nature in this way." When their scandalous love was discovered, Heloise's guardian sent her to a convent and had servants castrate Abelard in his sleep. Their tragic fate reflected the choice Christians were forced to make between a life of the body and a life of the soul.

Robert T. Francoeur, *The Erotic Impulse*, 1992.

His youth passed, and the worst of the burning, and Augustine evolved, as an African bishop beset by Donatists and Pelagians, a pessimistic theology that virtually identified human sexuality with original sin. Though Augustine's fiercer insistences (on infant damnation and predestination, say) reminded other Christians of the Manichaeism to which he had been a convert for a time, his theology became one of the foundations on which the church instituted a thousand-year war against the flesh—for saints, mortification, and for the laity, regulation.

Misguided Catholic Doctrine

It tests the patience of a Protestant to peruse the Catholic Encyclopedia's article on lust, with its fussy, imperturbable bureaucratic obstinacy and orderliness. An alleged order, described as natural and rational, is repeatedly invoked: "A lustful action is a disordered use or pursuit of sex pleasure not only because it defeats the biological, social or moral purpose of sex activity, but also because in doing this it subjects the spiritual in man to values of the grossly material order, acting as a disintegrating force in the human personality."

Lust leads to "blindness of mind, rashness, thoughtlessness, inconstancy, self-love and excessive attachment to the material world." The pitfall of venereal sin resides in "merely sensible" pleasures like "delight in the touch of a soft object," let alone a human kiss: "The Church has condemned a proposition that states that a kiss indulged for the sake of carnal pleasure and that does not involve danger of further consent is only venially sinful." That is, a kiss is *mortally* sinful. Sexual activity has but two legitimate ends, "the procreation of children and the promotion of the mutual love of spouses in marriage." Narrow and pedantic is the way; we are invited to consider two sinners against the sexual order, "a prostitute who plies her trade for monetary gain without any physical enjoyment, and . . . a married man enjoying normal conjugal intimacy but with no motive except that of physical pleasure." The first commits a sin "against the sex order without a sin of lust," the second commits "a sin of lust without a sin against the sexual order." With pleasure, without pleasure—the whole scene seems damned. What right-thinking man or woman would not quickly abandon so treacherous a mine field for the monastery or the nunnery?

Freudianism Has Triumphed

But, of course, the gospel of Freud has triumphed; the nunneries are drying up, and priests are being hauled into court for their numerous offenses against chastity. Sex is a great disorderer of society—the old ascetics were not wrong about that. The embarrassingly detailed religious prohibitions that strike the modern liberal as outrageous and ridiculous—against masturbation, contraception, homosexuality and so-called sodomy—were patchwork attempts to wall in the polymorphous-perverse torrents that, in our time, have conspicuously undermined those confining but as yet unreplaced institutions, marriage and the male-headed family.

Pornography and its slightly more demure cousin, advertising, present an ideal world, and the claims of the ideal strain and stress imperfect reality. Citizens' private sexual expectations do spill over into society, producing divorce, out-of-wedlock pregnancies and a rise in literally mortal venereal disease. The conscientious medieval lovers who in the throes of the sex act had to consider whether their concupiscent sensations (*concupiscentia*) were in line with "right reason" (*rectam rationem*) are matched by the modern lovers who must keep asking themselves which bodily fluids might infect what susceptible membranes with H.I.V.

The old naysayers were right at least in this: sex has consequences, it is not a holiday from the world.

The sin of lust was defined by St. Thomas as a misalignment with God's procreative purposes; another serene systematizer, Baruch Spinoza, wrote in his "Ethics," "Avarice, ambition, lust, etc., are nothing but species of madness." Madness, presumably, is to be avoided, as a deviation from an Aristotelian norm of sane moderation. Of the seven deadly sins, gluttony and sloth are sins of excess, of quantity rather than quality, since the human animal must both eat and rest. It must lust, also, one might say, or else sublimate.

Is lust, however, as simple, as marginal to our spiritual and mental being, as sleeping and eating? Is it not, as Freud and Augustine darkly agree, central to our Promethean human nature? Lust, which begins in a glance of the eye, is a searching, and its consummation, step by step, a knowing. Not only does the sexual appetite join us to "the beasts of the field" and to our chthonian mother—"the Mother of All Living," wrote Robert Graves, "the ancient power of fright and lust"—but it also calls into activity our most elegant faculties, of self-display, of social intercourse and of internal idealization. We are attracted not merely to the bodies of others but to their psyches, the shimmering nonmaterial identities that used to be called souls. Romantic love, which Denis de Rougement convincingly described as a pernicious heresy, rarefies lust into an angelic standoff, a fruitless longing without which our energizing circumambient dreamland of song, film and fiction would be bereft of its main topic. This endless celebration of love and its frustrations is a popular religion, giving dignity and significance to the ephemeral.

Love is eternal, whereas lust is a physical process that has an end. It rhymes with "dust," a number of poets have noticed. Andrew Marvell begs his "Coy Mistress" to succumb ere "your quaint honour turn to dust; / And into ashes all my lust." But William Shakespeare wrote the definitive treatise, in his Sonnet 129, beginning, "Th'expense of spirit in a waste of shame / Is lust in action." Lust is, he goes on, "a swallowed bait" and "A bliss in proof, and proved, a very woe; / Before, a joy proposed;—behind, a dream." Yet none, he concludes, "knows well / To shun the heaven that leads men to this hell."

Lust in the Bible

The Bible is actually rather soft on lust. Jesus' plea for the adulterous woman and his fondness for female company, high and low, give a genial tinge to his ministry. The Old Testament contains erotic poetry and a number of erotic episodes. King David's lust for Bathsheba, whom he spied at her bath from a rooftop, led to adultery and to the murder of her husband, Uriah the Hittite, but not to any permanent loss of David's status as God's favorite. "The thing that David had done displeased the Lord," and the Lord killed the illicit couple's firstborn child, but then Bathsheba gave birth to Solomon. Out of lust, wisdom. If God created the world, He created sex, and one way to construe our inexhaustible sexual interest is as a form of the praise of creation. Says the Song of Solomon, "The joints of thy thighs are like jewels / The work of the hands of a cunning workman."

In admiring another, and in yearning to make our flesh one with the other's, we are stepping out of our skins into a kind of selflessness and into a sense of beauty. Without lust on the planet, what would wax glad and lovely? Liberal truisms on the joy—nay, the downright goodness—of sex are very easy to write in this day and age. What we may lose in this ease is a sense of the majestic power the religious deniers felt—the power of sex to bind souls to this transient, treacherous world. Sex loses something when we deny its tragic underside.

T. S. Eliot wrote of [French poet] Charles Baudelaire, "He was at least able to understand that the sexual act as evil is more dignified, less boring, than as the natural, 'life-giving,' cheery automatism of the modern world. For Baudelaire, sexual operation is at least something not analogous to Kruschen Salts." Humanly enough, some sense of the forbidden—of what Freud spoke of as an "obstacle . . . necessary to swell the tide of libido to its height"—gives lust its savor, its keenness. Such is the confusion of this fallen world, where sins lie intermixed with the seeds of being.

"The Sexual Revolution . . . has come out into the open as a rejection of and attack on the sexual morality of Christianity."

The Sexual Revolution Is Immoral

Francis Canavan

The Sexual Revolution has ushered in popular attitudes that no sexual conduct in itself is wrong and that any sex between consenting adults is acceptable, Francis Canavan contends in the following viewpoint. Canavan argues that the source of this social revolution is the concept of separating sex from procreation, manifested in society's endorsement of abortion, contraception, and homosexuality. Canavan warns that such sexual liberation emancipates humanity from all moral norms and further unravels the social fabric. A Jesuit priest, Canavan is professor emeritus of political science at Fordham University in New York City and the author of several books, including *Edmund Burke: Prescription and Providence.*

As you read, consider the following questions:

1. What is the difference between individual and common human nature, according to Canavan?
2. Why is the author concerned about advances in biological technology?
3. Why will the Sexual Revolution be an important issue in the future, in Canavan's opinion?

Abridged from Francis Canavan, "The Sexual Revolution, Explained," *New Oxford Review*, November 1993. Copyright ©1993 *New Oxford Review*. Reprinted with permission from the *New Oxford Review* (1069 Kains Ave., Berkeley, CA 94706).

Western culture, the culture of what was once Christendom, is living through a vast change. The change is in itself nothing new, since it has been going on since the Enlightenment began some 300 years ago, and it has been enormously heightened by the Industrial Revolution of the past two centuries.

The part of this cultural revolution which is now referred to as the Sexual Revolution, however, has impinged upon our attention much more recently, although it, too, has roots far back in the past. But it is only in the last few decades that it has come out into the open as a rejection of and attack on the sexual morality of Christianity. I recall reading with some surprise only 30 years ago, in the British magazine *New Society*, "For the first time in centuries the Judeo-Christian code is under fire, not just from people who wish to break it for their own pleasure, but from people who believe that it is actually wrong."

Disturbing Numbers

Since then the Sexual Revolution has passed from what people think to what they do. Today, in the press, one constantly comes across statistics such as the following. According to the Alan Guttmacher Institute, more American teenagers (47 percent) regularly used contraceptives in 1988 than in 1982, when only 22 percent regularly used them. Yet the overall teenage pregnancy rate remained the same, because more teenagers were having sexual relations. Each year one of every 10 teenage girls in this country becomes pregnant, and of those who give birth, about 60 percent are unmarried. One of every four babies born in the U.S. is born out of wedlock.

The Guttmacher Institute also reports that more than one out of five Americans now suffers from a sexually transmitted viral disease. According to the Centers for Disease Control, sexually transmitted diseases are now at an all-time high among teenagers: Each year 2.5 million adolescents will contract a sexually transmitted disease.

All sources that I have read agree on a figure of about 1.5 million abortions every year in this country, and the number has held steady for a good many years now. Prof. Andrew Hacker of Queens College adds that about 82 percent of these abortions were performed on single women, yet out-of-wedlock births have steadily increased in number for the past 40 years.

These data may be, as we say in the social sciences, impressionistic. I am not in a position to vouch for their accuracy, and I don't pretend that they *prove* anything. Yet 30 years of reading about the sexual mores of the American people have left a firm impression on me: that among large numbers of Americans, young ones in particular, the sexual drive has slipped its moorings in Christian morality, and is now regulated, if at all, only

30

by certain vague principles such as respect for the feelings of other people. No sexual conduct is regarded as wrong in itself, but only insofar as it exploits others. In the contemporary mind, consenting adults can do no wrong sexually.

Separating Sex from Procreation

This change in attitudes and conduct, I submit, amounts to a sexual revolution. But I need not belabor that point because I doubt if many people today will disagree with it. My thesis, which surely will encounter some disagreement, is that this revolution began in the present century with growing social acceptance of the separation of sex from procreation. The revolution consists in the inexorable working-out of the implications of that separation.

It is true that people have always sought to separate sexual intercourse from procreation. But modern methods of contraception have now made this disjunction easily and widely possible. In so doing, they have changed the way in which we think of the nature and purpose of sex.

Contraception has called into question the definition of the sexual act itself. If it is permissible to sterilize the act of sex while performing it, one may ask why it is necessary to perform it with complementary organs of generation. And, if that is not necessary, why must sexual activity be confined to persons of opposite sex? Or, if they are of opposite sex, why must they be married to each other? These are questions that obviously have occurred to many people in our society. It is also obvious that many of us who do not like the questions have no convincing answer to them, once we have accepted contraception as morally permissible.

The Crying Game

At a deeper level, contraception changes our understanding of human nature itself. A good illustration of this change is the recent film, *The Crying Game*, which is in effect a piece of homosexual propaganda—and film critic John Simon has joined me in this judgment. The film teaches that sexual love can be disjoined from the distinction between the sexes, and that the distinction is therefore unimportant.

In the film, the Irish Republican Army captures a Jamaican-born British soldier and holds him captive to win the release of an I.R.A. man captured by the British. The British soldier, a charming man, wheedles the I.R.A. man assigned to guard him into agreeing to go to London to see his girl and tell her what happened to him, after the I.R.A. kills him, as he is sure it will.

In fact, the soldier is killed accidentally while trying to escape. The I.R.A. man goes to London nonetheless, meets the girl, and falls in love with her. When she takes her clothes off,

31

however, it becomes evident that she is really he, a transvestite homosexual male. The story ends with the pseudo-girl being the only regular visitor the I.R.A. man has when he is caught by the police and put in jail.

Sex as Fast Food

The astounding crassness of our own time is summed up in the phrase "safe sex," which reduces the most intimate human function to the level of fast food. The pursuit of orgasm is assumed to be an end in itself, limited only by the inconvenient health hazards that may attend it. The idea of the consecration of the person to a husband or wife is totally absent. Chastity is merely "abstinence," a purely negative option. We don't speak of fornication, but of being "sexually active." Husbands and wives, even boyfriends and girlfriends, are blurred with lechers, tramps, wolves, and whores in the all-encompassing vagueness of "sexual partners." If you have the same partner for more than a week or so, it's a "relationship." The filthiest vices are "alternative lifestyles." And of course if the worst should happen, you can always "terminate a pregnancy." The word "fetus" is used not to suggest a living being, but, on the contrary, to imply that it isn't much more than waste matter; I suspect there is some nebulous association between the fetal and the fecal.

Joseph Sobran, *The Wanderer*, December 12, 1991.

According to Neil Jordan, who wrote the script and directed the film, "This is a story of two people who manage to find whatever that thing is we call love, through everything in the world that separates us." Or, as the film's leading actor put it somewhat more crudely in an off-screen interview, "Well, if you are attracted [to someone of your own sex], why not deal with it? It is only a piece of meat, only flesh, and there are all varieties of flesh. If you are so inclined."

Debating Human Nature

Lying behind this story is a certain conception of nature. While the British soldier is in captivity, he charms his I.R.A. guard into friendship, and tells him, "You are a kind person. It is your nature." When the I.R.A. man goes to London and learns that the girlfriend is really a male, his first reaction is to get sick to his stomach and throw up. But the homosexual explains, "I can't help it. It is my nature."

Nature here is merely an individual essence, in the language of John Locke. My nature is the inclination, preference, orientation that I find deep within myself and can't help feeling. It is

32

what makes me *me*, distinct and different from all others. As I once heard a self-professed homosexual say in a public debate, "I find my personal identity through oral and anal sex." Or, as the "girl" says in *The Crying Game*, "I can't help it. It is my nature." Beyond "my nature" thus understood, there is no higher norm to which I must or can conform.

The alternative view, which is embodied in the Christian moral tradition, is that there is a common human nature, in which we all share, and which defines us as human beings and not merely as discrete individuals. We all have our individual personalities, and in that sense each of us is unique. But what makes us human beings and persons is our common human nature, not our mere individuality. I am an individual, to be sure, but so is my dog or my cat. What makes me a person, and not a dog or a cat, is my human nature.

The division of the human race into two sexes is an integral part of that human nature, not something adventitious and added on to it. There are no merely human beings; there are only men and women, because there is no other way of being human. Since we are animals and are therefore living bodies, our sex is a constitutive element of our being as humans. As the Book of Genesis puts it, "God created man in his own image, in the image of God he created him, male and female he created them."

Sexual Beings

The Bible's choice of words is highly significant. God created man, but He created man male and female. Made in the image of God though we are, we are not sexless souls that dwell in bodies and use them as instruments of the truly human part of us (our minds and wills). We are living material beings composed of both body and soul, and therefore endowed with our male or female sex as a natural and essential part of our humanity. Without our sex we would not be human.

In this view of human nature, the two sexes are twin principals of generation, or reproduction. Physically, the sexes are defined by their organs of reproduction, and they derive their psychological characters from their natural, built-in roles in the generation and rearing of children. Granted that reproduction is not the only or the highest function of human beings, it is the one that constitutes the two sexes as such. It is also the function that specifies and defines the structure of sexual intercourse as the natural act of sex.

Contraception implicitly denies that this natural structure of sex and of the sexual act is normative and binding. It acknowledges the undeniable orientation of the act of sex toward procreation, but reduces it to the status of a brute fact, a mere biological datum that it is permissible to counteract. Contraception

33

thereby releases sexual activity from any moral control that is based on the nature of sex and the sexual act.

That this result would follow was predicted in the debates on contraception that took place in the Church of England between the Lambeth Conferences of 1919 and 1929, when that church shifted its position on the morality of contraception. Today, however, the result is no longer a matter of prediction, but of observation. Western society has accepted contraception as a moral practice, and the predicted consequences have followed. They are what we now call the Sexual Revolution.

What Is Immoral

So, for example, masturbation is now widely regarded as morally neutral, simply a stage through which young people pass on their way to sexual maturity, but also as a practice which is always available as a way of relieving sexual tension. Recreational sex has become, in the words of a Broadway song, "just the friendliest thing two people can do." The practice of living together before marriage is increasingly common. It manifests the same attitude of mind that takes divorce and remarriage for granted, despite all the consequences of broken families that are causing more and more concern to social observers. For multitudes of people, marriage has largely lost its meaning as a lifelong union of man and woman ordered and ordained to the family.

I do not see homosexuality as sweeping the country, because most people find it repugnant, but our inability as a culture to say what is morally wrong with homosexual acts is obvious. We no longer know why anything that people choose to do with their sexual organs is unnatural, so long as they freely choose to do it. We do not know and we cannot know, because we have abandoned nature as the norm.

Abortion is widely accepted and practiced as a back-up to contraception. It is true that contraceptive methods (those which are not also abortifacients) only prevent conception, while abortion kills what has been conceived. Yet the slide from contraception to abortion has been remarkably easy. All that was needed was to undefine the fetus as a human being, and abortion was taken to be just another permissible form of birth control. The feminist movement, which seeks to free women from the burden of reproduction in order to pursue careers on the same terms as men, is particularly insistent on abortion as a basic human right.

Biological Technology

Finally, we must mention artificial insemination, in vitro fertilization, and similar ways of having children. These practices aim at, not against, conception. But they all separate conception from normal sexual intercourse, and often from marriage as well. Genetic engineering threatens to carry even further the process of splitting human nature into manipulable biological material and a conscious dominating will.

The root of this process is an idea of man as self-emancipated from all moral norms derived from his nature as a composite of body and soul, and therefore from his nature as a sexual being. Man is seen as a sovereign will who is free to make and remake himself according to his desires. But, given the increasing perfection of our biological technology, this is an idea with far-reaching implications, which Aldous Huxley, in his novel, *Brave New World*, and C.S. Lewis in *The Abolition of Man*, pointed out decades ago.

Humanity never has been very good at controlling its technology, as the history of weaponry demonstrates. Today, in the area of sexual biology, our technology, despite our illusion that we control it, more and more controls us by shaping the very way in which we think of ourselves and our sexuality. The emancipated self exploits its technology, but is ultimately exploited by it. As a 13-year-old girl in Irvine, Calif., wrote to *Time* (June 14, 1993), "Everything is based on sex today, and that's why I think during prom night, schools should hand out condoms." A true Daughter of the Sexual Revolution, she is, more than she knows, a product of modern applied science.

Questions of Public Morality

I said earlier that my thesis, that the source of the Sexual Revolution is the separation of sex from procreation, would meet with disagreement. I expect the disagreement. But it will not be enough for objectors to say that they are not convinced by the arguments offered to show that contraception is morally wrong. Those who reject the thesis will have to take a hard look at what contraception has wrought in modern society, and ask themselves what consequences follow in both logic and practice if contraception is right.

What clear and convincing proofs can they offer to show that contraception is permissible, but only between partners in marriage (assuming that they want to stop there)? If they discard the obvious procreative teleology of sex as a basis for moral argument, with what confidence can they fall back on the much less obvious "law of love" that makes sexual intercourse by its nature an expression of exclusive and lifelong love? Why should the Sexual Revolution stop with the legitimization of contraception, and not go on to work out all the implications of canceling the procreative effects of sexual acts? The answers to these questions had better be good ones, because they will be addressed to a world that clearly does not believe them and is not about to accept them.

These questions will become more and more urgent as we move into the 21st century. They will not be questions of personal morality alone, which can be left to individual judgment, but will heavily involve public welfare and therefore public morality. The Sexual Revolution is a social revolution whose effects cannot be isolated from the well-being of society at large. The breaking of the link between sexual activity and procreation has already changed relations between men and women, weakened the bond between husbands and wives, and contributed to the disintegration of the family. As this process continues, we may expect a further unraveling of the social fabric.

"Sexual behavior . . . should never be governed by a separate category of morality."

The Sexual Revolution Is Not Immoral

Judith Levine

In the following viewpoint, Judith Levine advocates the continuation of the Sexual Revolution—focusing on pleasure and new forms of relationships—as alternatives to traditional sexual relationships. Levine challenges the values of abstinence and heterosexual monogamy and the beliefs that homosexual and teenage sex are wrong. She writes that despite AIDS and sexually transmitted diseases, society should not fear sex but welcome it as a healthy and pleasurable part of everyone's life. Levine is a freelance writer and journalist who has written magazine articles on families, feminism, relationships, and sex.

As you read, consider the following questions:

1. According to Levine, how have progressives and feminists reacted to the Sexual Revolution?
2. What does the author mean by the "sexual hegemony" of the nuclear family?
3. How should children be taught about sex, in Levine's opinion?

Judith Levine, "Thinking About Sex," *Tikkun*, March 1988. Reprinted from TIKKUN MAGAZINE, A BI-MONTHLY JEWISH CRITIQUE OF POLITICS, CULTURE, AND SOCIETY. Subscriptions are $31 per year from TIKKUN, 251 W. 100th St., 5th fl., New York, NY 10025.

In the past we've witnessed sex the question transformed into sex the problem. The problem of teenage pregnancy has become the problem of teenage sex, so we try to teach abstinence instead of contraception and convince ourselves that teenagers have sex only because of peer pressure. AIDS is perceived not as a horrible disease of the body, but as the wasting away of the morals of the body politic. The cure is to contain, not the virus, but nonconventional, nonmonogamous sex.

But you don't have to travel far rightward to discover such attitudes. The middle is rife with them, too. No presidential candidate is unqualifiedly prochoice. No Congress member objects when Jesse Helms fulminates on the Senate floor about "safe sodomy." Bill Moyers speculates that promiscuity—too many undisciplined young cocks strutting around the inner city's roosts—is the cause of the black family's dissolution. Jesse Jackson, instead of refuting him, drops his economic analysis and preaches a return to the church and its sexual morality. On NBC's "Scared Sexless," host Connie Chung reacted quizzically to [former] Education Secretary William Bennett's remark that "AIDS may give us an opportunity to discourage [sex], and that might be a good thing." But she concluded that, plagues or no, less sex is better, especially for teenagers. She didn't say why.

Reactions to the Sexual Revolution

In response to all this, the left says nothing. In fact, it consistently puts sex at the bottom of the agenda (my mother has been fighting with my father, both of them old leftists, for forty years about the political centrality of abortion) or demonstrates downright antisex and antipleasure biases. In the 1980s, ever more squeamish about appearing unserious, it distanced itself from popular culture (which is all about fun) and from prosex feminists, gays, and other erotic minorities for whom sexual freedom is a fundamental struggle. This is more than an abstract problem: according to the Centers for Disease Control, in the 1990s AIDS may kill more Americans annually than were lost during the entire Vietnam War, yet no left group makes the epidemic a forefront issue.

Meanwhile, progressives dismiss the Sexual Revolution as a childish flight of caprice, and though they don't see AIDS as the scourge of God, they use the disease as a justification for endorsing certain kinds of sex and relationships and censuring others. Not as coldhearted as Bennett, but equally insulting to the people dying, these "progressives" find in AIDS the silver lining of newly "meaningful," committed sex. Even from the gay community a pious monogamism emanates—*vis* the mass marriage ceremony at the 1987 gay and lesbian march on Washington.

As for feminists, a small rowdy band of prosex guerrillas like

38

No More Nice Girls carries the flame of women's sexual freedom, but all around them the flame dims to a flicker. Influential moderates like Betty Friedan eschew public discourses on lesbianism and sex as "exhibitionist," and steer activism elsewhere. In the early 1980s, abortion is suddenly a "family" issue, and a secondary one at that. If there were good daycare and socialized medicine, the argument runs, we'd all want children, and the demand for abortion would disappear. Lately, abortion finds itself nestling under the antiseptic rubric of "reproductive freedom," with forced caesareans, *in vitro* fertilization, surrogacy, and other politics of modern motherhood. It's as if sex—which, if I'm not mistaken, is the cause of pregnancy—had nothing to do with it. In fact, the feminists most consistently passionate about cocks and cunts are Women Against Pornography—and they would wash my mouth out with soap for saying it!

Challenging Traditional Views

All this distresses me mightily, because, like Emma Goldman, who didn't want a revolution she couldn't dance to, I don't want one I can't fuck to. I consider pleasure a revolutionary goal. And I still endorse the commitment of the Sexual Revolution and the early women's movement to forging new personal alliances, new forms of love and friendship—including sexual ones. Though never a smash-monogamy zealot, I believe in destabilizing traditional sexual setups and struggling, as we did in the 1960s and 1970s, with the emotions that go with such a cultural upheaval.

At the risk of sounding "nostalgic," or, in the age of AIDS, either frivolous or mad, I contend that we can't change society if we don't challenge the sexual hegemony of the nuclear family and resist its enforcement of adult heterosexual monogamy and its policing of all other forms of sexuality within it and outside it. Supporting "alternative" families or giving lip service to gay rights isn't enough; we must militantly stand up for everybody whose sexuality falls outside "acceptable" bourgeois arrangements—even far outside of them.

But you can't do this without asking fundamental questions about sex. Questions like, is monogamy better? (My answer: not necessarily.) What's wrong with kids having sex? (Often, nothing.) Why is it worse to pay for sex than to pay for someone to listen to your intimate problems or care for your infant? (You tell me.) You can't ask those questions if you whisk sexuality to the bottom of the list of "serious issues" after peace, or childcare, or even AIDS.

Indeed, AIDS should have us thinking harder than ever about how to preserve pleasure in our lives. If the disease limits our options, at the very least we don't have to be sanctimonious about it! I may currently like having sex with only one person, but I don't like feeling I'd better sleep with him exclusively from now on, or death will us part. Fear of death is about as felicitous a motivation for monogamy as fear of impoverishment is for staying married.

A Libertarian Sexual Ethic

A libertarian sexual ethic frames sex as having multiple meanings. Sex may be a medium of pleasure, love or procreation, and sex is said to be legitimate in multiple social settings. Individual choice and consent are considered the guiding norms sanctioning sexual expression. Underpinning a libertarian ethic is a benevolent view of sex. Sex is seen bringing health, joy and happiness to the individual. Although libertarians insist that sex can have multiple meanings, there is an essentialist strain in much contemporary libertarian ideology. Sex is defined, in essence, as a mode of bodily, sensual pleasure. Unfortunately, according to libertarians, dominant social groups impose higher moral purposes on sex (e.g., procreation, love, family, spiritual growth) for social or political reasons. Imbuing sex with heightened social significance produces a cluster of legal and state restrictions and regulations. Sex loses its playful, erotic innocence as it becomes a sign of the moral state of the individual and society. Moreover, as sex accrues these surplus meanings and purposes, rigid moral boundaries crystallize that classify sexual desires and acts into "normal" and "abnormal," and categorize them as good, healthy and right versus bad, sick and wrong. Libertarians intend to free individuals of the excessive social controls that inhibit sexual expression and stigmatize transgressive desires and acts.

Steven Seidman, *Embattled Eros*, 1992.

We shouldn't be looking for meaning in sex at all, in fact, but rather trying to strip implicit meaning from sex. I don't mean pushing for casual sex, but allowing a separation of sex from commitment and then, by conscious decision only, rejoining the two. This would not only emancipate women to make the choices men have always made about what sex means in a given relationship, it would enhance the possibility for stronger alliances, both passionate and emotional.

In thinking about how that could be done, I recall a 1983 piece by Edmund White, "Paradise Found," about his circle of gay friends and lovers. Outside the rules and expectations of family, relationships were highly fluid. Unlike heterosexual couples, who date, become monogamous, marry, integrate into one another's families, have children, and adjust their sex lives accordingly, a gay lover could be anything from a trick to a husband, or over time, both. Though radical gayness singled out sexuality as an essence of identity, it also freed relationships from being defined by sex. In the novel *Dancing in the Dark*, Janet Hobhouse described "these loving friends, admitted into their Giotto heaven one by one as each 'came out' and professed the faith, free to touch and kiss like angels. . . ." If the meanings of sex were myriad, the use of sex was plain: pleasure.

Pleasure Amidst AIDS

Our task today is not to pine away in nostalgia, but neither is it to disavow the sexual liberation we fought for in the past decades. We need to keep pleasure as a vital part of the progressive vision at the same time as we confront AIDS, which vanquishes pleasure more powerfully than any repression the right or the left could ever dream up. We must help our children feel that sex is good in an era when sex can bring death, and learn how to relate sexually to each other when new relationships are short-circuited, and old ones sustained, by fear.

The first priority (and it's sickening that this doesn't go without saying) must be a unified fight against AIDS. We must demand government funds for research, medical treatment, and education, and oppose repressive policies on testing, employment, housing, and schooling. And since AIDS is becoming a disease of the poor and drug-addicted, we must redouble our efforts to eradicate poverty.

We have no choice but to teach children safe sex, but we must avoid hysteria, too. If a boy is gay, he is at high risk, but politicized awareness of his identity is his best defense. Vigorous education in the gay community has stabilized the spread of AIDS there. A lesbian child is virtually risk-free. Only one case of "apparent" female-to-female transmission has been reported. Now the media are sounding the alarm about heterosexual transmission—and indeed it is rising. Still, by far the most likely heterosexual carriers are poor, black, or Hispanic IV [intravenous] drug users and their partners; the most sensible AIDS-prevention technique, then, is to give kids real reasons and resources to stay away from serious drugs and away from sexual relations with people who use them. Excluding drug users, only four percent of people with AIDS are heterosexual. We are all fearful enough about sex; there's no point exaggerating the danger.

Aware but Ignorant

Nobody should make assumptions about what kids know about sex. Research shows that while they're highly aware of sex generally, they're often pretty ignorant about the details. Good sex education is safe sex education too. Helping kids to be aware of their bodies—of health and contraception, masturbation, sensual touching, and fantasy as well as intercourse—and of their feelings about sexuality can only make them better able to practice safe and egalitarian sex in what could be history's most honest chapter of sexual relations.

Sexual behavior, moreover, should never be governed by a separate category of morality. If we want our kids to balance their own desires with responsibility and consideration for others, to express their needs and objections freely but cooperate within a community, then we should practice and teach our kids these values in sex, too. Teaching abstinence as "right" is not only puritanical and ineffective in limiting sexual activity, but it fuels prejudice against people whose sexual expression may be more flagrant, and it implies that disease is a punishment for sin.

AIDS presents one of the biggest challenges in history to our survival as a loving community. Both safety and compassion require us to stop seeing those we've been taught to revile as the Other. When we are ruled by fear and alienation, it is easy for extreme attitudes and repressive policies to start sounding reasonable. On the day of the 1987 gay march in Washington, D.C., for instance, the *New York Post*'s lead story, headlined AIDS MONSTER, stereotyped the classic diseased and depraved homosexual, hunted by police for molesting what seemed like countless boys. It is easy to see through the *Post*'s bigotry, but the story plays on the same assumption that supports mandatory testing and disclosure: that people with AIDS lie, remain selfishly ignorant, and deliberately infect—murder—others, so desperate and devoid of social responsibility are they. When "they" are so unlike "us," Draconian measures like tattooing or quarantine seem necessary "for the greater good." In reality, the greater good demands reaching deep to find our human similarities and also respecting our sexual differences.

The antisex hysteria of the 1980s also presents a great challenge to us as lovers. Fear and malaise are counteraphrodisiac (the number one complaint sex therapists hear is lack of desire). We need not exacerbate them with self-righteousness. Married people, who these days seem to have no sensual outlet besides stroking Baby's cheek and watching the VCR, go around gloating about their maturity and security. Single people are home watching their VCR, too—and watching their backs. With movies like *Fatal Attraction*, it's no wonder. Once envied, singles are now blamed; once considered free, they're now portrayed as trapped.

Prosex Messages

Where can we look for prosex messages in the AIDS era? I found one in the most threatened quarter, the gay community, in the educational comic books [once] distributed by the Gay

Men's Health Crisis. These depicted sexual types from leather-men to clones, gorgeously built and hung every one, having phone sex, masturbating, or role-playing, all with minimum risk and maximum heat. Explicitly, humorously sexual, indeed happily pornographic, these pamphlets were pragmatic: they met their constituency where it lived, and did not try to preach living differently. But they implied more—that it's unnecessary to foment aversion to sex through moralizing or hyperbolizing. Death is aversion enough. It's driven many back into the closet and made celibates of countless more.

Instead, the lascivious comic-book hunks are saying: affirm sex. While death is all around us, let us nurture pleasure—for pleasure is life. Even now, especially now, just say yes.

"Homosexuality is sin whether committed in thought, word, or deed."

Homosexuality Erodes Moral Values

George Grant and Mark A. Horne

In debates on homosexuality and sin, clergy members and others often question what is sinful: homosexual sex or homosexual desire? In the following viewpoint, George Grant and Mark A. Horne argue that both thought and deed are sin according to God and the Bible, and that homosexuals, like all others, must be accountable for their sins. The authors maintain that regarding homosexuality as a sin—rather than a permanent genetic condition—provides hope that homosexuals can renounce their sexual orientation and become free of its sinful burden. Grant is a Presbyterian minister in Nashville, Tennessee, and executive director of Legacy Communications, a ministry and book publisher in Franklin, Tennessee. Horne is a writer/researcher and a contributing editor for Legacy Communications.

As you read, consider the following questions:

1. Why do Grant and Horne believe that God allows no exceptions for the sin of homosexuality?
2. How do the authors dispute John Shelby Spong's perspective of the Biblical story of Lot?
3. How are humans responsible for their sexual orientation, according to Grant and Horne?

Taken from: *Legislating Morality: The Homosexual Movement Comes Out of the Closet* by George Grant and Mark A. Horne. Copyright 1993, Mariposa Ltd. Moody Press. Used by permission.

What does the Bible teach about homosexuality? . . .
From the beginning of time, God's design for sexuality has
been a one man, one woman, lifelong, covenantal commitment.
Nineteenth-century theologian James Bricknell Houston Greg
asserts:

> The creation of gender—and thusly, sexual—differentiation by
> God from the beginning of the Genesis account clearly estab-
> lished chaste heterosexuality as normative for sexual impulses
> and acts. God the Creator gives the things of the earth their
> essential identity and function and He thusly defines man's
> proper relationships. Mankind's natural function in sexuality
> has been defined by God as male-female behavior.

And according to pastor William Brandt:

> The Biblical perspective of sexuality simply cannot be com-
> prehended apart from the bounds of holy matrimony—that of
> one man and one woman.

No Minced Words

God spoke from Mt. Sinai in a thunderous voice, "You shall
not commit adultery" (Exodus 20:14; Deuteronomy 5:18). Thus
did He prohibit all sex outside of the holy bounds of marriage.

This clearly enunciated standard was elaborated in the various
case laws He gave Moses—laws that applied the Ten Commandments to specific issues in the life of God's people. For instance,
"You shall not lie with a male as with a woman. It is an abomination" (Leviticus 18:22).

Strong words. But the Bible does not hesitate to use strong language when appropriate. Thus, it compares male homosexuals
to brutish animals:

> There shall be no ritual harlot of the daughters of Israel, or a
> perverted one of the sons of Israel. You shall not bring the hire
> of a harlot or *the price of a dog* to the house of the Lord your
> God for any vowed offering, for both of these are an abomina-
> tion to the Lord your God. (Deuteronomy 23:17-18)

In fact, this kind of covenantal violation is so serious in God's
eyes that He actually declared it subject to capital punishment:

> If a man lies with a male as he lies with a woman, both of
> them have committed an abomination. They shall surely be
> put to death. Their blood shall be upon them. (Leviticus 20:13)

Again and again, the absolute invariability and inescapability
of the prohibition is underscored. Through the years though,
many have tried to avoid the obvious significance of such passages. They have argued, for example, that the case laws were
only intended for the nation of Israel, and thus have no additional application whatsoever. This, despite the fact that God repeatedly indicates that the other nations were by no means ex-
empt. That is the very reason they fall under divine judgment:

And you shall not walk in the statutes of the nation which I
am casting out before you; for they commit all these things,
and therefore I abhor them. (Leviticus 21:23)

Indeed, once the Hebrews had settled in the land, God told
them that they were to be a witness to the nations around them,
which would be attracted by their laws (Deuteronomy 4:5-8).
Plainly, God intends His prohibition of homosexuality to apply
to the people of all cultures because God is the creator and sus-
tainer of them all and His Word is eternal and inviolate—it "will
by no means pass away" (Matthew 24:35).

Absolute Condemnation

Therefore God's condemnation of same-sex perversions is absolute and categorical—even homosexual partners who may be
"committed and faithful" fall under His immutable bar of justice. There is no hint in Scripture that there are exceptions or
aberrations to this standard—thus in the case laws, whereas any
form of extramarital sex was a capital offense, premarital heterosexual offenses were adjudicated with an option of covenantal marriage (Exodus 22:16-17; Deuteronomy 22:28-29). There is
no such option for homosexual offenses because God does not
recognize covenantal marriages between people of the same sex.

Even apart from the case laws, God's blanket condemnation of
homosexuality is evident in numerable passages throughout
Scripture—not the least of which is the story of His destruction
of Sodom and Gomorrah. Though the cities were judged for several sins, rampant unchecked homosexuality ensured their fate
(Ezekiel 16:49-50). According to Scripture, the divine judgment
poured out on the cities was meant to be "an example to those
who afterward would live ungodly" (2 Peter 2:6). Later, the entire Hebrew tribe of Benjamin was almost wiped out for behaving like Sodom (Judges 19-20). Still later, whenever the prophets
of the Old Testament accused Israel of severe apostasy they
would compare the nation to the city of Sodom (Isaiah 3:9;
Jeremiah 23:14).

The Gospel Upholds Moral Law

Many today would contend that there is a vast gulf of differen-
tiation between the harsh teaching of the Old Testament and the
fresh forgiveness of the New Testament—particularly when it
comes to the issue of homosexuality. Jesus, for instance, is silent
on the question, they say. But that is simply not the case. Not
only did Christ repeatedly endorse the teachings and commandments of the entire moral law of the Old Testament—He said
that "heaven and earth would pass away" before the statutes of
the Word passed away—He appealed directly to the creation account of one man and one woman as the sole model for covenant

marriage (Matthew 19:14-16). Additionally, He used the example of Sodom's sin as a warning to Israel of divine wrath in the same way the Old Testament prophets did. Christ was not the least bit ambivalent about this. In fact, He went so far as to assert that the only option for those who do not marry is celibacy (Matthew 19:11-12).

'Pride's a sin!'

First published in *The Spectator*, 1993. Reprinted with permission.

As the Christian faith began to penetrate into the surrounding promiscuous and perverse pagan culture, the apostles were forced to deal more directly with the issue of homosexuality. In Romans, Paul, under the superintendence of the Holy Spirit, condemned homosexuality as he discussed the consequences of suppressing God's revelation in creation:

> For this reason God gave them up to vile passions. For even their women exchanged the natural use for what is against nature. Likewise also the men, leaving the natural use of the

woman, burned in their lust for one another, men with men committing what is shameful, and receiving in themselves the penalty of their error which was due. (Romans 1:26-27)

And, furthermore, he wrote, "Knowing the righteous judgment of God, that those who practice such things are worthy of death," they, nevertheless, "not only do the same but also approve of those who practice them" (Romans 1:32).

Homosexual Desires

Notice here that the Scriptures condemn not only homosexual acts but homosexual desires. This principle takes what Jesus said about heterosexual lust at the Sermon on the Mount and applies it to homosexuality: "You have heard that it was said to those of old, 'You shall not commit adultery.' But I say to you that whoever looks at a woman to lust after her has already committed adultery with her in his heart" (Matthew 5:27-28).

Indeed, the Bible assumes that, contrary to popular opinion, men and women are responsible for their desires and are capable of controlling them (Job 31:1,9; Proverbs 6:25).

Again and again throughout the New Testament, homosexuality is listed among those unacceptable sins of the flesh from which the Gospel has liberated us:

Do not be deceived. Neither fornicators, nor idolaters, nor adulterers, nor homosexuals, nor sodomites, nor thieves, nor covetous, nor drunkards, nor revilers, nor extortioners will inherit the kingdom of God. (1 Corinthians 6:9-10) . . .

The Bible's Apologists

Whereas the defenders of homosexuality claim that they will tell us what the Bible *really* says about homosexuality, they inevitably reveal what they think about the Bible.

The fact is, most of these apologists just don't like what the Bible says. They are embarrassed by it. And so they attempt to explain it away—perhaps in a vain attempt to "defend" the honor and integrity of God.

Other apologists—with at least an increment of intellectual honesty—see through this ruse and simply confess that the Bible is wrongheaded on this issue. It is in error, they say, and thus we *ought* to be embarrassed by it. No need to go through exegetical gymnastics to prove otherwise.

Bishop John Shelby Spong's omnisexual manifesto, *Living in Sin? A Bishop Rethinks Human Sexuality*, opts for this course.

So, for instance, Spong's portrayal of the destruction of Sodom and Gomorrah is deliberately mocking. Noting that "fundamentalists" use the story as evidence of Scripture's condemnation of homosexuality, he remarks:

What a strange text to use for such a purpose. The biblical narrative approves Lot's offer of his virgin daughters to satisfy the sexual demands of the angry mob. It suggests that incest is a legitimate way of impregnating women when there is no man around save the father of those women. What society today would be willing to incorporate either of these practices into its moral code? Who among us is willing to accept the definition of women implicit in this account? If we reject the denigration of women as property or the practice of incest, both being based upon an inadequate view of morality, are we not also free to reject the society's faulty understanding of homosexuality as being also based upon inadequate moral grounds?

The text, of course, gives no hint that heterosexual gang rape or incest are morally acceptable practices. There is no sign of approval of Lot's offer of his two daughters to the mob. Given the fact that Lot was originally attracted to Sodom (Genesis 13:10-13) and ended up living out his days as a homeless vagabond (Genesis 19:30) seems to indicate that he was far from God's blessing. Though he was "oppressed" and "tormented" by the behavior of the Sodomites (2 Peter 2:7-8), his own moral character evidently suffered as well. The fact that Lot had to be intoxicated and tricked into impregnating his daughters (Genesis 19:31-36) strongly indicates that incest was viewed as immoral by him. Furthermore, though the descendants of those incestuous unions were initially accorded a degree of respect due to their relationship with Abraham's descendants (Deuteronomy 2:9,19), they were considered Israel's enemy because of their immoral deeds (Deuteronomy 23:3-6).

Of course none of this matters to Spong. He has already presuppositionally denuded the authority of Scripture. . . .

Control over Homosexuality

The whole testimony of Scripture, from the beginning of the Old Testament record, through the Gospels, and on to the end of the New Testament is absolutely clear: homosexuality is sin whether committed in thought, word, or deed. Furthermore, God holds homosexuals responsible for their sin—just as He does any other practicing sinner. Despite the dogmatic instance of those who believe that human beings are fated by either biological or behavioral determinism, Biblical faith insists that we have control over our so-called sexual orientation and are thus responsible for our lives.

As Christian counselor Jay Adams has stated:

One is not a homosexual constitutionally any more than one is an adulterer constitutionally. Homosexuality is not considered to be a condition, but an act. It is viewed as a sinful practice which can become a way of life. The homosexual act, like the act of adultery, is the reason for calling one a homosexual (of course one may commit homosexual sins of the heart, just as one may commit adultery in his heart. He may lust after a man in his heart as another may lust after a woman).

Of course homosexuality for some may not be a conscious and remembered choice any more than heterosexuality is for most. There may not have been any conscious process of deliberation, weighing the pros and cons and then finally coming to a decision. But that does not make sexual preference any less chosen. That does not make it any less voluntary or willful. The defense "I can't help it" is as indefensible as it is infantile.

Freedom from Sin

The Gospel's message of the sinfulness of homosexuality has been reviled by some as an awful bigotry. It has even been equated with the evils of racism—which are categorically condemned in Scripture. But the reality is that treating homosexuality as a sin is the very opposite of bigotry. For instead of simply stereotyping homosexuals as predetermined products of either their biology or environment, the Gospel treats them the same as every other sinner who needs to repent and believe.

Calling homosexuality a sin may well seem to be a cruel, insensitive attitude—perhaps even a "homophobic" response of condemnation rather than of concern. But the truth is that it is the beginning of true freedom and joy for the homosexual. For if sexual preference were either a genetically encoded human condition—such as height or skin color—there would be no real hope. The homosexual would be shackled to his lusts forever, with no possibility of release. But once we can freely admit that homosexuality is just a sin, we can also see the way of deliverance and redemption.

This is the message of the Gospel: Christ died for sinners—to set them free from sin.

The apostle Paul knew this well. After listing homosexuality among other sinful practices that exclude people from the kingdom of God, he wrote to the church in Corinth:

> And such were some of you. But you were washed, but you were sanctified, but you were justified in the name of the Lord Jesus and by the Spirit of our God. (1 Corinthians 6:11)

The New Testament church, apparently, was filled with repentant ex-homosexuals who had found new life in Christ.

May it be so once again.

"Homosexuality, far from being a sickness, sin, perversion or unnatural act, is a healthy, natural, and affirming form of human sexuality."

Homosexuality Does Not Erode Moral Values

C. Robert Nugent and John Shelby Spong

Neither God nor the Bible regards homosexuality, in and of itself, as a sin, C. Robert Nugent and John Shelby Spong argue in the following viewpoint. Nugent and Spong maintain that although the possibility of sin exists equally in homosexuality and heterosexuality, a faithful and loving homosexual relationship has the blessing of God. Trained as a Roman Catholic priest, Nugent is a graduate of the Yale University Divinity School, cofounder of the New Ways Ministry (Mt. Rainier, Maryland) for gays and lesbians, and a consultant for the Center for Homophobia Education in New York City. Spong is an Episcopalian bishop in Newark, New Jersey, and the author of eleven books, including *Living in Sin? A Bishop Rethinks Human Sexuality*. The following viewpoint is excerpted from a survey of theologians made by the Federation of Parents and Friends of Lesbians and Gays (P-FLAG) in Washington, D.C.

As you read, consider the following questions:

1. According to Nugent, what type of sexual behavior is sinful?
2. Why does Spong disagree with a literal interpretation of the Bible's views on homosexuality?
3. In Nugent's opinion, how could a homosexual couple build a relationship and family?

In your opinion, does God regard homosexuality as a sin?

Spong: Some argue that since homosexual behavior is "unnatural," it is contrary to the order of creation. Behind this pronouncement are stereotypic definitions of masculinity and femininity that reflect the rigid gender categories of patriarchal society. There is nothing unnatural about any shared love, even between two of the same gender, if that experience calls both partners into a fuller state of being. Contemporary research is uncovering new facts that are producing a rising conviction that homosexuality, far from being a sickness, sin, perversion or unnatural act, is a healthy, natural, and affirming form of human sexuality for some people. Findings indicate that homosexuality is a given fact in the nature of a significant portion of people, and that it is unchangeable.

Our prejudice rejects people or things outside our understanding. But the God of creation speaks and declares, "I have looked out on *everything* I have made and 'behold it (is) very good.'" (Gen. 1:31) The Word of God in Christ says that we are loved, valued, redeemed, and counted as precious no matter how we might be valued by a prejudiced world.

God Is Where Love Is

Nugent: I do not believe that God regards homosexuality as a "sin" if homosexuality means the psychosexual identity of lesbians or gay persons, which we know from contemporary scientific studies is within the boundaries of healthy, human psychological development, and which seems to be as natural for some people as heterosexuality is for others. If homosexuality means the emotional, intimate bonding in same-gender relationships of love and friendship, I believe that since God is love, where there is authentic love, God is present.

Where God is present, there can be no sin. If homosexuality means same-gender erotic, physical expressions of union and pleasure, the possibility of personal sin exists in homosexuality—as it does in heterosexuality—depending on the interplay of three factors including the physical behavior itself and its meaning for the person, the personal motives and intentions of the person acting, and the individual and social consequences or results of the behavior. For many people, sexual behavior which is exploitative, coercive, manipulative, dishonest, selfish or destructive of human personhood is sinful; for all people "sin" means freely acting contrary to one's deeply held moral or ethical convictions, whether these come from organized religion or a personally developed value system. In speaking of the "sinfulness" of same-gender genital expression, the Roman Catholic Bishops of Washington [state] say that ". . . no one except Almighty God can make certain judgments about the personal sinfulness of acts."

In your opinion, do the Scriptures object to homosexuality?

Spong: There are few biblical references to homosexuality. The first, the story of Sodom and Gomorrah, is often quoted to prove that the Bible condemns homosexuality. But the real sin of Sodom was the unwillingness of the city's men to observe the laws of hospitality. The intention was to insult the stranger by forcing him to take the female role in the sex act. The biblical narrative approves Lot's offer of his virgin daughters to satisfy the sexual demands of the mob. How many would say, *"This* is the word of the Lord"? When the Bible is quoted literally, it might be well for the one quoting to read the text in its entirety.

Leviticus, in the Hebrew Scriptures, condemns homosexual behavior, at least for males. Yet, "abomination," the word Leviticus uses to describe homosexuality, is the same word used to describe a menstruating woman.

A Misuse of Scripture

We simply have no way of knowing what the biblical authors would have said about the type of homosexuality we know today. Had they known the caring adult human relationships we see today, who knows what they would have written? When the bible is used as a bludgeon to attack homosexuals it is a misuse of scripture and reveals both a serious lack of scholarship and a strong hidden cultural and social agenda. This is not scriptural scholarship, nor good pastoral practice. It is a lazy and ignorant approach to a most significant matter for all of us, whose lives are affected by homophobes all around us.

Robert S. Perkins, *Gay & Lesbian Times*, August 27, 1992.

Paul is the most quoted source in the battle to condemn homosexuality (in Rom. 1:26-27 and in I Corinthians 6:9-11). But homosexual activity was regarded by Paul as a punishment visited upon idolaters by God because of their unfaithfulness. Homosexuality was not the sin but the punishment.

In I Corinthians 6:9-11, Paul gave a list of those who would not inherit the kingdom of God. That list included the immoral, idolaters, adulterers, sexual perverts, thieves, the greedy, drunkards, revilers and robbers. Sexual perverts is a translation of two words; it is possible that the juxtaposition of *malakos*, the soft, effeminate word, with *arsenokoitus*, or male prostitute, was meant to refer to the passive and active males in a homosexual liaison.

Thus, it appears that Paul would not approve of homosexual behavior. But was Paul's opinion about homosexuality accurate, or was it limited by the lack of scientific knowledge in his day and infected by prejudice born of ignorance? An examination of some of Paul's other assumptions and conclusions will help answer this question. Who today would share Paul's anti-Semitic attitude, his belief that the authority of the state was not to be challenged, or that all women ought to be veiled? In these attitudes Paul's thinking has been challenged and transcended even by the church. Is Paul's commentary on homosexuality more absolute than some of his other antiquated, culturally conditioned ideas?

Three other references in the New Testament (in Timothy, Jude and II Peter) appear to be limited to condemnation of male sex slaves in the first instance, and to showing examples (Sodom and Gomorrah) of God's destruction of unbelievers and heretics (in Jude and II Peter respectively).

That is all that Scripture has to say about homosexuality. Even if one is a biblical literalist, these references do not build an ironclad case for condemnation. If one is not a biblical literalist there is no case at all, nothing but prejudice born of ignorance, that attacks people whose only crime is to be born with an unchangeable sexual predisposition toward those of their own sex.

Scriptures Are Only One Source

Nugent: Catholicism uses four major sources for principles and guidance in ethical questions like homosexuality: scripture, tradition (theologians, church documents, official teachings, etc.), reason, and human experience. All are used in conjunction with one another. Scripture is a fundamental and primary authoritative Catholic source—but not the *only* source. Biblical witness is taken seriously, but not literally. An individual scriptural text must be understood in the larger context of the original language and culture, the various levels of meanings, and the texts' applications to contemporary realities in light of the role of the community's and its official leadership role in providing authoritative interpretations. Both Jewish and Christian scriptures do speak negatively of certain forms of same-gender (generally male) sexual *behavior* (not same-gender *love*), especially when associated with idol worship, lust, violence, degradation, prostitution, etc. Whether scriptures condemn all and every form of same-gender sexual expression *in and of itself* for all times, places and individuals is the topic of serious theological and biblical discussion and debate. Same-gender expressions of responsible, faithful love in a covenanted relationship between two truly homosexually oriented people not gifted with celibacy is not something envisioned by scriptures. Whether this form of homosexuality violates biblical or anthropological principles of sexuality and personhood—especially in light of current scientific knowledge and human experience about the homosexual orientation—is a key issue facing the churches and religious groups today.

In your opinion, does God approve of two gay or lesbian individu-

*als pledging their love to each other in a religious ceremony and rais-
ing children who may be born to them or adopted by them?*

Spong: I regard the blessing of gay or lesbian couples by the
church to be inevitable, right, and a positive good. We must be
willing to relinquish prejudice and turn our attention to loving
our gay and lesbian brothers and sisters, supporting them, and
relating to them as a part of God's good creation. That will inevitably include accepting, affirming and blessing those gay and
lesbian relationships that, like all holy relationships, produce
the fruits of the spirit—love, joy, peace, patience, and self-
sacrifice—and to do so in the confidence that though this may
not be in accordance with the literal letter of the biblical texts,
it is in touch with the life-giving spirit that always breaks the
bondage of literalism.

This is a step the church must take *for the church's sake,* to be
cleansed from our sin of complicity in their oppression. We
need to affirm God's Word in creation that "it is not good for
man (woman) to live alone." It is this Word of God that calls us
to act now.

"In Christ," said Paul, "shall all be made alive." Yes, *all,* including the gay and lesbian couples who have become in Christ
one flesh. *Now* is the time to break the bondage of this prejudice that prevents that gift of life promised to all by the Christ
from being realized.

Modifying the Norm

Nugent: Catholic teaching is that genital sexual union has its
true meaning in the context of heterosexual marriage grounded
in the procreative and unitive dimensions of gender differences
and sexual identity. This is the "norm" or what sexuality *ought* to
be. It is the ideal form for full genital expression which is approved by God. Where we got this norm, whether it should be
the only norm, and how or whether it applies to gay and lesbian
people are critical questions today for some church groups and
theologians. A norm can be upheld in general, but modified
when applied to special unique cases. Behavior which goes
against the general norm might be acceptable for some people in
unique and individual and exceptional cases as exceptions or ac-
commodations. Gay and lesbian individuals who do not fit the
heterosexual norm might be encouraged to embrace and affirm
their own sexual reality and strive for the most human, loving
and religious way to live their lives in keeping with fundamental
values of stable family life, sacrificial love, faithful and life-
giving relationships. A religious ceremony would say clearly that
the couple took their relationship with God seriously and would
also witness to the social impact of their relationship on others of
the faith community. Caring for children born of prior heterosex-

ual unions, adopted or foster children by a same-gender couple would not only be "approved" by God, but would be a serious religious obligation coming from one's belief in and commitment to God. The issue of procreation in a same-gender relationship through technology (artificial insemination, test tube babies, third-party donors, surrogate motherhood, etc.) raises more complex and serious ethical and legal issues about personal dignity, the nature of human sexuality and the rights and limitations connected with human life and technology.

Periodical Bibliography

The following articles have been selected to supplement the diverse views presented in this chapter.

Michelle Bearden	"Single Catholics: Can We Talk About S-E-X?" *U.S. Catholic*, August 1993.
Lisa Sowle Cahill	"Abortion, Sex, and Gender: The Church's Public Voice," *America*, May 5, 1993.
Jim Castelli	"Abuse of Faith: How to Understand the Crime of Priest Pedophilia," *U.S. Catholic*, August 1993.
Robert George	"Sexual Morality's Positive Goals and the Problem of Legalism," *Origins*, April 22, 1993. Available from the Catholic News Service, 3211 Fourth St. NE, Washington, DC 20017-1100.
Peter J. Gomes	"Homophobic? Re-read Your Bible," *The New York Times*, August 17, 1992.
Stanton L. Jones	"The Loving Opposition," *Christianity Today*, July 19, 1993.
Mark Matousek	"Addicted to Sex," *Common Boundary*, March/April 1993. Available from 4304 East-West Hwy., Bethesda, MD 20814.
R. Walker Nickless	"Priestly Sex Scandals and Media Lust," *The Wall Street Journal*, November 30, 1993.
The Ramsey Colloquium	"Morality and Homosexuality," *The Wall Street Journal*, February 24, 1994.
Heather Rhoads	"Cruel Crusade: The Holy War Against Lesbians and Gays," *The Progressive*, March 1993.
Thomas H. Stahel	"'I'm Here': An Interview with Andrew Sullivan [the gay Catholic editor of the *New Republic*]," *America*, May 8, 1993.
Sheryl Temaat	"Lust Darkens the Mind," *Fidelity*, December 1992. Available from 206 Marquette Ave., South Bend, IN 46617.
William Tucker	"Monogamy and Its Discontents," *National Review*, October 4, 1993.
Michael J. Ybarra	"Going Straight: Christian Groups Press Gay People to Take a Heterosexual Path," *The Wall Street Journal*, April 21, 1993.

2 CHAPTER

How Should
Society Regard
Gays and Lesbians?

Chapter Preface

Gays, lesbians, and issues related to homosexuality are garnering more exposure in public, particularly in the media, than ever before. For example, gay characters are regularly portrayed in popular television series such as *Melrose Place* and motion pictures such as *Philadelphia*. In real life, singer k.d. lang, actress Sandra Bernhard, and other entertainers have openly discussed their homosexual or bisexual lifestyles. Media giant Time Warner, publishers of *Time* and *Life* magazines, announced in January 1994 that it was creating a magazine aimed at gays and lesbians.

Such media visibility, particularly on television, has prompted debate about the effects of such exposure on the public. For example, homosexuals and their supporters welcome the positive portrayals of gay and lesbian characters on television as a step toward greater tolerance. According to Newton Deiter, executive director of the Gay Media Task Force, "The more TV reveals the truth of gay life and that relationships are no different no matter the gender, the more it promotes tolerance and shows that gay stereotypes are not real." However, critics argue that these portrayals of gays and lesbians promote a perverse and destructive lifestyle. Regarding the 1993 children's special "Other Mothers," about a teenage boy who lives with his lesbian mother and her lover, columnist Brent Bozell charged, "Not once was a rational argument against gay rights, the homosexual lifestyle, or even the detrimental effects of same-sex parents presented."

Increased media focus on gays and lesbians may reflect the homosexual activist slogan "We're here. We're queer. Get used to it"—a trend long overdue in the minds of many Americans. Others, however, assert that a biased media is spreading propaganda that homosexual lifestyles are acceptable and normal. The authors of the following viewpoints debate how society should regard homosexuality.

*"While I've seen homosexuality through [others']
eyes—having been raised to do so—they've never
seen it through mine."*

Homosexuality Is Normal

Bruce Bawer

Homosexuality is simply a matter of being, Bruce Bawer argues in the following viewpoint, and homosexuals have no more and no different problems than anyone else. Bawer rejects arguments that homosexuality is wrong or a personality disorder, as well as words such as homosexual "activity" or "practice" that dehumanize homosexuals. He contends that labeling homosexuality wrong or abnormal is largely due to homophobia and ignorance. Bawer writes regularly for the *Wall Street Journal* and is the author of *A Place at the Table: The Gay Individual in American Society*, from which this viewpoint is excerpted.

As you read, consider the following questions:

1. According to Bawer, why is homophobia powerful and irrational?
2. Why did many gays of past generations suffer from mental disorders, in Bawer's opinion?
3. Why does the author reject criticism of homosexual behavior?

Excerpted from Bruce Bawer, *A Place at the Table: The Gay Individual in American Society*, pp. 81, 94-97, 150-52. Copyright ©1993 by Bruce Bawer. Reprinted by permission of Poseidon Press, a division of Simon & Schuster, Inc.

Homophobia. In a world of prejudice, there is no other prejudice quite like it. Mainstream writers, politicians, and cultural leaders who hate Jews or blacks or Asians but who have long since accepted the unwritten rules that forbid public expression of those prejudices still denounce gays with impunity. For such people, gays are the Other in a way that Jews or blacks or Asians are not. After all, they can look at Jewish or black or Asian family life and see something that, in its chief components—husband, wife, children, workplace, school, house of worship—is essentially a variation on their own lives; yet when they look at gays—or, rather, at the image of gays that has been fostered both by the mainstream culture and by the gay subculture—they see creatures whose lives seem to be different from theirs in every possible way.

Irrational Prejudice

Peter J. Gomes, an American Baptist minister and professor of Christian morals at Harvard University, has described homophobia as "the last respectable prejudice of the century." Certainly there is no other prejudice in which people feel more morally justified; no other prejudice that reaches so high into the ranks of the intelligent, the powerful, the otherwise quite virtuous; no other prejudice, therefore, more deep-seated and polarizing. There is, one would wager, no other prejudice that takes more irrational forms. One sees Christians hatefully reviling homosexual love in the name of Christ, whose supreme commandment was to "love one another." And one sees defenders of "the family" citing gay rights as the greatest threat to "family values"—as if homosexuals didn't have families by whom they longed to be accepted, as if anything that deserved the name of "family values" didn't include the idea of parents responding humanely to the news of their child's homosexuality, as if it somehow served the cause of "the family" to heap abuse on the idea of same-sex couples (the obvious alternative to which, of course, is gay promiscuity). . . .

The most striking fact about anti-gay prejudice in America is not that it has endured for so long; it is that Americans who disapprove of homosexuality have refused to face the deep contradictions inherent in their attitudes. But of course doing so would involve *thinking* about those attitudes, and homosexuality is something that many people simply don't want to think about.

Moral Attitudes

For many, these attitudes seem to come terribly easily. Most people who engage in anti-gay rhetoric, while claiming to speak from profound religious or moral conviction, haven't put much serious thought into their censures. The widely held view of homosexuality as "wrong" is not unlike antebellum Southern whites' notion that slavery was morally defensible: both attitudes are long-established, socially entrenched, taken for granted. One would think that any Christian halfway sincere in his religious beliefs—which demand of him that, above all else, he love and not hate—would be anguished at the thought of having to condemn millions of people for their sexual orientation. One would think that such a person might examine the relevant scripture in order to see if there was some basis for acceptance instead of condemnation; one would think he might read a book like John Boswell's *Christianity, Social Tolerance, and Homosexuality* in order to understand how it is that many good, intelligent people, straight and gay alike, sincerely see no contradiction between homosexual life and Christian belief. But such serious reflection and soul searching on the topic of homosexuality appear to take place far less often than they should. On the contrary, when it comes to discussions of the moral dimension of homosexuality, illogic, closed-mindedness, and the reiteration of age-old formulas are the order of the day.

Where Is the Wrong?

What underlies most of this prejudice? Opponents of homosexuality use different words. They contend variously that they find it "evil," "wrong," "sick." "Evil" is a religious person's verdict; "wrong" is a secular person's verdict; "sick" is the verdict of a person with pretensions to psychological expertise. Each verdict is the result of someone reaching for the nearest available term to label, and to damn, something that confuses him or makes him uncomfortable.

What can someone mean when he says that "homosexuality is wrong"? That to be born homosexual makes one automatically a malefactor? Or could it be that the crime lies in accepting one's sexuality and in trying to lead a loving and committed life with another human being? Or does the crime not begin until your hands touch? Your lips? Your genitalia? Moreover, if homosexuality is wrong, who is wronged by it—the homosexual person? Society in general? Young people who are in danger of being "recruited"? Do these questions sound frivolous? They're not. What's frivolous is to state unequivocally that homosexuality is "wrong" without asking oneself such questions and figuring out exactly what one means.

The Disorder Myth

And what of the argument that homosexuality is not wrong but "sick"—a psychological disorder? This popular view is expressed by one D. L. Forston, M.D., of Gary, Indiana, who in a letter to the *New Republic* argues that "the depression, mental illness and substance abuse associated with the lifestyle cannot be fully accounted for by reaction to societal isolation and hostility. In short, homosexuality is a personality disorder at best and a mental illness at worst." "Cannot be fully accounted for"? How can Dr. Forston possibly know this? He obviously has no idea what most homosexuals have to go through day by day in the way of inadvertent reminders that they are considered evil, depraved, emotionally disturbed, or just plain anomalous. Dr. Forston's views notwithstanding, it has for many years seemed remarkable to me that, given these daily assaults, there aren't *more* gay alcoholics and depressives and so on.

The Highest Form of Life and Friendship

Plato says that the highest form of human life is one in which a male pursues "the love of a young man along with philosophy," and is transported by passionate desire. He describes the experience of falling in love with another male in moving terms, and defends relationships that are mutual and reciprocal over relationships that are one-sided. He depicts his pairs of lovers as spending their life together in the pursuit of intellectual and spiritual activities, combined with political participation. (Although no marriages for these lovers are mentioned, it was the view of the time that this form of life does not prevent its participants from having a wife at home, whom they saw only rarely and for procreative purposes.)

Aristotle speaks far less about sexual love than does Plato, but it is evident that he too finds in male-male relationships the potential for the highest form of friendship, a friendship based on mutual well-wishing and mutual awareness of good character and good aims.

Martha Nussbaum, *The New Republic*, November 15, 1993.

Of course, if one considers homosexuality a personality disorder or mental illness, then every homosexual is by definition an emotional cripple, however sane and stable he may be in comparison to the average heterosexual. But to make such a blanket diagnosis is preposterous. Medical science has always classified psychological phenomena as disorders, rather than as mere variations, on the basis of their consequences in the real world. In other words, a given psychological phenomenon cannot be objectively classified as a disorder unless it gives rise, of itself, to some sort of maladjustment. A generation and more ago, in a time when one could not even go to a gay bar without fear of arrest, homosexuals suffered severe neuroses—or even psychoses—at a rate higher than they do now and manifested higher rates of alcoholism, drug addiction, and suicide. They suffered these problems not because they were gay but because they had been raised to think that homosexuality was an abomination, because they had to live with the knowledge that virtually everyone around them considered them morally corrupt, and because the fear of ostracism, denunciation, and imprisonment forced them to keep their sexual orientation a secret. Only the most uncommon individuals could live with perfect sanity and serenity under such circumstances; most could not. So it was that psychiatrists designated homosexuality as a psychological disorder.

No Worse Problems

The almost universal opprobrium with which homosexuals once lived has not entirely dissipated. Yet homosexuals are now permitted to live more openly and with less fear of persecution, and are accordingly more productive and more emotionally balanced than ever before. It is clear that self-respecting homosexuals who live openly among accepting people have no more problems or different problems than anyone else; in an accepting society, they can lead lives that are, in every respect but sexual orientation, indistinguishable from the lives of heterosexuals. This is not true of schizophrenics, psychotics, and other people classified as suffering from psychological disorders. Such people suffer real problems of adjustment that are caused entirely by their psychological disorders and that could not be avoided by any modifications in social attitudes or behavior. Given this simple practical fact, to label homosexuality a "sickness" or a "psychological disorder" is simply name calling—an attempt to pigeonhole and patronize something that the pigeonholer may well find threatening for reasons having to do with his own psychological problems. Certainly if homosexuality were a psychological disorder, it would have to be considered a unique one: for the "sufferers" who experience the greatest emotional health are those who confidently reject the idea that it is a psychological disorder, while the greatest psychological damage is suffered by those homosexuals who have allowed themselves to be persuaded that they're suffering from a sickness. . . .

Dehumanizing Words

When two heterosexuals meet each other, it usually doesn't occur to one of them to imagine the other having sex. But when a heterosexual who doesn't know many homosexuals meets someone whom he knows to be gay, that person's sexuality becomes, for the heterosexual, the cardinal fact about him, subsuming every other attribute. The heterosexual can't *help* imagining the homosexual in bed—and he doesn't like what he sees.

Because the thought of homosexual sex affects so many heterosexuals so strongly and negatively, it is in the interests of opponents of homosexuality and gay rights to focus attention on bedroom matters. By using such dehumanizing words as "practice" and "activity," anti-gay activists reduce profound personal relationships to graphic peep-show images. These words isolate the sexual act; they strip it from the context of life and love and partnership and hold it up for all to see, naked, scandalous, and clinically explicit. Most homosexuals want to fall in love, to be part of a couple, to make a life with someone else. Sex is usually an important part of the picture, but it's *only* a part. Yet heterosexuals who speak of "activity" either can't see, or don't want others to see, beyond that part. Words like "activity" and "practice" also accomplish something else: they downplay recognition of the homosexual as a kind of person whose sexual orientation cannot be changed, while implying a connection between homosexuality and such objectively self-destructive (and reversible) behavioral phenomena as heavy drinking and drug taking. "Rehabilitation" model[s] to the contrary, homosexuality is not a bad habit or addiction of which a gay person can and should be broken; it's about the whole way that one experiences love and human attachment in this world, if one happens to be gay.

Anti-Gay Hypocrisy

For all the propagandists' emphasis on "activity," moreover, in reality such institutions as the armed forces, the Boy Scouts, and the clergy of many Protestant denominations terminate membership on the basis not of sexual activity but of sexual orientation. If a soldier is discovered having sex with another man, he may be permitted to stay in the Army so long as he testifies that he's not homosexual—that the liaison, in other words, was an example of what is called "situational homosexuality." If a soldier is not discovered having sex with another man but simply admits that he is homosexual, he will be discharged. Such policies point up the hypocrisy of the anti-gay activists' emphasis on "activity"; for, in one institution after another, the real target is not individuals (gay or straight) who may have done certain things in bed but individuals whose natural sexual orientation differs from that of the majority.

Many heterosexuals use words like "behavior" to describe homosexuals' personal lives in a way at which they would take grave offense if someone spoke thus about them. In a *Commentary* essay on the homosexual English novelist E. M. Forster, for example, Cynthia Ozick writes that "the Gay Liberation argument that homosexual activity is a positive good in a world afflicted by overpopulation would not have won Forster over." Her opinion of Forster and "the Gay Liberation argument" aside, what startles one about this sentence is the phrase "homosexual activity." What Ozick shares with her husband is, one presumes, a loving home; what two men living together share is "homosexual activity." One is dismayed to see Ozick, a sensitive and intelligent writer, using so unspeakably cruel, insulting, and diminishing a phrase.

Natural Behavior

Some opponents of gay rights follow the Roman Catholic Church's formula: the Church, recognizing that homosexuals are born gay and can't do anything about it, opposes "homosexual conduct," not "homosexual orientation." Referring to [his deputy's] position paper on homosexuality, Captain Larry H. Ellis, the Marine Corps chaplain, said that it was not intended to be "hostile toward persons who are homosexuals—just hostile toward homosexual behavior." Yet to recognize homosexual orientation as naturally occurring and morally neutral, while insisting that acting upon that orientation is, in every instance and without exception, abnormal, unnatural, and perverse, makes no sense. If homosexual "behavior" comes as naturally to gays as heterosexual "behavior" comes to straight people, then how can heterosexual sex in marriage be seen as a blessing, a virtue, and a force for good, while homosexual sex within a committed long-term relationship is seen as an evil, deviant urge that must be resisted?

When decent, well-meaning people say that they don't mind homosexuals but are simply "opposed to homosexual behavior," all I can think is that such unintentional heartlessness could only be the result of a failure to consider, or an inability to imagine, how things look through my eyes. After all, I have a pretty good idea how things look to them, because like most homosexuals I've had to make my way from their point of view, which was thrust on me, to the one I have now, as my need to understand myself demanded. In short, while I've seen homosexuality through their eyes—having been raised to do so—they've never seen it through mine.

Homosexuality, at the deepest, truest level, is not a matter of *doing* something. It's a matter of *being* something.

"Homosexuality is not an inborn, normal, alternative lifestyle."

Homosexuality Is Abnormal

Roy Masters

Homosexuality is a psychological disorder that society must neither condemn nor condone, Roy Masters argues in the following viewpoint. Masters theorizes that homosexual orientation is "seeded" in many young children when they become victims of taunting or sexual abuse. He maintains that these traumatic events are so powerful that a child's identity can be involuntarily transformed to embrace homosexuality. Society can help victims overcome or prevent homosexuality, he contends, by helping them understand the true nature of the affliction and by addressing their resentment toward their violators. Masters is an expert on stress management and has hosted the syndicated radio show *How Your Mind Can Keep You Well*.

As you read, consider the following questions:

1. What are the building blocks of trauma conditioning, according to Masters?
2. How has society reacted to homosexuals and why have these responses failed to help them, in the author's opinion?
3. Why does Masters believe it is important for victims to forgive their violators?

Roy Masters, "Sex and Power: Inside the Secret World of Homosexuality and Trauma Conditioning," *New Dimensions*, January 1990. Reprinted with permission.

"This [homosexual urge] was not a matter of chance attraction to a forbidden object," explained former U.S. Representative Robert Bauman. "This was a frightening force from deep within my being, an involuntary reaction to the sight, smell, and feel of other boys. I neither understood it nor accepted it."

The above admission by Congressman Bauman is evidence of a classic case of trauma conditioning. Also referred to as Pavlovian conditioning, trauma conditioning commits the victim to a life of compulsion, wherein he has no control over his own actions, even when the compulsion is personally repulsive to him. To make matters worse, the struggle against any aberrant behavior only feeds the slavishness of that behavior—like throwing fat on a fire to extinguish the flames.

Trauma-Induced Conditioning

Homosexuality is not an inborn, normal, alternative lifestyle. It is the result of trauma-induced conditioning, from which a person can recover if he can come to understand the causative mechanisms responsible for his affliction. Most victims of homosexuality, in order to cope with the pressure and guilt involved, eventually find release by completely embracing their condition, as though it were a virtue. That is the final stage of the illness, wherein cure becomes almost impossible. And it is this conflict with which Congressman Bauman, and others like him, wrestle.

All self-destructive compulsions have a common denominator. The following explanations will make clear that the root causes of all emotional and psychological compulsions are the same as those that led to Bauman's homosexuality.

To understand this process, we must examine the building blocks of all trauma conditioning. In order for a person to be conditioned there must first be a specific type of emotional environment within him that allows the vicious domino effect of conditioning to occur. That inner environment is formed only when the victim is made to react with extreme hatred, resentment, or suppressed frustration. Experiences that produce strong negative emotions in a person create a fertile environment for the trauma conditioning/suggestion process to begin. The upset reaction in itself acts like a vacuum, drawing in negative outside suggestions from others that later on will be unknowingly acted out by the victim. He will eventually come to believe the suggestion to be his own idea. Here is an example:

Let us consider a young child who is slight, gentle, sensitive, and different, as many of us are. Put into a school environment the child starts receiving degrading comments and put-downs from other children. At first he is puzzled by this, but eventually he starts to take the insults personally. At a certain point, he starts to resent the other children for their constant degrading. . . .

If the boy has been called a "homosexual" or "weirdo," the thoughts and suggestions implanted by such cruelty now whirl around in his mind. He tries to suppress the thoughts, but the struggle of his own resistance and self-condemnation somehow lends strength to the now constant parade of internalized mental images and suggestions. Being unable to remain objective to these thoughts and see them for what they are—just thoughts—he reacts to them, mentally reliving the scene of the children taunting him. The implanted thoughts themselves now become a hypnotic reinforcement, having the same effect as the cruel children actually being there—except now they are inside of him, and there's no place to hide.

The Normal Do Not Need the Abnormal

The only parallel with a normal thing is a complementary normal thing. The homosexual is no more like the heterosexual than illogic is like logic. . . .

To put it another way, the abnormal need the normal, but the normal have no need of the abnormal. Logicians don't need the advice of the illogical. Those who don't know what four and three make are forever at the mercy of those who do. The illiterate have nothing to tell the literate about Shakespeare.

The homosexuals exist at all, in other words, only because heterosexuals beget them; the favor can't possibly be returned. And this would be true even if homosexuals were the majority. So it is beside the point to ask whether homosexuality is caused by nature or nurture. Many deformities are caused by nature; so are baldness and diabetes. We nevertheless recognize them as undesirable.

Joseph Sobran, *The Human Life Review*, Spring 1993.

The more he reacts to the thoughts, the more they bond to his psyche. In other words, the more he rebels and tries to reject the suggestions implanted in him through his reactions to cruelty, the more that very struggle gives power to the suggestion. The ultimate conquest of those suggestions over the boy comes with his final and total acceptance of the implanted identity that was projected into him by others by way of his original upset/angry reactions. . . .

Consider a similar example, but let's say now that a young boy is raped by an older boy. Humiliated, the rage he feels, of which he may not be conscious, immediately awakens sexual feelings for the violator in the same way as described above, only with greater intensity. Hating himself only amplifies the sexual hunger for the violator. Loving what he hates, hating what he loves, he eventually evolves into the very thing he hates—a violator and molester himself. . . .

Homosexual Relationships

Homosexual relationships are formed through the need for identity—a sense of being whole. But one simply becomes more completely homosexual, and never completely one's true original self. Strangely enough, the compulsion a kleptomaniac has to steal carries with it the same aphrodisiac effect, as though stealing objects were a kind of love fulfillment.

A little-known fact is again presented for your personal examination: All violations are sexual (although, of course, not all sex is violation). All traumas produce sexual feelings toward the violator or toward the object through which the violation came. Many of us are sexual "love slaves" of another person for the sake of identity.

We have looked at how homosexual orientation can be "seeded" into an innocent person through violation. Now, when the violator rewards or gratifies this implanted need in another, i.e., has homosexual sex with him, he completes the sexual identity of his victim. The reason: Homosexual "love," the fulfillment of the "seed"-need implanted by the violator, is as much a violation, only in a different form, as the cruel destruction of original innocence was itself. Therefore, the second violation (sex) now intensifies the sexual feeling of sensual love (fulfillment) for the violator, ending in the very emotion that caused the sexual feelings originally—hatred.

The Victim's Life

This need to be love-violated is transferred to familiar forms—to persons, places, and things throughout the victim's life. The sight, the smell, the touch, the look, the "wicked glint in the eye," all awaken in the victim the compulsion to seek completion, through the acceptance and support of another, of an identity gone wrong. Sights, smells, noises, memorabilia, colors, look-alike people, objects that were originally present in forgotten trauma scenes, secretly govern the lives and strange loyalties of violated people.

The terrible forces controlling Congressman Bauman [who stated he was violated at age six by an older boy] are also the forces that control our own lives. Some of us are still alive inside as true identities, fighting a life and death struggle for the survival of who we really are.

There are two distinct sides to most people: the original self identity, and the side that has been conditioned to act out a

70

whole set of unnatural behavior patterns. These implanted or imprinted behaviors originated in the wills of violators, who themselves were most probably violated. Later in life those behaviors are reinforced by exploiters, to whom we unconsciously hand over our lives, thinking our relationship to be love.

Even in the case of extreme perversions, such as homosexual pedophilia or bestiality, one must remember there are two distinctly different groups that engage in such activity. One group consists of those who are truly unwilling slaves of compulsion, created through anger and trauma, as described earlier. The other group, however, consists of hard-core, egotistical deniers of reality—decadent, militant individuals who have justified their own sickness to the point of thinking perversity is a virtue. These people think backwards. Whatever their original substance was before the conditioning process exists no longer. What we are dealing with here is human evil. Organizations such as the Rene Guyon Society and the well-known North American Man-Boy Love Association (NAMBLA), which regularly march with their own banners in Gay Pride parades, also publish literature instructing people how to have sex with infants.

How Society Reacts

There have always been two ways, it seems, that society or individuals have dealt with these deviants. The first has been a strong reaction, based on fear or anger, which leads to the horror of extreme treatment of the offender. The second way starts off as an extreme reaction, but turns into the embrace of the abnormal behavior of the offender. This is accomplished when our guilt (from reacting so angrily) turns into false compassion. Either extreme fails to cope with the underlying reasons for the problem. And, believe it or not, the "compassionate" way of dealing with the offender may be the more dangerous of the two, because "compassion" in today's society is often false and guilt-based, and tends to make problems worse.

Anger, reaction, and violence on the one hand, or false compassion on the other, can never solve the problem. The extreme of one way reinforces and hardens the extreme of the other.

There is a third way. Society has traditionally lumped homosexuals, pedophiles, and criminals together. (In Thomas Jefferson's day, the punishment for rape, sodomy, or bestiality was death. In what he believed to be a merciful gesture, Jefferson asked the Virginia legislature in 1777 to at least make the punishment mere castration.) But if such people can be handled with true compassion—a compassion that is not motivated by a desire to prove that you are fair, or by false guilt—then those offenders who want to return to their original selves can be helped. Such people can and do learn to come back to innocence through being taught how to deal with rage, how to forgive, how to understand those who violated them. Through giving up anger, we are released from the strange hypnotic conditioning that permeates our lives.

Disordered Behavior

We do not doubt that many gays and lesbians—perhaps especially those who seek the blessing of our religious communities—believe that theirs is the only form of love, understood as affection and erotic satisfaction, of which they are capable. Nor do we doubt that they have found in such relationships something of great personal significance, since even a distorted love retains traces of love's grandeur. Where there is love in morally disordered relationships we do not censure the love. We censure the form in which that love seeks expression. To those who say that this disordered behavior is so much at the core of their being that the person cannot be (and should not be) distinguished from the behavior, we can only respond that we earnestly hope they are wrong.

The Ramsey Colloquium, *First Things*, March 1994.

This third way of dealing with the strange, aberrant behavior is true, calm compassion. True compassion shows others where they are wrong by your not responding wrongly. True compassion does not condemn, nor condone. It gives space, allowing the sincere victim of compulsion to see the true nature of his affliction, and thereby be freed from it. At the same time, this type of compassion cannot be manipulated by a hardened offender. Rather, such people experience great guilt and conflict when they discover that they cannot justify and excuse their position by confusing you into becoming sympathetic to their sickness. (This is similar to the way a troubled child feels when he cannot convince his parents that he is right, when he is actually wrong, and they know it. The child probably feels that the parents are being cruel and unreasonable, but who is *really* being unreasonable?)

Abnormal Behavior

In the case of homosexuality in our society, too long were these unfortunate deviants ridiculed and driven underground by an overreactive, angry, and pseudo-religious populace. Little attempt has been made to deeply understand the roots of their abnormal behavior. Instead a guilty, overreactive populace has now gone to the opposite extreme, coddling this behavior and compounding the sickness. Instead of helping homosexuals, false compassion drives them further into their own perversion, robbing them of the opportunity to truly overcome their problem.

It is important, in learning to deal with these troubled people, to realize the trauma/conditioning nature of their affliction. Without that understanding and true compassion, we are all in danger of embracing and confirming their lifestyles, which will condemn them to the hell of empty relationships and self-condemnation, or celebrating their disease as a virtue. If one becomes angry and violent with homosexuals, like the skinheads, that response merely consolidates the self-righteousness gays feel in being unfairly persecuted. But the flip side of this anger against homosexuals is guilt, which can be manipulated into pseudo-conversion, and ultimately approval and support. This type of extreme emotional swing is commonly used and manipulated by politically astute homosexual activists to support a growing political power base held by a minority of troubled individuals (homosexuals).

Since this question has never really been dealt with openly in society, the problem has now become critical. As noted earlier, homosexuality is not a "normal, healthy, alternative lifestyle"; it is the result of a seldom-discussed Pavlovian conditioning process. And it is important to remember that most homosexuals have been deeply traumatized and suffer a sort of hypnotic amnesia of the event. They can, therefore, say with "perfect honesty" that they were born that way, not having any memory of being normal. Indeed, their trauma could have entered and imprinted them soon after they came into a too cruel world.

Destructive Condemnation

Some gays don't want to be that way, but are driven by some deep implanted drive. In Congressman Robert Bauman's own words, "Some inner force drove me, and repeatedly pursuing this insane conduct made it more difficult to resist each time I was tempted again. . . . Each time I would feel a great guilt and head for Saturday confession at St. Peter's or St. Joseph's on Capitol Hill so I could make amends with God . . . always vowing to myself and God I would never do it again." Do you see the terrible suffering of this man? Unable to find release from his affliction, even from his church, the only honest thing left to do, it seemed, was to completely surrender to the affliction itself, to accept his homosexuality and be accepted for it. Being accepted for it, however, is the end of the road, the ultimate cruelty for the suffering Congressman, robbing him of the chance to find true understanding, and through this the ability to forgive those who traumatized him, which would be the resolution of his problem.

But to condemn him would be the extreme horror. Have you ever had a bad habit like biting your nails or smoking, and had someone condemn or nag you about it? What happened? You rebelled and got worse, or, motivated by rage, you struggled to get better, but the very rage you used in trying to overcome the problem only aggravated it. Eventually you gave in to the problem, which overwhelmed you using your own energy. Therefore, moral support, "feeling sorry," supportively accepting someone in their sick condition, homosexual or whatever, is destructive, just as extreme condemnation is destructive.

Watching for Resentment

Very often good people resent those who sympathize with their faults. They somehow sense they are being robbed of personal growth, through which they might have overcome their faults. The resentment they feel towards this type of coddling has the same effect on them as the resentment they experience when someone condemns them; either way, their problem is compounded.

Here is a simple secret for all those who would overcome any conditioning: Become objective. Watch for that subtle resentment rising when you are coddled, and also when you are ridiculed and degraded. No traumatic experience could ever become traumatic without your hatred towards the offender. Resentment towards the effect of the trauma, say, biting nails, smoking, an ulcer, even homosexuality, is exactly the same as hating the person who violated you and caused you to have those symptoms. Forgiving those who violated you and letting go of the hatred towards the offender is a cleansing process that eventually restores the individual to his original self. In addition, becoming objective to your compulsion—neither hating yourself, nor agreeing with the condition—will also have the same cleansing effect.

Struggling within yourself with resentment and self-loathing feeds the cycle. Resentment causes the problem to enter, and resentment towards the problem reinforces the trauma, making the problem bigger. This holds true, as well, when people offer you false compassion. This type of unhealthy nurturing encourages us to continue failing as though it were a virtue. So we die in the process of living.

Society needs to come to grips with homosexuality. It has swung from one extreme of hatred and condemnation, to the opposite extreme that we are now witnessing—of not only acceptance, but even special privilege and reverse prejudice. Homosexuals will be the unfortunate victims either way.

"The homosexual 'rights' movement is proceeding with its assault upon what remains of America's sexual morality."

Gays and Lesbians Are a Danger to Society

William Norman Grigg

Homosexuals and their campaign for gay rights and for tolerance toward gays and lesbians are a serious threat to religion, education, and the rest of American society, William Norman Grigg argues in the following viewpoint. Grigg describes how vehement homosexuals verbally and physically attack the religious community for any opposition to homosexuality. The author also contends that homosexuals are targeting schools to garner support for their deviant lifestyle. Grigg is a contributing writer for the *New American*, a biweekly conservative magazine.

As you read, consider the following questions:

1. How are homosexuals using the media to win public support, according to Grigg?
2. What tactics do homosexual activists use against the religious community, in the author's opinion?
3. According to Grigg, what has been the result of the Massachusetts pro-gay school program?

Abridged from William Norman Grigg, "The Lavender Revolution," *The New American*, January 24, 1994. Reprinted with permission.

During the 18th-century French Culture War, which ended in the French Revolution and the Napoleonic dictatorship, Christian writer Guillaume Francois Berthier described the fashion in which cultural debates had been framed: "The custom has been to call 'philosophers' those who attack revealed religion, and 'persecutors' those who battle for its defense." In contemporary America a similar custom presently prevails, in which leftists—however violent—are said to represent the forces of "tolerance," and traditionalists—however peaceful—are portrayed as agents of "hate" and "violence." This double standard is most visible in the campaign to normalize homosexuality.

A Media Campaign for Gays

In the late 1980s, media analysts Marshall K. Kirk and Erastes Pill outlined a media campaign designed to win public support for the "gay rights" revolution. Noted the authors, "The first order of business is the desensitization of the American public concerning gays and gay rights. To desensitize the public is to help it view homosexuality with indifference rather than keen emotion. . . . You can forget about trying to persuade the masses that homosexuality is a good thing. But if only you can get them to think that it is just another thing . . . then your battle for legal and social rights is virtually won."

According to Kirk and Pill, once the public has been persuaded that moral indifference is a virtue, homosexuals would be able to use the mass media to "portray gays as victims, not as aggressive challengers. In any campaign to win over the public, gays must be cast as victims in need of protection so that straights will be inclined by reflex to assume the role of protector." Once the public has been beguiled into believing that "decency" requires support for "gay rights," public hostility must be focused upon those who remain committed to traditional morality:

> At a later stage of the media campaign for gay rights . . . it will be time to get tough. To be blunt, [traditionalists] must be vilified. . . . The public should be shown images of ranting homophobes whose secondary traits and beliefs disgust middle America. These images might include: the Ku Klux Klan demanding that gays be burned alive or [tortured]; bigoted southern ministers drooling with hysterical hatred to a degree that looks both comical and deranged.

With a calculated dishonesty that would have won the admiration of [Nazi propaganda leader] Joseph Goebbels, the homosexual movement and its media allies have followed this strategy. In contemporary popular culture, any expression of opposition to homosexuality, no matter how temperate and intellectually sound, is immediately free-associated with violent bigotry. Having defined the rules of engagement in America's Culture

War, the homosexual "rights" movement is proceeding with its assault upon what remains of America's sexual morality.

Urvashi Vaid, former executive director of the Gay and Lesbian Alliance Against Defamation, issued the following directive to the "gay rights" movement in the December 14, 1993, issue of *The Advocate* magazine: "The Gay and Lesbian religious movement has to come out politically and create a national religious council to promote tolerance, oppose theocracy, and fight monotheism."

Britt/Copley News Service. Reprinted with permission.

A key figure in the lavender jihad may be the "Reverend" Mel White, who presides over the Cathedral of Hope Metropolitan Community Church in Dallas (the Metropolitan Community Church is a homosexual denomination). White made a reputation for himself as a ghostwriter in the employ of such Evangelical leaders as Billy Graham and Jerry Falwell. Even as he lent his pen to the expression of biblical principles, White surrendered himself to the indulgence of his sexual impulses. He eventually descended into the homosexual "lifestyle," leaving behind his wife of 25 years. . . .

On the August 13, 1993, edition of CNN's *Larry King Live*, White stated: "I'm a member of ACT-UP [AIDS Coalition to Unleash Power]. I know what we do and what we don't do." White must certainly be aware that ACT-UP frequently disrupts religious services and conducts campaigns of harassment, violence, and intimidation. He should also be aware that ACT-UP/DC [in Washington, D.C.], arguably the organization's most influential chapter, was organized by activists who used Adolf Hitler's *Mein Kampf* as their tactical bible. Predictably, nobody in the Establishment media saw fit to examine the implications of White's admitted membership in ACT-UP.

Using the Cathedral of Hope as a base of operations, White intends to conduct a "personal war" against the Religious Right, which he describes as "the enemy . . . a threat to the warp and woof of American society." Speaking on *Larry King Live*, White charged that Christian conservatives "use gays to make money, and the suffering from their rhetoric trickles down and causes death—literally."

The "trickle-down" metaphor was given fuller development by White in this statement he made to the *Washington Post*:

> We [homosexual activists] have gone underground and we have people in every one of the Religious Right's organizations. We're on their mailing lists. We're reading everything they're putting out. We think the words from their mouths trickle down into violence. And when our evidence reaches a critical mass, we're going to use the best attorneys in this country to bring a class action suit in 50 states to have it stopped.

What exactly do White and his allies seek to "stop," and how would they "have it stopped"? Would they ask the federal government to suppress "homophobic" speech, or—in the fashion of White's ACT-UP comrades—disrupt "homophobic" worship services? Clearly, White's crusade against the Religious Right should be looked upon as a threat to what remains of America's religious liberty. . . .

A Gay Mob Riots

On September 19, 1993, a mob of homosexuals surrounded the Hamilton Square Baptist Church in San Francisco. They had been aroused to action by two newspaper articles announcing that the service on the Sunday night in question would feature an address by Reverend Lou Sheldon of the Traditional Values Coalition. Reverend Sheldon has been an outspoken defender of the biblical teaching that homosexuality is an abomination before God.

Dr. David Innes, pastor of the Hamilton Square Church, noted in a press release that before the local press publicized Sheldon's visit, "Only the church's membership and regular attenders were notified of this service, through the church's own Sunday bulletin." During the week before the September 19th meeting, Innes received two phone calls demanding that Sheldon be disinvited. The church was also visited by two homosexual activists who told the building's caretaker that Sheldon would not be allowed to speak on the following Sunday. Fearing for the safety of his congregation, Dr. Innes formally requested protection from the Northern Station police division. "You must understand," Dr. Innes was told, "this is San Francisco." Innes persisted until he received assurances that police would "monitor" the Sunday evening gathering.

The mob began to assemble around the church at 5:00 p.m. Sunday evening; an hour later the protest had evolved into a full-scale riot. The protesters essentially seized control of the church grounds and attempted to prevent worshippers from entering the chapel. Church property was damaged; obscene handbills were plastered on the building's walls and windows; worshippers were assaulted with obscenities and pelted with stones. A group of the protesters tore down the Christian flag that had been on display in front of the church and replaced it with the rainbow flag of the "Queer Nation.". . .

Death Threats

Shortly after the protest, Dr. Innes received an anonymous phone message containing a bomb threat. Pastor Charles McIlhenny, who was in attendance at Hamilton Square Church on September 19th, can testify that such threats are not to be lightly dismissed. In 1983, McIlhenny and his family narrowly escaped death when his First Orthodox Presbyterian Church was fire-bombed. Although the assailant was never captured, the McIlhenny family suspects that the murder attempt was made in reprisal for McIlhenny's public opposition to the homosexual lobby. Since 1977, the McIlhenny family has received numerous death threats from radical homosexuals. The problems began when Pastor McIlhenny dismissed a church organist who was an unrepentant homosexual. . . .

McIlhenny recalls receiving phone calls "describing our children—by name, appearance, where they attended school, when they got out of school, and what sexually deviant behavior was to be practiced on the children before killing them." Not surprisingly, McIlhenny has urged parents to understand the implications of what he calls the "homosexualization" of public education.

Gay Youths and Suicide

In a column published in *The Advocate* magazine, lesbian activist Donna Minkowitz urged her comrades to "take the offensive for a change, whether the issue is promiscuity or recruiting the previously straight. . . . Ten percent is not enough! Recruit, recruit, recruit!" Increasingly, the "gay rights" movement is pursuing recruiting efforts through the public school system—in the name of "suicide prevention."

In January 1989, the Department of Health and Human Services published a four-volume report on the problem of teen suicide in America. That report contained a brief polemical essay entitled "Gay Male and Lesbian Suicide," written by an obscure San Francisco social worker named Paul Gibson. The article was not an empirical study, yet it has been cited ad nauseam by the "gay rights" movement and its apologists to prove that "homophobia" is a murderous social pathology.

Gibson began with the now-universally discredited Kinsey premise that ten percent of the population is innately homosexual. On the basis of that fraudulent statistic, Gibson offered this contribution to apocryphal social science: "Given the higher rates of suicidal feelings and behavior among gay youth in comparison with other young people this means that 20–30 percent of all youth suicides may involve gay youth." Gibson cited no studies, adduced no clinical evidence, and offered no documentary support to fortify this claim.

Perverse and Promiscuous

Recent studies indicate that male homosexuals average between 20 and 106 partners every year. The average homosexual has 300 to 500 partners in his lifetime. Thirty-seven percent, it is reported, engage in sadomasochism and at least 20 percent have sexual relations with more than 1000 men. Compared to heterosexuals, male homosexuals are more than 8 times more likely to have had hepatitis, 14 times more likely to have had syphilis and 5000 times more likely to have contracted AIDS.

Allan C. Brownfeld, *The Washington Inquirer*, April 23, 1993.

Gibson blamed the traditional home and conventional religion for the problems experienced by suicidal homosexual youth. He described religion as a "risk factor in gay youth suicide because of the depiction of homosexuality as a sin and the reliance of families on the church for understanding homosexuality." Gibson's essay—which was included in a taxpayer-funded federal report—censured "traditional (e.g., Catholic) and fundamentalist (e.g., Evangelical) faiths [which] still portray homosexuality as morally wrong or evil."

Gibson's unsupported conclusions are contradicted by Professor Edward Wynne of the University of Illinois-Chicago, who offered the keynote address at the 1987 national Youth Suicide Conference. According to Wynne, traditional religious belief is perhaps the single most effective deterrent to youth suicide. . . .

In early 1992, Republican Governor William Weld of Massachusetts created a "Governor's Commission on Gay and Lesbian Youth." Appointed as head of that body was David LaFontaine, a homosexual activist and political lobbyist. In February 1993, the Governor's Commission inaugurated the nation's first state-wide effort to eradicate "homophobia" from public schools.

In announcing the program, Weld declared: "We must free our schools from violence. . . . We must free our schools from hate as well. Words of hate can quickly become weapons of violence." Weld was not reacting to an epidemic of anti-homosexual violence or harassment. Hattie McKinnis, chairwoman of the Citywide Parents Council in Boston, told the *Boston Globe* that the "harassment of gays is not a problem in Boston schools. But it could become a problem if you bring it to the attention of the kids and they start looking around and asking 'Who's gay?'"

Learning About Gays

In February 1993, the Governor's Commission published a report entitled *Making Schools Safe for Gay and Lesbian Youth: Breaking the Silence in Schools and in Families*. The report was essentially a repackaged version of Paul Gibson's totalitarian recommendations.

According to the Governor's Commission document:

> The Higher Education Coordinating Council should facilitate changes in teacher-training standards so that all certified teachers and educators will receive training in issues relevant to the needs and problems faced by gay and lesbian youth. Such training should be a requirement for teacher certification and school accreditation. . . . Schools should be required to schedule in-service diversity training in order to receive accreditation from the appropriate professional associations.

Being "sensitized" to homosexuality is also a mandatory requirement for all public school students: "Learning about gay and lesbian people, including their experiences and contributions to society, should be integrated into all subject areas. School systems should urge teachers . . . to integrate gay and lesbian themes and issues into all subject areas," including "literature, history, the arts, and family life." Classroom re-education also includes "inclusive human development education, which addresses issues of sexual orientation.". . .

Experimenting with Homosexuality

One predictable result of the Weld/LaFontaine program has been a noticeable increase in the willingness of Massachusetts youngsters to experiment with homosexuality. The November 8, 1993, issue of *Newsweek* reported that in Massachusetts, "National Coming-Out Day" is "an autumnal rite every bit as gala as graduation day." In the Commonwealth, according to *Newsweek*, "multiculturalism has come to embrace multisexualism." As a result, "more students seem to be coming out, and they're coming out younger. A climate of greater tolerance is making it

81

possible for teens to explore more openly what they've historically sampled in secret."

Nor is this trend confined to Massachusetts. A July 15, 1993, *Washington Post* story reported that in the Washington, DC, area many public school students were not only discussing "gay rights" issues in school, but "declaring their own bisexuality or homosexuality, a step some said they were taking to be trendy or cool." According to one teen interviewed by the *Post*, some kids professed homosexuality or bisexuality "to protect themselves from just being normal."

Although public school systems throughout the country have begun to include material on "sexual orientation" as part of multicultural education, the Weld/LaFontaine program is indisputably the most ambitious of its kind. If Weld's political fortunes continue to flourish, he may have the chance to impose a similar program upon the entire country. Weld is a member of "Empower America," an establishment think-tank whose membership includes such neo-conservative luminaries as Jack Kemp and Bill Bennett. It is possible that Weld may soon emerge as an early favorite for the 1996 GOP [Republican] presidential nomination. It is thus conceivable that family-oriented conservatives may face the worst of all possible worlds in 1996: A choice between Democrat Bill Clinton and the man acclaimed by *The Advocate* as "the nation' s most pro-gay governor."

The AIDS Plague

Teaching "acceptance" of homosexuality as a means of suicide prevention is murderously irrational. Disease, violence, and early death stalk the homosexual subculture. The persistence of the AIDS plague among homosexuals offers proof that use of the human body in a manner forbidden by its designer voids its warranty.

The December 11, 1993, *New York Times* reported that San Francisco displays "ominous signs of a second wave of AIDS infection" in spite of that fact that it is "a city where virtually everybody knows that [homosexual] intercourse without a condom spreads AIDS." (It should be pointed out that the "protection" offered by condoms is at best extremely unreliable.) According to the *Times*, many in the city's male homosexual population pursue suicidal sex because they are "unwilling to face a measure of sexual deprivation and eager for the attention showered on the sick and dying."

According to Dana Van Gorder, who was identified by the *Times* as an "AIDS educator," "We need to give guys more meaning, so they'll commit to wanting to live." The *Times* left this question untouched: What is it about the "gay" lifestyle that leaves its practitioners devoid of the will to live?

Many in the homosexual mecca find themselves caught in the tightening coils of nihilism. Notes the *Times*, "With homosexual identity and AIDS so tightly intertwined, particularly in gay enclaves like the Castro [District], some men said they were attracted to the idea of getting sick because it would deepen their sense of belonging." Bear in mind that this is the community from which Paul Gibson issued his prescriptions to "heal" American society of "homophobia."

Jewish tradition describes Sodom, Gomorrah, and the "cities of the plain" as dismal, heartless communities in which violence and depravity reigned. Governed by corrupt, tyrannical civic authorities, the residents of Sodom and her sister cities surrendered themselves to the unfettered indulgence of every variety of vice and selfishness. Those who sought to promote Godly standards of behavior were punished with gleeful severity.

We have not reached Sodom yet—but we can see its suburbs from here.

*"What gay people need to demonstrate is that
their existence, their visibility, their out-ness are
in fact* good *for society."*

Gays and Lesbians Are Not a Danger to Society

Richard Schneider Jr.

In the following viewpoint, Richard Schneider Jr. argues that opposition to homosexuals thrives on homophobia and the lie that gays are insidious threats to society. Schneider asserts that despite homophobes' desire to keep gays "in the closet," the best thing for homosexuals—and society as a whole—is for gays to take pride in themselves and increase their visibility. The author contends that homosexuals benefit society through their roles as advisers and supporters of families and communities. Schneider lives in Boston and is the editor of the quarterly *Harvard Gay & Lesbian Review*.

As you read, consider the following questions:

1. According to Schneider, what is the rationale behind the two versions of the "bad for society" argument?
2. How could homosexuals' increased visibility work against them, in Schneider's opinion?
3. What is the logical response to the argument that the gay lifestyle is unhealthy, according to the author?

Abridged from Richard Schneider Jr., "Homophobia's Last Stand," *Christopher Street*, September 1993. Reprinted with permission.

The world is rapidly conceding what we've been saying all along, that being gay is just a given fact, not something that can be either eliminated through punishment or wished away through metaphysical sleight of hand (as in "We forgive the person but condemn the deed"). As it does so, the world—the world of Homophobia, at any rate—finds itself grappling for a more plausible battering ram with which to assault the claims of gay people for equal rights. And that calls for a different kind of response on the part of the gay community.

It all comes back to origins. The question of where we came from becomes critical to the kind of rights we seem to be entitled to. The Movement had always maintained an official silence on the matter, insisting that *why* someone is gay or lesbian should not matter when justice and rights are at stake. All at once colonels' sons and politicians' daughters were coming forward and saying, "I don't know why I'm gay, I just am." Where has Homophobia to go? . . .

Homophobia's Last Stand

Homophobia finds itself in a bind: The military and most of straight America have recognized the existence of the gay person as a fixed and unfragile identity. (Even putting anti-gay initiatives on ballots would seem to presuppose acknowledging the existence of this class of person.) Grasping for a last resort, one final argument to ward off this person's claims to equality, they come up with a scenario that parallels the military's justification for maintaining the closet: What disturbs the order of things is not the mere existence of homosexuals but instead their being open about it, their "flaunting it" in public, their participation in something called "the homosexual lifestyle," not to be condoned. Homosexuals "looking" in the base showers become gay men cruising there and everywhere—especially in places where young recruitables hang out.

What the homophobes mean by "the gay lifestyle" has much more to do with public display and play than with the sex act itself. Inevitably, in our age, the message is conveyed in visual images rather than verbal polemics. These images shift the condemnation from the gender of one's sex partners to their number and variety, from the bedroom to the barroom and bathhouse and, oddly, to the Gay Pride parade. Ads in Colorado depicting scenes of moral turpitude had nothing to say about the issue on the [November 1992 state] ballot, which asked drily whether a certain classification of person should be singled out *not* to be officially recognized as a protected minority.

The argument on this higher ground is not absolutist but utilitarian: What they are saying is that gay people should be denied recognition because the pursuit of their "lifestyle" has adverse ef-

85

fects upon society—an extraordinary claim that ought to give many people and groups pause. In youth *veritas:* A now-infamous publication [*Peninsula*, October/November 1991] put out by some Harvard students states the right's new position in bold terms:

> We believe that homosexuality is bad for society and that it can harm even those who might not otherwise seem affected by it. More importantly, we think it is bad for individuals; submitting to the homosexual "lifestyle" can destroy individuals emotionally, physically, and spiritually.

The fate of the individual turns out to be a minor concern in this 56-page diatribe, as the reader can imagine; but rest assured, the theme of submission to temptation plays a relentless role throughout. The dominant metaphor is invariably that of being overpowered by a superior force. Could it be (in the Church Lady's voice) *Satan?*

©Milt Priggee. Reprinted with permission.

There are two versions of the "bad for society" argument, as *Peninsula* reveals, one that might be called sacred, the other profane. In the profane version, gay people are seen as responsible for spreading disease, corrupting minors, using drugs, and just generally staying up too late. In the sacred version, the antics of homosexuals contribute to the moral degeneration of society, threatening everyone with the judgment of God and hastening doom.

Eventually, all its instincts tell the Right to assign moral responsibility to the practicing queer (in *their* sense of the term). In the profane version, the gay person has elected to hang out with deviants whose lifestyle violates the norms of decency in our society: The upshot is that these norms, coded as "traditional/family values," are being undermined. The family takes the place of the military unit of "unit morale" fame; again the social structure appears to be peculiarly fragile, vulnerable to the mere presence of a tiny minority of outsiders—or, rather, to the public exhibition of that minority's "lifestyle." It is straight society's *awareness* of their existence, once again, that constitutes the danger.

The sacred version veers irresistibly back to biblical scenarios of damnation and doom. Nevertheless, if only as a [public relations] measure, we find the Christian Right shifting away from the blanket condemnation of certain abominations, sexual acts explicitly defined in their law, to a more selective censuring of those vaguely conceived but graphically depicted goings-on that they equate with "the gay lifestyle." The person isn't being condemned for having wicked desires or even for acting upon them; instead he or she is being despised for having taken up with a lifestyle that undermines, somehow, the righteousness of everyone else, inviting the judgment of God and all that *that* implies. Forgiven are those famous and forgotten homosexuals of the past who suffered in silence, even those who may have engaged in some homo sex in their time; condemned are those living "the gay lifestyle."

Thus is the sacred version of the "bad for society" argument rendered as morality play: Those enacting The Gay Lifestyle, demonized as Vanity and Lust, become the high priests of decadence reigning over Sodom and Gomorrah, their sinfulness threatening everyone with Armageddon. The very theatricality of Gaydom plays into this argument's hands, as costumed occasions such as Pride parades and Castro streetlife become the stuff of mass-mailed videos and pre-referendum TV commercials.

Power and the Faustian Bargain

Arguments melt into images as we go from the intrinsic sinfulness of homosexuality to its social consequences. The Right discovers that a few choice snips from "the gay lifestyle" are worth a thousand Biblical injunctions or catechismic guilt trips—as witness their success in states where anti-gay referenda have been passed. Who cares about abstract questions of rights, these ads are implicitly saying, when the fate of the family, of civilization itself, hangs in the balance?

But what power gay people have in this scenario! Look who stoops to conquer now! So much for gay men as ineffectual sissy boys. Suddenly the Right *likes* those hunky hulks in leather as seen in their chosen venues, those dark dens of iniquity. Or, rather, the Right would have it both ways. It is out of weakness that boys and men surrender to temptation in the first place, but the surrender is voluntary in this Faustian bargain; what they are promised and given in return for their souls is access to a secret and dangerous world, a world so wondrous that someone can become its instant devotee and potent enough to endow its practitioners with the power to bring down civilization as we know it.

Fundamentalists speak explicitly of people selling their souls to you-know-who in their pursuit of forbidden knowledge, as Faust sought a "variety of experience" hitherto unknown. And when Faust comes, can the whole archetype of temptation and original sin be far behind? For Adam and Eve (or is it Steve?), as for Faust, it was for the sake of forbidden Knowledge that the plunge was taken. For the First Couple this knowledge included *carnal* knowledge—as, needless to add, it does for gay men in the corresponding mythology. It is indeed the promise of sex—sex for its own sake, in lurid quantity, in various venues, always *in extremis*—that furnishes the magic charm with which others are lured into this wild, wild world.

The Fearful Right

Thus are they fruitful, and do they multiply. This power to seduce gives gay people a strange ability to reproduce themselves, almost to procreate. Fittingly enough, it is sex that furnishes the source of this unnatural fecundity. In the Right's utopia, of course, gay men would go back to being priests and other epicenes, attendant drones that neither mated nor procreated. How frightening for them to witness the emergence of a sexual minority that declares openly its intention to pursue sex for its own sake!

It is a fear easily exploited by sermonizers who spend their time spinning mythologies that both justify their holy book and keep their flock in line. A more sinister interpretation would be that gay people are merely filling a preconceived slot in their little morality pageant, a slot filled by groups like Jews and Communists in the past. Rational argument breaks down here, as *any* manifestation of the group's existence provides evidence of its insidious intent. Images of gay men pairing off and settling down as suburban couples are no less frightening than those of sadomasochistic sessions in leather bars. Each confirms the insidious presence of the group—there on the margins of society leading lives of perpetual indulgence, here in our midst, infiltrating our neighborhoods and schools.

The Right's willingness and ability to exploit both images—both the June-and-Ward [Beaver Cleaver's parents in the traditional-family sitcom *Leave It to Beaver*] couple lacking only "the boys" *and* the professional queens camping it up in the city— renders the public relations debate between assimilation and cultural separatism largely irrelevant. Doubtless images of clean-cut couples play better at hearings on gays-in-the-military. But the logical extension of such relationships by the churches' own law, marriage for gay men and lesbians, strikes horror in their hearts and provides fuel for the fire and brimstone on Sunday mornings. "Get used to it" sums up the radical response to any attack on the here-and-queer world, regardless of what "it" may be in the slogan. The sentiment is admittedly thrilling; the risk is that it tends to confirm their contention that the foe is waging a "cultural war" specifically *against* them, nay against all good churchgoing folks and their way of life.

The Same Needs

Gay people have the same needs that nongay people have. We too need to feel worthwhile, to feel safe, to feel free of pain and suffering. We too need to achieve and acquire. We too need to love and be loved. We too need to do for others and to generate projects that will endure beyond our own lifetime. These are the internally generated needs that motivate most of human endeavor, including involvement in the nuclear family drama.

Where we *are* different is in some of the mechanisms we are developing to meet our needs for affiliation, security, altruism and immortality. For instance, we have replaced the straight marriage with the same-sex lover partnership. Many of us have replaced or supplemented our straight family of origin with a gay and lesbian friendship/support group with whom we can more easily share the joys and struggles of our gay lives. The gay movement itself is a resource for support and positive identification, offering opportunities for involvement in a collective effort to change the quality of life for gay and lesbian people in our lifetime and beyond.

Betty Berzon, *Positively Gay*, 1992.

Thus does the very act of being out come to be identified as an act of war in their mythology. The war is a self-fulfilling prophesy, for it cannot be waged except insofar as gay people are out *en masse*. Yet the more visible gay people are, the more justified homophobes feel in their fear and loathing, and the more determined to suppress the gay subculture and restore the closet. We would dismiss this as a textbook case of paranoia; but we know very well how potent a force paranoia can be in the promotion of intolerance.

Each of the arguments coming out of Gaydom preserves the moral neutrality of the gay subculture (or -cultures). "Get used to it" immediately rules out any moral argument at all: simply, "We're here." June-and-Wardism, declaring "We are everywhere," wants to level the moral playing field by minimizing the differences between gay and straight. The first position finds the gay subculture at root a "culture of desire" (as Frank Browning's opus calls it) founded on deeply rooted predilections; the so-called "secondary" characteristics of Gaydom, including the ones the Right equates with the gay lifestyle, are seen as merely derivative and carry little moral baggage. The second alternative, in trying to sanitize the image of gay people for straight consumption, plays down the subcultural elements and tries to pass off the gender of one's "partner" as an unimportant detail.

Underlying this moral neutrality is in both instances a denial that free will plays much of a role in the state of being gay. To the extent that we acknowledge the existence of a gay subculture, we are reluctant to take responsibility for its manufacture or to furnish it with ethical justifications. We retreat to the no-fault position that has served us so well in the past, giving up moral choice in favor of inalienable rights.

Gays Are Good for Society

Grudgingly, creakily, the established order is conceding that being gay is not just a bad habit, let alone an ultimate moral choice. Fewer and fewer people believe that homosexual yearnings are chosen from a menu of desires. It is for this reason that the ideologues of Homophobia have shifted from individual moral responsibility to the collective social good. The self-confirming loop that would keep gay people in the closet is not defeated by recitations of "not by choice" or "just like everyone else." What gay people need to demonstrate is that their existence, their visibility, their out-ness are in fact *good* for society, that they improve things on balance, leaving the world a better place.

What form this counter-argument will take is at this point a matter of speculation. To give a handy example, though: One of the Right's constant themes is that the gay lifestyle is inherently unhealthy, its members for the most part drugged, drunken, sex-crazed, diseased, and dying. Such arguments are effective because health has become the ultimate Good in our time, the healthfulness of something the true measure of its worth. The logical response would be to show that gay people are actually the bearers of a revived "health culture" marked by fit bodies and physical beauty, cleanliness, clearheadedness, a love of nature, protection of the environment, the defense of life itself. Why not? Is such a claim so farfetched?

Once the straight world has accepted the deeply ingrained nature of homosexuality, it is forced to confront the existence and persistence of gay people as a social fact. Perhaps gay people are actually on this earth for a reason! The evolutionist E.O. Wilson starts with the premise that homosexuality is present in all societies and survives as a genetic trait along with other successful adaptations. By not procreating, speculates Wilson, homosexuals give their communities a selective advantage over communities lacking a gay member or two. Freed from the burdens of child-rearing and other social commitments, the gay person can apply surplus resources to help support her brother's children or come to the rescue of a cousin in need. Often the gay person plays a special role as shaman, collecting and redirecting resources while sometimes furnishing medical know-how or spiritual counsel. Many societies in the anthropological annals have created special roles to accommodate homosexuals and, as it were, institutionalize their generosity.

Experience and Wisdom

It seems to me that gay people, freed from the closet's constraints, often play a corresponding role in contemporary society, albeit without stepping into a set social role. We are the prodigal sons and daughters who have traveled outside the community to learn new things and, upon our return, to impart new ways. Often a gay person ends up traveling to a distant city in search of a new life, along the way gaining experience of the outside world that straight people miss. The latter have "stayed behind" in order to preserve resources and raise kids. Gay people, having acquired an education in the ways of the world that others lack—often more formal education, too—serve their families and communities as career counsellors and financial advisors, legal executors, and marriage counsellors, experts and facilitators of all kinds. It is as outsiders that gay people assume the mantel of sage—but only insofar as society is prepared to accept what they have to offer.

Whatever form the argument takes, demonstrating that gay people are beneficial to society provides the strongest argument yet for gay men and lesbians to come out of the closet and be seen. Doing so immediately disarms the Right's paranoid tautology, in which the very out-ness of gay people is taken as proof of their insidious intent. Don't ask, *don't tell* is the best they can do at this point. On the other hand, if being out means being able to play a uniquely positive role in society, why *wouldn't* one choose "the gay lifestyle" on its own merits, as something *worthy* of being chosen?

In shifting from individual responsibility to the collective social good, the Right is giving up its traditional line of defense in favor of a profoundly collectivist argument. Accordingly, if gay people are deemed inevitable yet harmful to society, then "society" should act to minimize their power and presence. That is why homophobes take such pains to diminish the number of gay people—why, for example, they latched onto that study reporting that only one percent of American men are gay. How breathtaking to imagine a time when society accepts the presence of its gay minority as beneficial!

For now, the acceptance of a gay population, whatever its size, opens new possibilities for gay people to seize the moral high ground. That "We're here" is a claim that the straight world seems poised to accept as fact. Who knows but that one day we could find ourselves chanting, in place of "Get used to it," something closer to "Don't mention it!"?

"The struggle for legal rights for lesbians and gay men is, for good reason, at the heart of our revolution."

The Civil Rights of Gays and Lesbians Should Be Protected

William B. Rubenstein

William B. Rubenstein is the director of the American Civil Liberties Union (ACLU) Lesbian and Gay Rights Project in New York City. In the following viewpoint, Rubenstein argues that unjust laws and the lack of gay rights laws discriminate against homosexuals by criminalizing their sexual behavior, failing to protect their employment and housing rights, and denying them family rights and privileges that heterosexuals enjoy. Rubenstein concludes that the law is a vital force in the construction of society and one that can and should provide equal rights for homosexuals.

As you read, consider the following questions:

1. In Rubenstein's opinion, how do governments sanction discrimination against homosexuals?
2. Why does the author believe that the *Hardwick* decision was a major blow to the gay rights movement?
3. According to Rubenstein, what family rights have been denied to homosexuals?

Excerpted from William B. Rubenstein, *Lesbians, Gay Men, and the Law* (pp. xv-xxi), ©1993 by William B. Rubenstein. Reprinted with permission from The New Press.

The struggle for equality by lesbians and gay men has moved to the center of American life at the outset of the 1990s, and during the coming decade lesbian and gay issues will form a greater part of the American political scene and public consciousness than during any other era in American history. With Bill Clinton's election and his first presidential directives a heated debate has erupted regarding the presence of lesbians and gay men in the U.S. military. Nearly every religious organization in the country is struggling with questions ranging from gay marriage to the ordination of openly gay ministers. And at no time in American history have gay people been more visible: with lesbians and gay men battling in Congress, in the streets, and in courtrooms for civil rights, well-known figures publicly discussing their sexual orientation, and gay characters on prime-time television shows, few Americans can continue to claim that they do not come into contact with gay people.

At the same time, lesbians and gay men face stiffer opposition than ever before. A well-organized and well-funded religious right has pledged that "gay rights will be the 'abortion' issue of the 1990s"—the message being that its adherents will vehemently challenge advances by gay people. And more and more lesbians and gay men are attacked every year simply for being gay: antigay violence rose 31 percent between 1990 and 1991 in five major cities (Boston, Chicago, Minneapolis/St. Paul, New York, and San Francisco), with more than 1800 incidents of anti-gay/lesbian violence reported in these cities alone.

Sexuality and the Law

The law is a primary arena in which the struggle for gay rights has been, and will continue to be, played out. Throughout American history, sexual relations have been a concern of the secular legal system, as well as an issue of religious morality and medical "science"; American society has long maintained laws that directly dictate what combinations of individuals may have sex with one another and in what manner. For example, sex outside of marriage was traditionally proscribed by most states, as was sex between people of different races. It was not until the late 1960s that the United States Supreme Court struck down as unconstitutional laws that criminalized interracial marriages. In addition to these direct prohibitions, the state has long maintained various mechanisms to channel sexual relations indirectly. For example, government jobs could be denied to individuals whose sexual practices were not approved by the state.

For lesbians and gay men, state regulation of sexuality has been particularly harsh. State sodomy laws have criminalized one way in which gay people express their love for one another. Discrimination against lesbians and gay men exists in employment and housing, and gay people are often denied access to programs and public places solely because of their sexual orientation. No state has recognized lesbian and gay relationships, and sexual orientation has often been used to deny gay people custody of, or visitation with, their own children. Lesbians and gay men have been legally barred from adopting children or becoming foster parents.

Not only has the law typically failed to redress discrimination against gay people but such discrimination is often sanctioned by the government itself. The federal government, for example, has openly denied lesbians and gay men the opportunity to serve their country in the military, effectively denied employment to gay people in the FBI, CIA, and other security-related positions, and placed burdens on gay applicants for security clearances.

Alongside this stark picture of the barriers faced by lesbians and gay men lives another image, however. This portrait is of a constantly growing movement to eradicate these barriers, of lesbians and gay men and their advocates who, in the past forty years, have made enormous strides in abolishing some of the barriers to equal participation by gay people in American society. . . .

Sodomy Laws

In modern American society, sodomy laws have served as a legal basis for the regulation of lesbian and gay sexuality and of lesbians and gay life generally. Discrimination against lesbians and gay men is often predicated on the existence of laws prohibiting lesbian/gay sex, and thus sodomy laws are understood as criminalizing not merely homosexual acts but lesbians and gay men themselves. Sodomy laws were not always understood in this way. Historically, sodomy laws were drafted in order to proscribe sexual behavior that did not lead to procreation, including oral and anal sex between people of the same or opposite genders.

In 1961 every state in the United States had a sodomy law. While most of these laws outlawed heterosexual as well as homosexual sodomy, every one of them criminalized the manner in which gay men and lesbians express love for one another—even if the acts took place between consenting adults in the privacy of their home.

Today fewer than half the states have sodomy laws. Nearly all of the 26 states that no longer have sodomy laws abolished their law through legislative action rather than through a court decision declaring it unconstitutional. . . .

In 1986 the United States Supreme Court rejected a constitutional challenge to Georgia's sodomy law in the *Bowers v. Hardwick* case. Michael Hardwick was arrested for having sex with another man in his own bedroom. Although the state did not criminally prosecute him for this act, Hardwick brought a civil suit challenging the sodomy law as violating his constitutional rights. He was joined in this effort by a heterosexual couple who complained that they feared that the Georgia law—which applied to *all* oral and anal intercourse—could be enforced against them as well. By a 5-4 vote, the Supreme Court ruled against Hardwick. Despite the Georgia law's ban on all oral and anal intercourse, the Court focused only on *homosexual* sodomy: it held that the "right to privacy" recognized under the federal constitution did not encompass a right to engage in homosexual sodomy and, therefore, that states are free to criminalize such conduct.

A Time to Be Equal

The next great leap forward in our struggle as lesbians and gay men, as bisexuals and transsexuals and queers of any color, is to radically alter the prism through which the world views us by radically altering the prism through which we see ourselves. We need to move from "other" and outcast to conscious subjects capable of joining with other progressive people to lead this nation; from gender benders who defy gender constrictions to conscious beings who obliterate gender roles. It is our time to be equal, not other, to be not oppressed but righteously furious. It is our time to say we refuse to respond to the indignity of the question: Why are you gay? We are.

Carmen Vásquez, *The Third Pink Book*, 1993.

The *Hardwick* decision was a major blow to the movement for lesbian and gay rights in the United States. It means that despite the progress made in the past few decades, late in the twentieth century, in nearly half the states in the United States of America, it is still illegal for lesbians and gay men to express love to one another. To lesbians and gay men, this means, as [homosexual and AIDS activist] Larry Kramer has written, "We are denied the right to love. Can you imagine being denied the right to love?" Worse still, the U.S. Supreme Court has condoned this oppression, ruling in the *Hardwick* case that our love for one another has no place in American constitutional jurisprudence.

Despite its harsh outcome, the *Hardwick* decision has not retarded the movement for gay rights; in fact, some argue that the decision activated many in the lesbian/gay community and solidified support for this fight among many nongay people. Not withstanding *Hardwick*, for example, the effort to eradicate sodomy laws has continued, based on challenges brought in state courts under *state* constitutional theories. Since *Hardwick*, sodomy laws have been declared unconstitutional by lower courts in Michigan and Texas, and by the highest court in Kentucky. Nor has *Hardwick* impaired gains in other areas. . . .

Discrimination Against Gays

Although the argument for the repeal of sodomy statutes has been based on an argument of "privacy," privacy has been only one of the goals of the lesbian/gay rights movement. Beyond wanting to be left alone by the government regarding the most intimate decisions, lesbians and gay men also want to be able to "come out"—to be open about our sexual orientation—without fearing discrimination or worse. By contrast to sodomy's argument for privacy, the argument for civil rights protections for lesbians and gay men is one of "publicness."

In 1971 there was not a single law, ordinance, or policy prohibiting discrimination against lesbians and gay men. No one had ever heard of, nor had any public or private entity ever adopted, a policy that prohibited discrimination on the basis of sexual orientation.

Today, seven states, the District of Columbia, and more than 100 municipalities ban discrimination against lesbians and gay men. These laws generally ban discrimination on the basis of sexual orientation in employment, housing, and places of public accommodation. In 1981 Wisconsin became the first state to pass a lesbian/gay rights law on a statewide level, but for the next nine years no state followed. Since 1990, however, six states have done so—Massachusetts, Hawaii, Connecticut, New Jersey, Vermont, and California. (Interestingly, these laws are sometimes passed *before* the state repeals its sodomy law. Wisconsin passed its gay rights law in 1981 but did not repeal its sodomy law until 1983. Massachusetts enacted a gay rights law in 1990 even though it still has a sodomy law.)

Notwithstanding these advances, in 43 states it remains perfectly legal for a private-sector employer to deny employment or refuse to serve or to rent to lesbians and gay men based solely on their sexual orientation—unless one happens to be in a municipality that has a gay rights ordinance. In 1991 a restaurant chain, Cracker Barrel, fired all of its lesbian and gay employees, announcing that it was a "family" restaurant where such employees were not welcome. Although Cracker Barrel operates in many states throughout the country, its actions were in no case subject to a locale that protected against discrimination on this basis.

Government Sanctions Prejudice

Not only do 43 states and the federal government permit this discrimination, though; even worse, in many places government itself sanctions the prejudice. Governmental actions are policed by the constitution, and in some instances the constitution has furnished protections to lesbians and gay men. For instance, courts have ruled that the government generally cannot simply fire lesbians and gay men without first articulating some nexus between the worker's sexual orientation and his or her ability to do the job; this "nexus" requirement is also a part of the federal civil service regulations protecting federal employees. At the same time, though, the federal government has successfully prohibited lesbians and gay men from serving their country in the armed forces, banned lesbians and gay men from working for the FBI and CIA, and created extra burdens for lesbians and gay men who apply for security clearance. State and local governments are often no better: often, they openly ban lesbians and gay men from holding jobs ranging from teaching to police work. Despite the nexus requirement and other constitutional standards, courts have with near and unique uniformity ruled that such government line-drawing that discriminates against gay people does not offend the constitution. The courts have condoned the military's bias against lesbians and gay men as well as that of the FBI, CIA, Foreign Service, Defense Department Security Clearance office, and many school boards and police departments. The constitution has been little more than a promise to lesbians and gay men.

Thus, in most areas of the United States lesbians and gay men are not protected from the reach of the criminal law in their homes, and they are left, in effect, legally naked if they chose to come out publicly. With such minimal legal protection—and often confronted by employers who frown upon them—gay people must negotiate how open to be about their sexual orientation in the workplace. . . .

Family Rights

Lesbians and gay men form relationships with one another in much the same way heterosexuals do. Unlike heterosexual unions, however, lesbian and gay relationships are not recognized by law. In seeking protection for relationships, lesbians and gay men are looking both to guarantee the privacy and autonomy society provides to heterosexual couples—particularly to marriages—and to gain the public recognition and economic responsibilities and benefits that go with marital status.

In 1981 no public or private entity in the United States recognized lesbian/gay relationships. Indeed, until the early 1980s few advocates within the lesbian and gay rights movement prioritized family issues. The exception was the many lesbian and gay parents—especially the former—who were losing their rights to their natural children in custody and visitation battles with their former (heterosexual) spouses. In the 1980s the concept of "domestic partnership" was invented as a basis for the recognition of lesbian and gay relationships.

Today dozens of municipalities and many more private institutions recognize lesbian and gay relationships through "domestic partnership" programs, according different types of benefits to these newly acknowledged unions. Additionally, the highest court in the state of New York recognized gay couples as "family" in a 1989 decision. Similar developments have permeated parenting law, as well, with state courts less and less considering a parent's sexual orientation as a pertinent factor in custody and visitation decisions. Moreover, courts in about half a dozen states have recognized "second-parent adoptions," permitting a lesbian/gay coparent to adopt his or her partner's biological children.

Losing a Partner

Among many developments, two central events of the 1980s for lesbian and gay men helped spur this family rights movement—AIDS and the Sharon Kowalski case. AIDS has made the lack of a legal relationship crushingly apparent to lesbian and gay couples: for instance, a gay man whose partner is dying may have difficulty inquiring about his condition or visiting him in the hospital because the men have no legal relationship to one another. Once the lover dies, his surviving partner will not automatically share in his estate, nor enjoy the tax benefits of so doing, and may indeed lose control of property the couple purchased together. He may also face eviction from his home. The survivor, moreover, could well face legal challenges from his partner's biological family regarding a will or even the disposition of his lover's remains.

The situation of Sharon Kowalski and Karen Thompson has similarly focused attention within the lesbian and gay community on family rights. Kowalski and Thompson lived together as partners for four years when, in 1983, Kowalski was in a tragic car accident, leaving her physically and mentally disabled. After the accident—for more than nine years—Thompson had to fight with Kowalski's biological family for the right to be Kowalski's legal guardian. The plight of the couple received a great deal of attention within the lesbian/gay community and highlighted the consequences of the legal system's failure to recognize our relationships.

Legal Protection for Gays and Couples

Because of AIDS, because of Sharon Kowalski, and because of many similar though less publicized cases, lesbian and gay couples have become increasingly sophisticated about preparing legal documents to secure their relationships to one another. But for many, such second-class attempts to make a relationship resemble a marriage do not go far enough. A number of gay couples around the country have filed challenges to their states' marriage statutes; statutes have also been introduced in state legislatures that would change the definition of marriage to include gay couples. Other activists strongly believe that marriage is not the answer, based on their belief that lesbian and gay couples should not appropriate the mechanisms of oppression—particularly of the oppression of women—in order to secure legal recognition of our relationships. These activists have focused their attentions more on the domestic partnership movement.

Despite significant gains over the past decade, lesbian/gay couples' legal situation remains abysmal. Not one state recognizes lesbian and gay relationships by permitting gay people to marry one another—not one. Lesbians and gay men continue to be deprived of custody of, or visitation with, their own children solely because of their sexual orientation. In some states, lesbians and gay men are explicitly legally barred from adopting children or becoming foster parents; in others, they are prohibited in practice from doing so. Even as they develop new family structures with one another and with the assistance of emerging technological advances, lesbians and gay men still have no legal protection for the families they form. We remain a strange anomaly to the area of family law, challenging the very structure of an edifice constructed upon the model of a mother, father, and 2.4 children. . . .

Hope and Promise Through Law

Lesbians and gay men have been forced to fight for the right to fight for their rights. This struggle will continue to be just that in the 1990s. New efforts to deprive lesbians and gay men of legal protections are keeping pace with the enactment of those protections. In late 1992, for example, the voters in the state of Colorado amended that state's constitution to prohibit the enactment of laws that would ban discrimination against lesbians and gay men. Similarly, voters in Tampa, Florida, repealed that municipality's gay rights law. . . .

The law is in no way a domain separate and apart from society itself but, rather, is always already part of and a constituent force in the construction of society. The law represents a unique promise to members of our society and, at the same time, can reflect the basest desires and most repulsive instincts of human beings. Despite this tension, the struggle for legal rights for lesbians and gay men is, for good reason, at the heart of our revolution—because the law holds out the hope that our society is capable of treating *all* of its citizens, including lesbians and gay men, with the dignity and respect that each deserves.

"The homosexual movement has transformed itself into the homosexual menace."

The Civil Rights of Gays and Lesbians Should Not Receive Special Protection

Dennis A. Wheeler

Many Americans are opposed to laws specifically designed to protect the civil rights of gay and lesbian persons, as voters in Colorado proved in 1992 when they amended the constitution to prohibit the state from protecting homosexuals against discrimination. In the following viewpoint, Dennis A. Wheeler asserts that homosexuality is an antireligious, antisocial, and vile behavior that should not be given civil rights protection. He maintains that America must abolish the philosophical ground of civil rights on which the homosexual movement stands. Wheeler is an assistant editor for *World News Digest*, a bimonthly conservative magazine.

As you read, consider the following questions:

1. Why does Wheeler believe that homosexuals are an affront to religion and society?
2. How does the civil rights legal system coerce people, in Wheeler's opinion?
3. According to the author, how has the homosexual movement been welcomed by recent U.S. presidents?

Dennis A. Wheeler, "The Legacy of Sodom," *World News Digest*, October 19, 1993. Reprinted by permission of Soundview Publications, 1350 Center Dr., Suite 100, Dunwoody, GA 30338.

A new idea has thrust itself onto the American social and political scene this past decade—the idea that homosexuals are cheerful, productive, poetic victims of unjust persecution. Most Americans have never thought of them like that. In fact, even the subject of homosexuality has been perceived as shameful and generally received the silent treatment. Is the new view really an accurate description of homosexual life?

Historically, it certainly doesn't fit. Looking at the most popular and accurate history book in the world, we can see how a group of homosexuals acted 4,000 years ago. The setting is the city which so characterized homosexuality that its name is now used to describe homosexuals' perverted style of sexual intercourse.

> Genesis 19:1-10. The two angels arrived at Sodom and Lot was sitting in the gateway of the city. When he saw them, he got up to meet them and bowed down with his face to the ground. "My lords," he said, "please turn aside to your servant's house." . . . [H]e insisted so strongly that they did go with him and entered his house. . . .
>
> Before they had gone to bed, all the men from every part of the city of Sodom—both young and old—surrounded the house. They called to Lot, "Where are the men who came to you tonight? Bring them out to us so that we can have sex with them." Lot went outside to meet them, "No, my friends. Don't do this wicked thing. . . ."
>
> "Get out of our way," they replied. "This fellow came here as an alien, and now he wants to play the judge! We'll treat you worse than them."
>
> They kept bringing pressure on Lot. . . . But the men inside pulled Lot back into the house and shut the door.

This cheerless tale is preserved for us in the Bible. Lot, the nephew of Abraham, found himself in a culture where all the men had degenerated into homosexuals and bisexuals. These men were not the least bit interested in "sexual relations between consenting adults," but were aggressive and forceful in their erotic pursuits. They were also vengeful and violent in their actions toward Lot, threatening to do worse to him than to their intended victims, because he opposed their actions.

This is how things were back then. But haven't things changed? Aren't modern homosexuals an "enlightened," civilized people who are far removed from such barbaric behavior? Let's examine the record.

Destructive Behavior

Homosexuals argue that they are a peaceful and gay people who only want to be accepted for what they are and who they are. Yet, according to the *Washington Times*, 8 out of every 10 homosexuals the U.S. Army court-martialed for sexual misconduct between 1989 and the fall of 1993 had engaged in sexual assaults against their victims. Of these 102 assault cases, nearly half involved the molestation of children.

Jeffrey Dahmer is a homosexual who wasn't concerned about the consent of his partners. He lured young men to his apartment, drugged them, raped them, killed them, and ate them. This was not an isolated occurrence of homosexual behavior, either. According to Dr. Paul Cameron who writes the *Family Research Report*, "the top six U.S. male serial killers were all homosexuals." John Wayne Gacy raped and killed 33 boys in Chicago. Patrick Kearney murdered 32 young men, cutting them into small pieces after sex and leaving the bodies in trash bags along L.A. freeways. Juan Corona, the migrant worker in California, was convicted of murdering 25 migrant workers. He testified at the trial that he had "made love with the corpses."

Even those homosexuals who don't make a *career* of mutilating their "lovers" are known for an astounding degree of savagery when they become violent. Among law enforcement officials, homosexuals are infamous for the overwhelming violence they employ against each other when they discover their partners have been unfaithful or want a "separation."

Gay Affirmative Action?

What's wrong with gay-rights laws? Gay activists argue that they are neutral, merely guaranteeing rights already enjoyed by the straight majority. But don't they actually create a special protected class? A lot of bigots voted against gay-rights legislation in Colorado. But as Virginia Postrel, editor of *Reason* magazine, writes, the swing vote was provided by nonbigots who "simply said 'Stop' to the seemingly endless proliferation of protected categories that divide people into favored and disfavored classes. . . ."

Creating these categories has consequences. This path, taken for blacks, a truly victimized group, isn't necessarily appropriate for other groups. And we are not sure where it would lead. Could it provide the legal scaffolding for gay affirmative action and quotas, or attempts to establish same-sex marriages? No one knows.

John Leo, *U.S. News & World Report*, May 3, 1993.

And the incredibly promiscuous behavior of the Sodomites hasn't changed either. According to Dr. Paul Cameron, "Our surveys show that the average homosexual has around 100 sex partners in a lifetime. Now some have thousands. But the average is around 100."

Homosexual behavior, you see, is no different now than it was in the days of Lot.

Homosexuals, bisexuals, lesbians, and others have joined hands in a political alliance across America and throughout the "civilized" world. The license to practice their "lifestyle" has gone virtually unprotested. But that is not enough for them. The homosexual lobby is now working to use the Civil Rights Act to gain for themselves "protected minority status." They are moving forward on another front as well. They want to stifle all resistance to their foul deeds by making opposition to them illegal. . . .

The homosexual movement has defined itself as a persecuted minority whose basic civil rights are being denied by people, groups, and governments who discriminate against them. These equalitarian concepts have proven very difficult for typical Americans and Western Europeans to contest. Author Samuel Francis noticed this during the Roberta Achtenberg hearing, "This, then, is the position in which the nation now stands: a senator who objects to the nomination of an open homosexual to a high public office is condemned by his colleagues as a fearmonger, a bigot, and an exponent of hatred, and is told he is a disgrace to the Senate, while the pervert herself is held up as a moral paragon." [Achtenberg was confirmed by the U.S. Senate to a Department of Housing and Urban Development post in 1993.]

The reason for this dilemma is that America has accepted the equalitarian philosophy of civil rights. According to this paradigm, all men are assumed to be "men of good will" except those who are infected with the twin "evils" of nationalism (patriotism) and theism (belief in God). The further you stand from patriotism or a belief in God, the more righteous you are assumed to be because of your tolerance, acceptance, and openmindedness.

The homosexual who has overcome his conscience is guilty of neither patriotism nor theism. His time and energy is spent fulfilling his carnal desires. He admits no obligation towards his community and society. In fact, the homosexual lifestyle is invariably anti-society, because it destroys any possibility that society can endure and continue.

Besides this, the unrepentant homosexual must ceaselessly make conscious attempts to deny the existence of God, or any lesser authority who makes moral judgements on his choices. Homosexual "churches" have nothing to do with worshipping the true God, as He makes very clear His *intolerance* of them in the scriptures. Instead, they worship a god of their own imagination who is not affronted by their total perversion of the created order.

Reject Homosexual Civil Rights

There is only one answer to the philosophical dilemma posed by the homosexual movement: totally reject civil rights as a valid legal concept. "Civil rights" have proven utterly incapable of propagating the just and peaceful coexistence of men in society. Instead, they have instigated unprecedented strife and injustice. We must return to our historic, efficacious, and proven common law if we are ever to regain peace in our country.

The common law upon which America was built protected the citizens against *force* and *fraud*. This was the essence of the laws regulating relations between citizens. No one could use force against a fellow citizen. And no one could defraud anyone else. The simplicity of this law system allowed for great liberty.

The civil rights legal system is entirely different. This system *uses* force, in the form of coercive state powers, to make people associate and enter into financial relationships with others, whether they want to or not. Freedom of association is forcibly taken from the citizen and the government becomes a participant in most financial and social interactions.

Applying the civil rights paradigm to the homosexual implies that the state will now force businesses to overlook homosexuality in all hiring decisions. Landlords must do the same in housing. And, to be logically consistent, churches must overlook homosexuality in all membership decisions. In fact, anyone who discriminates against a homosexual on the grounds of his behavior becomes a criminal.

This is a drastic reversal in roles for American governments. As it now stands, 24 states list consensual sodomy as a statutory crime. Society has judged it to be such a serious breach of morality that the state is empowered to use force in subduing it. Applying civil rights status to homosexuals makes a mockery of our statute law. It places the government in the compromising position of having to use force against the very people it has heretofore used force to protect from the homosexuals.

Pedophiles and Pornography

Another item to remember is this: If taken to its logical conclusion, the granting of civil rights status to homosexuals produces another absurdity. If homosexuals get it, how will pedophiles be excluded? Many homosexuals are pedophiles—in fact, they have an advocacy group to agitate for their "right" to molest young boys. It's called the North American Man Boy Love Association (NAMBLA).

Pedophiles have also learned to speak the language of equalitarianism. A spokesman for NAMBLA recently said his group's main function was to change the laws in the country to allow adults to have sexual relations with children. A NAMBLA press release stated, "These quiet events provide a space for men who love boys to talk about their feelings and their struggle for justice in a society that fails to understand the form of love es-

105

teemed in ancient Greece and in many other cultures throughout history."

Pornography must also be allowed under the civil rights motif. And child porn certainly cannot be discriminated against. All behavior, no matter how vile and perverse, is allowed in the civil rights scheme of things, as long as this behavior demonstrates no patriotic loyalty and no belief in God.

The Homosexual Agenda

In May 1993, President Bill Clinton, with apparent glee, announced to the American people that "gays" had always served in the American military. He was merely putting forth a policy which respected the great contributions they had made. His goal was to establish a standard of judgement wherein a sailor or soldier was judged by his standard of performance rather than his sexual orientation.

The President was probably correct in his assessment that "gays" had always served in the military. But that is not the issue. The issue is: "What is society's judgement on homosexual conduct?" Will such conduct be held up as worthy of special protection, will it simply be tolerated, or will it be punished? Any answer we choose will have far-reaching consequences.

Until the mid-1960s, homosexuals stayed hidden from sight in this country. When they began to emerge and thumb their noses at American society, they were opposed by singer/beauty queen Anita Bryant. The violent and vituperative campaign they carried on against Mrs. Bryant was simply dreadful. Eventually, though, the homosexuals prevailed, and when Bryant lost, America lost. Still, very few realized what was in store for the country at that time.

After this victory, the homosexuals began peppering radio and TV call-in shows, spreading the message that they were wonderful Americans who had rights. Gradually they worked their way into the corridors of American society. Massachusetts elected two homosexuals to Congress. Homosexuals became judges. They became talk-show hosts. They even became the boy next door.

The Gay Nineties?

In 1990, President George Bush climbed into political bed with the homosexual movement and gave the cause tremendous political impetus. Bush became the first President of the United States to invite homosexual activists to the White House and a presidential bill signing. The momentous occasion for this was the placement of his signature on the Hate Crimes Statistics Act.

With the triumph secured in Washington, the battle then moved to California. That state is governed by a Fair Employment and Housing Act which outlaws discrimination against any members of minority groups listed in the act. In 1991 the legislature took up a bill to add homosexuals to that list. Republican Governor Pete Wilson supported the bill and the debate in the California Assembly was loud and acrimonious.

A Moral Distinction

Blacks have been discriminated against for what they are and homosexuals have been discriminated against for what they do. This in no way exonerates gay-bashing or gay-baiting, let alone such evils as the Nazi or communist incarcerations of gays. But it does mean that a moral distinction between discrimination against behavior and discrimination against color is possible. For example, there is no moral basis to objecting to blacks marrying whites, but there is a moral basis for objecting to homosexual marriage.

Dennis Prager, *The Public Interest*, Summer 1993.

One of the most disputatious speeches was made by a freshman Assemblyman named David Knowles. Reading a report from the Centers for Disease Control, Knowles alleged that it was common for homosexuals to urinate on each other and play with each other's feces. He concluded, "I believe that it is the right of every Californian to know the specifics of the lifestyle that a vote for this bill would advocate."

Assemblyman Knowles was scorned and ridiculed by both the press and opposition lawmakers. But in the end, the bill failed and the homosexuals were rebuffed.

This same scene has been replayed in scores of states, counties, and cities across the country. Despite the setback in California, the homosexual movement marches on. It has won great victories in Oregon, Atlanta, New York City, and other places. It has been beaten most notably in Colorado and Cobb County, Georgia. The issue has not been settled, and the fight continues.

We should salute those valiant souls who have ventured into the public arena to fight them, for this is done at great price. The pro-homosexual media makes it a point to vilify and intimidate those who oppose the homosexual movement.

Clinton Yields to Gays

With the ascent of Bill Clinton to the presidency, 1993 has proved a banner year for the homosexuals. One of Clinton's first executive actions was the ill-fated attempt to remove the restrictions on "gays" in the military. He has nominated at least one known lesbian—Roberta Achtenberg. Also, credible evidence of both lesbianism and moral turpitude has surfaced concerning

[U.S. Attorney General] Janet Reno, though she denies it.

The homosexual "March on Washington" carried the queer clamor to a higher decibel level. By some estimates, 300,000 homosexuals invaded America's capital and flaunted demands for their civil rights. This was the "movement" in full flower: lesbians strolling topless, men totally naked, anti-Christian and anti-capitalist signs everywhere, and vile language pouring shamefully forth in overflowing abundance.

The cat was let out of the bag concerning two members of the President's team. First, Larry Kramer, one of the founders of ACT-UP [AIDS Coalition to Unleash Power], "outed" (exposed as a lesbian) Secretary of Health and Human Services Donna Shalala. Kramer denounced Shalala for failing to admit she was one of them and joining the march. To this day, Shalala denies the charge.

Second, Hillary Clinton was referred to in the dearest of terms. One of the masters of ceremonies, a lesbian, was thrilled that the United States finally had someone in the White House who she could have sex with. Curiously, neither Hillary nor her husband has bothered to deny the charge that she is a lesbian.

By taking up residence in the White House, the homosexual movement is now in a position to project political, legal, and social pressure on American society for years to come. Perverted politicians concoct perverted laws. And perverted judges pervert justice. The homosexual movement has transformed itself into the homosexual menace.

A Menace to Society

To fail to stop the "menace" means that America will become like Sodom in the days of Lot. We will have no peace, but will be hounded by the homosexuals night and day. This is what awaits our society once they receive a full measure of civil rights.

We must oppose their evil onslaught. Yet, in order for our opposition to be effective, we will have to sweep away the philosophical ground on which the homosexual menace stands. And that philosophical ground is something very dear to millions of Americans—the concept of civil rights.

The application of civil rights to one person or group necessitates the removal of common law rights to another. It can never be any other way.

In this light it becomes evident that the homosexual menace is a part of a much larger problem. How will America be governed? By the common law in a constitutional republic? Or by the civil rights law in an anarchic democracy?

Our fight with the homosexual menace is a fight for the soul of America. We had better get to it.

"It is terrible to tell people they are unfit to serve their country, unless they really are unfit, which is not the case here."

Gays and Lesbians Should Be Allowed to Serve in the Military

Richard A. Posner

Richard A. Posner is a U.S. Court of Appeals judge for the Seventh Circuit and a senior lecturer at the University of Chicago Law School. In the following viewpoint, Posner considers four arguments against allowing gays in the military, and concludes that only one, the harm to heterosexual morale, has any merit. But even in this case, Posner points to the large number of homosexuals already serving without difficulty as a reason to doubt that military morale would be seriously harmed. In conclusion, Posner proposes an experiment to keep a ban on the recruitment of homosexuals but not to expel them after entry.

As you read, consider the following questions:

1. Why does Posner disagree with the argument that homosexuals would be blackmailed to reveal military secrets?
2. In Posner's opinion, why is it wrong to assume that declaring gays fit for service would create no morale problems?
3. According to the author, how do both sides of the debate use the argument of effective military performance?

Reprinted by permission of the publishers from *Sex and Reason* by Richard A. Posner. Cambridge, MA: Harvard University Press, copyright ©1992 by the President and Fellows of Harvard College.

The question whether homosexuals should be permitted to serve in the armed forces is part of the larger question whether discrimination on the basis of sexual preference should be forbidden. The reason for taking the more specific question first is that the arguments for excluding homosexuals from the armed forces are stronger than the arguments for excluding them from most other jobs. Thus, if the former arguments fail, the ground is laid for a comprehensive principle of nondiscrimination.

Four Arguments Against Gays

The principal arguments that are made against homosexuals in the military are fourfold. I list them in ascending order of persuasiveness. First, homosexuals are likely to be blackmailed into giving up military secrets. This is a weak argument. Not only is it inapplicable to persons who acknowledge their homosexuality—and those who conceal it can in fact rise to the highest levels of command in the armed forces, as in government generally—but only a tiny fraction of military personnel have access to military secrets.

The second argument is that homosexuals are on average less stable than heterosexuals. This point may be correct, but its relevance is unclear, and this on several counts. First, the artistic, often effeminate homosexual who is most likely to have a problem of psychological adjustment is least likely to find the military an attractive career—a decisive consideration when, as now, all our service personnel are volunteers rather than conscripts. Second, if male homosexuals are on average less suited psychologically to a military career than male heterosexuals, lesbians are more suited to such a career than heterosexual women. Corresponding to the effeminacy of a male heterosexual, as a trait that distinguishes the average homosexual from the average heterosexual, is the mannishness of a female homosexual, which makes her better soldier material than her feminine sister and which may explain why lesbians are a larger fraction of female soldiers than male homosexuals are of male soldiers. Third and most important, the military does not hire on a first-come, first-served basis. It screens its applicants to determine their fitness for military service. Unless the screen somehow fails to identify the maladjusted homosexual, there is no reason to have a cruder filter that excludes all homosexuals. The 1957 Crittendon Report contains the flat statement, apparently by the chief of naval personnel, that there is no correlation between homosexuality and either ability or attainments.

The third argument against allowing homosexuals to serve in the armed forces is that homosexual superior officers may coerce their subordinates for sexual favors; this is the ground on which the admiral commanding the Atlantic Fleet has urged the

rooting out of lesbians. The broader point is that sexual intrigue can reduce operational effectiveness. But this bridge was crossed when the armed forces admitted women over the same objection. Whenever there is sexual interest between a superior and a subordinate employee, there is a potential for sexual harassment. That potential is rarely thought an impressive ground for sexual segregation, and it seems no more impressive as a ground for excluding homosexuals. This is not to deny that there are lesbian cliques in the navy and in the other services, lesbians preying on nonlesbian subordinates, and all the rest. Sexual harassment is a reality. It just is not ordinarily thought a sufficiently serious problem to warrant the blanket exclusion of a whole class of workers, especially when, as in the case of the navy's lesbians, they appear to be of above-average ability. Likewise the fact that sexual interest between co-workers can distract them from their tasks: [political philosopher] Herbert Marcuse's point about the subversive potential of Eros, writ small.

Heterosexual Morale

The fourth argument for excluding homosexuals seems the worst but is the best. It is that the morale of heterosexuals, and hence the effectiveness of the military services, would suffer if homosexuals were allowed to serve. It seems the worst argument because it has the identical form as the argument for racial segregation of the armed forces, which was not ended until 1948. Because whites do not want to serve with blacks, blacks should be confined to all-black units; because heterosexuals do not want to serve with homosexuals, homosexuals should be kept out of the armed forces altogether. One might think that before giving the slightest credence to the argument, we should investigate the basis of the heterosexuals' hostility. Does it rest on ignorance and prejudice? Do they think that homosexuals cannot or will not fight, or that they will rape or seduce heterosexuals, or that homosexual preference is contagious? There is no reason to believe that homosexuals who want to join the armed forces and who pass all the physical, mental, and psychological tests that the armed forces administer to recruits are militarily less effective than heterosexuals, or cause trouble, or otherwise degrade military performance. Many homosexuals are known to have served in the American military in the Second World War, the Korean War, and the Vietnam War, and studies of their military records show that they did as well on average as the heterosexuals. It may seem that they must have been rather a select group, inasmuch as they were able to conceal their homosexuality. But in fact homosexuals are not required to conceal their homosexuality in order to join or remain in the armed forces; mostly they need only not flaunt it.

Although complete data are not available, it appears on the basis of a study conducted by Congressman Gerry Studds that outside Great Britain and the nations that once were colonies of Great Britain (including the United States, India, Australia, New Zealand, and Canada), a majority of nations do not attempt to exclude homosexuals from their armed forces, including several nations whose armed forces are highly regarded, such as France, Germany, Switzerland, and Sweden. During the Second World War the German army was considered, not despite but because of Nazi persecution of homosexuals, a refuge for them, because the military command was too busy to worry about trying to root out homosexuals; evidently they were not considered a threat to effective military performance. The idea that homosexuals will not or cannot fight seems a canard, on a par with the idea that Jews or blacks will not or cannot fight. And even if the presence of homosexuals did degrade military performance, one would have to ask how much it degraded it before deciding that the costs of allowing homosexuals to serve in the armed forces outweighed the benefits. Among the benefits to the military would be saving the cost of administering a policy of excluding homosexuals, expanding the supply of soldiers, reducing the incentives to fake homosexuality when a draft is in force, and bolstering the self-esteem of homosexuals by deeming them fit to serve their country in positions of responsibility and danger.

A Good Argument

So why do I say that the argument about the impact on heterosexuals' morale of allowing homosexuals to serve is a good argument for exclusion rather than a despicable argument that should be dismissed out of hand? Because the question of morale is separable from the question of the merits of the exclusion. Suppose American soldiers harbored the irrational but unshakable belief that to attack on Friday the thirteenth would bring disaster. This belief would be a fact that their commander would be obliged to take into account in scheduling attacks. If it was very important to attack on Friday the thirteenth, he might try to educate the soldiers out of their superstition; but if it was not very important or if the superstition was extremely tenacious, he might think it best to yield. It is the same with the homosexual question. By 1981 the percentage of Dutch people who thought homosexuality was dirty, deviant, or abnormal had fallen below 10 percent. It is no surprise that the Dutch do not exclude homosexuals from their armed forces. The corresponding figure for Americans would probably be 70 percent. In one survey 62 percent of the heterosexual veterans in the sample said that homosexuals should not be permitted to serve in our armed forces, and only 12 percent that they should (the rest were uncertain). A principal reason was that heterosexuals were upset at the prospect of being seen in the nude by a homosexual. However silly a reason this may seem, one cannot simply *assume* that declaring homosexuals fit for service in our armed forces would create no morale problems. Remember that the armed forces were integrated only after the blacks had proved themselves in all-black units during the Second World War, and that women still remain segregated to some extent from men in our armed forces. And there is the larger public to be considered: would it become hysterical at the prospect that some of the soldiers manning our nuclear missile silos might be homosexual?

It is true that not all of the nations that allow homosexuals to

113

serve in their armed forces are as tolerant as the Netherlands, Denmark, and Sweden. Switzerland has a conservative sex ethic, similar to that of the United States. Finland is distinctly less tolerant of homosexuals than Sweden. Spain is sexually conservative in many ways, though contemptuous tolerance of homosexuality is, as we know, a characteristic of Mediterranean cultures. None of these armed forces is anywhere as powerful as ours, however, and maybe that makes a difference (the finger-on-the-nuclear-trigger point). On the whole, it is the more tolerant nations that permit homosexuals to serve and the less tolerant that do not. The United States is among the least tolerant.

Patriotic Gays and Lesbians

For the first 150 years of our country's history, gay and lesbian Americans served in our country's military. And for the past 50 years, these same Americans, regardless of their conduct, devotion, and their accomplishments, have been told they need not apply to any branch of the Armed Forces. Fortunately, this has not stopped brave, patriotic gay and lesbian Americans from serving their country. But these brave Americans put themselves at risk twice every time they answer a call to service. First, they put their lives on the line for their country. Second, they risk being disgracefully cashiered if their sexual orientation is discovered. We should be thankful that they have ignored this stupid policy.

Patricia Schroeder, statement to the U.S. House of Representatives, May 19, 1992.

Another strut beneath the policy of our armed forces is the anxiety, itself a result in part of the hostility to homosexuality in our society, that many heterosexual men feel concerning their heterosexuality. There is a lurking fear that at bottom one may be one of *them*. The fear is exacerbated in a homo-social setting such as traditionally characterized the military (and still does in combat units, from which women remain excluded). In these settings men develop strong emotional, though generally not erotic, bonds. It is important to them that the line not be crossed. An official policy against retaining any "line crossers" helps to reassure that the line will be maintained.

But there is more to the story. In a 1989 Gallup Poll 60 percent of the respondents opined that homosexuals should be allowed to serve in the military. Police forces are quasi-military, yet the New York City, San Francisco, and Los Angeles police have opened their ranks to overt homosexuals without incident. And the experience with coed dorms and bathrooms in colleges is that sexual desegregation is not eroticizing but often the opposite.

The most important reason for doubting that dropping the ban on homosexuals in the military would cause serious morale problems is simply that a large number of homosexuals already serve without significant difficulties. Some of these men and women conceal their homosexuality from their heterosexual comrades and superiors, but many do not. Yet for the most part they are accepted, generally without fuss, unless they get arrested or otherwise misbehave in ways that would land heterosexuals in trouble for corresponding forms of sexual misconduct. It is as if, before 1948, a large number of black soldiers had served in integrated units under the fiction that they really were white men.

So there are good arguments for dropping the ban against homosexuals in the armed forces, but there are also bad arguments, such as the argument that there would be a significant educative effect, which would in time erode heterosexual soldiers' hostility toward homosexuals and indeed public hostility generally. True, the homosexuals would not do as badly as the heterosexuals expected, and might indeed do just as well as the heterosexuals. And there is evidence that working with homosexuals promotes tolerance, though the evidence is difficult to interpret because the causality could run in the opposite direction: the tolerant are more apt to work with them. But what weakens the point is precisely that homosexuals *already* serve in the armed forces in considerable number. The incremental educative effect of formally acknowledging their existence might be slight. And even if it would be large, this would merely pose, not answer, the question whether the armed forces should be required to serve as an agency for public enlightenment at some unknown cost in military effectiveness. Notwithstanding its excellent performance in the Persian Gulf War, the American military has a long history of problems in achieving military effectiveness, and such problems can of course be immensely costly in lives and money. If we give the military social assignments, we also give it an excuse for failing to achieve combat effectiveness, and perhaps we risk giving it a taste for meddling in nonmilitary affairs generally.

The Issue of Performance

That excellent performance, by the way, is a two-edged sword in the debate over whether to continue the prohibition against homosexuals in the armed forces. On the one hand, it allayed many of the concerns about the effectiveness of our armed forces and also demonstrated their ability without loss of effectiveness to integrate large numbers of blacks and other racial and ethnic minorities and women—so why could they not do the same with homosexuals, and with equal success? (And no doubt there were a number of homosexuals in our Persian Gulf expeditionary force, performing unexceptionably.) On the other hand, the better the performance of the armed forces, the stronger the argument for civilian deference to military judgments, one of which is that homosexuals should be barred from military service.

Even though homosexuals *can* serve in the American military, despite the formal bar against them, provided they are discreet, the removal of the bar would do much for their self-esteem—for it is terrible to tell people they are unfit to serve their country, unless they really are unfit, which is not the case here—and would be a step forward in social justice. At what cost? This is impossible to estimate with any confidence, because of the counterfactual character of the analysis. We need an experiment, and this leads me to propose that we adopt Canada's approach and, without relaxing the bar against recruitment of homosexuals to serve in our armed forces, permit them once in to remain (with or without career restrictions), provided of course that they do not engage in the sorts of misconduct that would get them kicked out if they were heterosexuals. Such a difference in treatment between new applicants and existing employees would be analogous to amnesties for illegal immigrants and to the greater scope allowed for random drug testing of job applicants than of the already employed. Experience would show whether military morale or other factors affecting military effectiveness suffered from the acknowledged presence of known homosexuals, and would therefore provide guidance for a definitive resolution of the debate over whether to allow homosexuals to serve.

The Blackmail Myth

However we ought to proceed, we should at least drop the weak arguments for excluding homosexuals from the military, for those arguments are used to bar them with even less justification from other jobs. A combination of the blackmail and instability concerns supplies the traditional rationale for excluding homosexuals from positions, whether in the government or in the private sector, requiring a security clearance. The rationale is weak, not only in theory but also in evidence. For when one searches the literature on espionage, sabotage, and other forms of treason, one finds—despite lurid claims, redolent of the time when homosexuality and treason were thought two sides of the same coin—little evidence that homosexuality is particularly widespread among traitors. It is difficult to make a persuasive argument that a known (hence blackmail-proof) homosexual who satisfies all intellectual, psychological, and other criteria for a security clearance should be denied one.

"The pursuit of the homosexual lifestyle [is] intrinsically harmful to the military community."

Gays and Lesbians Should Not Be Allowed to Serve in the Military

Melissa Wells-Petry, interviewed by Allan H. Ryskind

Melissa Wells-Petry is a U.S. Army major and lawyer at the Pentagon in Washington, D.C., and the author of *Exclusion: Homosexuals and the Right to Serve.* In the following interview, Wells-Petry argues that allowing homosexuals in the armed forces would be detrimental to America's military because of the impact on morale and health. Not only would such a move harm morale, the author contends, but it could also compromise the health of personnel through exposure to sexually transmitted diseases and HIV infection, a great concern and burden to soldiers who might require blood transfusions. Wells-Petry maintains that the military should avoid these problems by keeping its ban on homosexuals. Allan H. Ryskind is the Capitol Hill editor for *Human Events*, a weekly conservative publication.

As you read, consider the following questions:

1. What does Wells-Petry mean by her statement that the law sees no difference between status and conduct?
2. In the author's opinion, what is the difficulty in regulating a homosexual's conduct?
3. According to Wells-Petry, why should America be concerned with its own military policy rather than those of other nations?

Abridged from Melissa Wells-Petry, interviewed by Allan H. Ryskind, "The Dangers of Lifting the Military's Gay Ban," *Human Events*, June 5, 1993. Reprinted by permission from Human Events Publishing, Inc., 422 First St. SE, Washington, DC 20003.

Ryskind: Why should homosexuals be excluded from the military?
Wells-Petry: Homosexuality is clearly incompatible with military service. The military policy goal is to ban homosexual conduct in the ranks because of the social, political and health impact. Yet the homosexual community has made it known that they are not fighting for the right to remain celibate, even though their sexual conduct is what produces this adverse impact.

The basic policy of the military is to draw from groups of people that have the highest potential for successful soldiering, and to exclude groups that have a low potential for successful soldiering. And so you have to ask yourself, do homosexuals, as a group, have a high potential for successful soldiering?

Intrinsic Harm

Well, first of all, the conduct they are fighting to legitimize is against military law. So do they have a high probability of breaking military law? Yes. True, you can "fix" that just by changing the law, but then there's still the moral and practical dynamics of this conduct. This homosexual conduct, including sodomy and all the other sexual practices, and the pursuit of the homosexual lifestyle are intrinsically harmful to the military community.

Such conduct has terrible health consequences by exposing individuals who engage in it not just to HIV, but to a whole variety of communicable diseases and infections—such as hepatitis, other complications such as anal cancer and so on—and it eventually exposes the military community to these health problems, for one thing, because the Army has an obligation to take care of sick soldiers.

Then, of course, homosexual social conduct—striking up relationships, dancing, kissing and wanting to do all that sort of stuff—has a deleterious effect on the morale of the overwhelming majority of military personnel. In fact, the No. 1 concern of our soldiers, sailors, airmen and Marines is this social impact, the impact on their privacy.

How do we deal with a sexual dynamic normally? We deal with it in the military and most of society with gender segregation, in such areas as showering, using the latrine, all the sleeping arrangements and so on.

Well, that breaks down when you have homosexuals. Then you would have men together with men for whom there is potential sexual attraction, so maybe you might want to resolve the problem through segregation. But the homosexual community is adamantly opposed to such a solution, and the truth is you wouldn't want to put homosexual men together in the same barracks, either, because they would be quite likely to strike up sexual relationships. You can't give everyone his own room, especially not on ships or when you're going to war, so there are a lot of practical reasons for banning them from the military in the first place.

President Clinton insists there's a difference between status and conduct. Many homosexuals, he points out, have served both ably and heroically, so what's wrong with his recommendation that we allow open homosexuals into the armed forces, but exclude them only when they engage in homosexual conduct?

Look, we're talking about minimizing risk here. First of all, the law says there is no such thing as a difference between status and conduct. When a person labels himself a homosexual, the law says that you are perfectly entitled to presume that that person has some basis and experience for doing that, for either having engaged in homosexual conduct, wanting to engage in it, or intending to engage in it in the future. So we're talking about minimizing risk.

This status concept just doesn't make sense. For example, there's a case where a guy wanted to be in ROTC [Reserve Officer Training Corps] and he told the ROTC recruiter that he was a Nazi. And the Army didn't say, well, you know, that's a very interesting status. The Army said, well, you have identified yourself as a member of a group whose behavior is incompatible with the military and he was excluded. And that's exactly the same process here.

The law says that when you're a homosexual, you are identifying yourself as a member of a group whose behavior is incompatible with the military service. So you can't have this in the abstract.

If you allow homosexuals to serve, you have to face reality, that they are not going to be celibate. Celibacy is not popular, that's not realistic and that's not their goal. So if you're trying to avoid conduct and all its associated effects—and even our commander-in-chief has agreed that homosexual conduct can present problems to the military—the question is, why bring in a person and make him a soldier when he has a very high probability of engaging in conduct that's going to be incompatible and have a detrimental effect on the military?

Restraints on Admission

Right now, the law and rules and regulations forbid people from coming into the military who are homosexuals, but even this restraint has not prevented gays from entering the armed services.

Well, no rule is unbroken. We have a prohibition against single parents, for example, but we have a constant problem with people not telling the truth about their status as parents.

My point is, if the Administration finally allows open homosexuals into the military, removing all restraints on their admission, don't you believe there would be a major increase?

119

We've seen that with the single parent policy. There was a time when we said this was okay, and we had a significant increase of single parents coming on board, and a significant increase of the problems associated with the conflict between what was best for the child and meeting Army requirements.

It's completely indefensible to say they're in the service now, so what's the big deal? We're not talking about now, when we have *some* problems with homosexuals who are breaking the rules to come in and are living under the restraints of the law. We're talking about removing the restraining hand of the law.

A Burden on the Military

I looked at that [homosexuals in the military] issue when I was secretary of defense and decided not to lift the ban on gays serving in the military. The burden that is already imposed on folks who sign up voluntarily in military units did not justify putting an extra added burden and saying, "Oh, by the way, you've also got to accommodate people who are avowedly gay." It would affect the units' morale and cohesiveness and make it more difficult for them to accomplish their assignments. I didn't have the right as secretary to impose that burden.

Dick Cheney, *The Washington Times*, February 2, 1994.

So you do fear a big increase?

Yes, over time. Remember, we're not talking about what happens the day after a policy change. You have to assume a policy change is *forever*. What will be the cumulative effect of the change down the road?

Right now, homosexuals in the military, like everyone else who's breaking the rules, have to take care, keep their activities under wraps to make sure their co-workers don't know about it. And that is one good effect of the law.

But if a homosexual can come into the service and you say you can only regulate his conduct, what are we talking about here? Only his sexual conduct? Is he going to be able to dance with his boyfriend at the NCO [noncommissioned officer] club? Is he going to be able to talk to people about his homosexuality, ask them for dates? Where are you going to draw the line? That's why, over the years, experts on and in the military say we need to draw the line at the front gate. Because why should we bring in people who we are just going to have to kick out if they can't walk what, for them, is a very fine line?

Isn't it likely that many in the homosexual community would want to join up with the military, if you remove the ban against gays, be-

cause (1) homosexuality will be under some form of legal protection, and (2) gays will have the kinds of health care benefits they may not be able to get now?

I think that's a distinct possibility. I think, too, it's such a high visibility issue that I'm sure if the ban were lifted, you'd see camera crews going into the recruiting station and somebody following Joe and Bill through basic training, smooching on the tapes. I think it's completely predictable that the whole cadre of legal defense kinds that have been supporting the homosexual "rights" movement would continue to push their agenda within the military.

They would argue that now that it's legal to enter the military, therefore you have to legalize the conduct associated with it.

You know, there's this doctrine in the law called the assumption of the risk, and it says if you know the risk, and you take that risk, and the harm happens, you get what you deserve, you've got to live with it.

I think it's completely predictable because the seeds are sown in the proposed change. When conduct is discovered, the argument for the homosexuals will be, well, what did you think I was going to do? And surely we could not go to court and say, "I thought all homosexuals were celibate." We couldn't do it.

Health Concerns

So what would be the added health costs of opening the armed forces to homosexuals?

Homosexuals are vulnerable to a whole variety of sexually transmitted diseases, some you don't even see in other groups in the population. If you use the figure $200,000 for the cost of seeing a soldier through HIV, through medical retirement to his death and burial, it would only take 10 additional soldiers to get HIV on active duty to ring up a bill of $2 million. Now $2 million is small change in terms of the defense budget, but that's for a mere 10 soldiers.

There's another cost, and that's the cost of protecting the overall force. Hepatitis is a disease that is frequently found in the homosexual population. It's contagious. Maybe you'd have to immunize the whole force. How much does that cost, maybe $2 a pop, maybe $5? But it costs, and ask yourself what are you getting in return for your money.

I think you're going to have to go to increased HIV testing. Now bear in mind that the homosexual community has already put us on notice that they are going to challenge our HIV testing policies. They've been against mandatory testing. I saw a copy of a transition document which said the homosexual community was opposed to mandatory testing.

Even for the military?

121

Yes. From my point of view, you'd have to test more, however, because how else are you going to be able to safeguard the blood supply? What you're going to have to do is what I call console people, give them a confidence factor that the military is doing every single thing it can to minimize the risk that the blood supply will be tainted with HIV. There are, as you may know, gaps in the testing.

What are the inadequacies of the testing procedures? I've heard homosexuals say that there's nothing to worry about because they are being tested all the time in the military.

My understanding of how the test works is that they test for the antibody to the HIV virus and a person may have the virus and be infected, but not yet have developed sufficient antibodies to show up as a marker for the test.

So the point is that many people could totally pass the test, even though they are HIV-positive?

Yes. And they might have been infected with the virus for several months. . . .

Battlefield Risks

What about battlefield transfusions? Combat soldiers have to give blood under certain conditions, and surely, in this case, heterosexuals would have every reason to fear receiving blood from a homosexual combatant.

Soldiers do receive transfusions on the battlefield from their buddies in a combat unit when they don't have time to get blood that has been specially screened. The transfusions might be necessary as part of a mass casualty situation where soldiers are lined up and there's no time for getting blood that has been already checked.

You'll hear people say, "Oh, technology can fix that; we won't have soldier-to-soldier transfusions in the future" or "we'll be able to get quick tests on the blood." I wouldn't bet my life on such sure-fire technical progress, however. Nor are such transfusions "old hat." I heard they had a situation in Somalia where they had to draw five units of blood from soldiers, and then give immediate transfusions.

The important point is we would be introducing an added risk to the military if you say it's okay for homosexuals to serve in the military and you're kind of winking at their conduct. That's what we would be doing here.

Maybe they will develop a test that can detect HIV immediately. But technology will never solve the fear that people feel in coming in contact with another person's blood, especially if they know or have reason to suspect that that person is engaging in homosexual conduct.

I understand that today in the National Basketball Association, if you get cut, they pull you out of the game. Magic Johnson, as I recall, retired permanently, saying, when he got out, he saw the fear in the eyes of his fellow players. I mean, HIV-infected blood is poison. Now think about this for a moment. You can get HIV from a needle stick, and not even see any blood on the needle or on your finger. But in the military, there is blood all over the place.

Discord in Every Case

General Norman Schwarzkopf echoed what I have been telling you for years: "The job of the military is to go to war and win, not to be instruments of social experimentation."

General Schwarzkopf says that although homosexuals have no doubt served honorably in the military, in every case he knows about, their units have become divided when others learn of their sexual orientation. *Every* case!

Rush H. Limbaugh III, *See, I Told You So*, 1993.

If you were in a foxhole with someone who is homosexual, and if the guy gets hurt or wounded, you'd wonder if you should touch him or even give him mouth-to-mouth resuscitation. I think you'd be worried all the time that you were with some ticking time bomb, a lethal comrade-in-arms, when you should be concentrating on the enemy. And the blood, one assumes, flows freely even in non-battlefield situations.

Absolutely. I mean soldiers are always getting hurt and that's the nature of the business. It's a very dangerous profession. And it's an extra burden you're putting on young men and women if you allow homosexuals in the armed services. How are you going to give them the confidence factor they need? They're not naive. If someone is engaging in homosexual conduct, they are going to wonder about their blood, and so on. And I think that is something that technology cannot fix.

Foreign Militaries

What about foreign countries, such as Israel and Holland?

Israel, on a very restricted basis, does allow some homosexuals into the military.

But you have to remember that because of religious and cultural reasons, Israel does not have a friendly environment for homosexuals. As I understand it, in Israel, if you don't make it through your military service, you are dead meat in that society. You can't go to college, you're not welcome at the synagogue, mom and dad are ashamed of you. But their society frowns on homosexual behavior, and homosexual soldiers do not rise to high positions.

We don't have the same kind of cultural and religious restraint in our society. We don't have a social brake on homosexual conduct. We have a very militant homosexual population that is determined not only to pursue this conduct, but to gain social legitimacy for it.

We're also in a different situation because we are a very litigious society and it's very easy to use our legal system as a vehicle for a political agenda. When your social restraints are ineffective, then your need for an official, explicit policy barring homosexuals in the military is much greater.

As far as I've seen, the Israeli military has the same goal as we do, to avoid and minimize homosexual conduct. In fact, when they know you're a homosexual, you won't get advanced and they won't let you live in the barracks.

In Holland, there are studies showing that parents are more reluctant to allow their teenage sons to join the military if they know they would be living in close quarters with gays. And an internal study shows that they're still having problems with the acceptability of homosexuals within the ranks. So if there is still a problem in the Netherlands, which we think of as very liberal, why should we buy such a headache for ourselves?

Keep the Exclusion Policy

Look, the bottom line is not what any foreign country does, but what is best for the United States' military, given our national values and mores. We have the best military in the world, and we shouldn't embark on a policy that will tend to weaken it. . . .

I think one of the important things is to ensure that people understand what we're getting into. A vote for changing the exclusion policy—a vote of confidence for changing the exclusion policy—is a vote for homosexual conduct. People need to know we're not talking about status, we're not talking about lifestyle, and we're not talking about some kind of abstract concept.

We are talking about homosexual conduct, and we are talking about, of course, steps for legalizing and legitimizing that conduct. It might be a baby step, it might be an express bus, all the way to that end, but we just need to keep in mind what we're being asked to buy here. If people want to buy it, that's the democratic process at work. They need to know what's for sale.

Periodical Bibliography

The following articles have been selected to supplement the diverse views presented in this chapter.

The Advocate	"Us vs. Them," November 23, 1993.
The CQ Researcher	"Gay Rights," March 5, 1993.
John Finnis and Martha Nussbaum	"Is Homosexual Conduct Wrong? A Philosophical Exchange," *The New Republic*, November 15, 1993.
Christopher Hill	"Colorado in the Gay Nineties," *National Review*, September 6, 1993.
Stan Karp	"Trouble over the Rainbow," *Z Magazine*, March 1993.
John Leo	"Gay Rights, Not Approval," *U.S. News & World Report*, May 3, 1993.
Michael Lerner	"Curing Homophobia and Other Conservative Pathologies," *Tikkun*, September/October 1993.
David Link	"I Am Not Queer," *Reason*, August/September 1993.
Tony Marco	"Oppressed Minorities, or Counterfeits?" *Conservative Review*, November/December 1993. Available from 1307 Dolley Madison Blvd., Room 203, McLean, VA 22101.
Keith Meinhold	"The Navy vs. Me," *The New York Times*, December 16, 1993.
The Nation	Special issue on homosexuality, July 5, 1993.
Dennis Prager	"Homosexuality, the Bible, and Us—A Jewish Perspective," *The Public Interest*, Summer 1993.
Sara Rimer	"Gay Rights Law for Schools Advances in Massachusetts," *The New York Times*, December 8, 1993.
Eloise Salholz	"The Power and the Pride," *Newsweek*, June 21, 1993.
Joseph P. Shapiro	"Straight Talk About Gays," *U.S. News & World Report*, July 5, 1993.
Randy Shilts	"What's Fair in Love and War," *Newsweek*, February 1, 1993.
The World & I	Special section on homosexuality, October 1993.

Is Pornography Harmful?

Sexual
Values

Chapter Preface

Chuck had been separated from his wife for one year when he got high one day on alcohol, heroin, and marijuana and watched a pornographic movie. "It was a guy coming up behind a girl and attacking her and raping her. That's when I started having rape fantasies." That night, Chuck attempted his first rape but got scared and ran home. On his second attempt, he raped a girl in a college restroom and was finally arrested after attempting rape twice more. Chuck insists that pornography caused him to rape. "You look at these movies and think, 'Wow, I wonder what it would be like to go out and rape somebody!' I know five or six guys who saw pictures of rape in a dirty book and believed [rape] was all right."

Of course, many men who view pornography do not commit or condone rape—an argument made by experts who find no direct causal relationship between pornography and rape. These psychologists and other experts contend that other factors, unrelated to pornography, must also be considered. In Chuck's case, they would cite his chronic substance abuse or his intense hatred of his adulterous wife and abusive stepmother—hatred that he admittedly acted out against other women. According to conservative scholar Ernest van den Haag, "If there is a disposition to sex crimes, an almost infinite variety of things may trigger the criminal action."

Such factors notwithstanding, some argue that images of violence, rather than the sexual images in pornography, are more likely to provoke violence against women. But other experts disagree and argue that pornography—whether portraying violence or not—is at fault. According to the 1986 report of the Attorney General's Commission on Pornography, "Substantial exposure to [nonviolent] materials bears some causal relationship to . . . sexual violence, sexual coercion, or unwanted sexual aggression." Such acts, antipornography activists charge, are the direct result of pornographic images that, while not explicitly violent, degrade women and convince men that women enjoy being abused.

Violence against women is only one issue in the pornography debate. Others include the effects of pornography on women, religion, and society as a whole. The authors in this chapter focus on these issues as they debate whether pornography is harmful.

"Pornography is ruining homes and families."

Pornography Harms Society

Bob Navarro and Bob Peters, interviewed by Robert Selle

Bob Navarro is a sergeant and Bob Peters a detective in the Los Angeles Police Department's administrative vice division. In the following viewpoint, Navarro and Peters describe pornography as a moral plague afflicting more and more Americans. Pornography, they contend, contributes to many of the nation's social ills: organized crime, exploitation of women and violence against them, as well as unhealthy male sexual attitudes and sexual dysfunction. Navarro and Peters argue that America can help stop pornography from corrupting society by declaring, as Canada did, that anything that degrades women sexually is obscene and subject to censorship. Robert Selle is an editor of *The World & I*, a monthly magazine that covers culture, politics, and science.

As you read, consider the following questions:

1. According to Navarro, what threat do sexually explicit movies on cable television pose?
2. How can addiction to pornography have negative effects, in the police officers' opinion?
3. Why do Navarro and Peters believe that soft porn is a stepping-stone to hard-core pornography?

Abridged from Bob Navarro and Bob Peters, interviewed by Robert Selle, "The Pornography Industry Today: An Interview with Two Detectives." This article appeared in the December 1992 issue and is reprinted with permission from *The World & I*, a publication of The Washington Times Corporation, copyright ©1992.

Robert Selle: What sort of day-to-day work do vice officers such as yourselves do?

Bob Peters: Basically, our responsibility is gathering information on the pornography industry and putting together obscenity cases. We check the bookstores, arcades, and other pornography outlets on a regular basis, find out the type of material that's on the market, the type of product that's selling and not selling, magazines that are coming on the market.

We try to find material that we feel is prosecutable under our obscenity statutes. After that, we look for the people who are supplying it.

Selle: Does that involve undercover work as well? Electronic surveillance?

Peters: We don't do a lot of electronic. We do some. Also, we might respond undercover to ads, and we do undercover operations on the distributors.

Bob Navarro: There are also many companies that distribute primarily by mail order, so we'll order material that we think may be prosecutable. And, because of the obscenity laws, we have to keep abreast of changes in community standards, especially any changes that tilt against the presence of pornography in the community. . . .

The Porn Capital

Selle: Would it be accurate to say that America has become the porn center of the world?

Peters: Definitely.

Navarro: You could even go further and say Los Angeles.

Peters: I think we're probably the porn capital of the United States, but America is definitely the distributing point for pornography in the entire world. A lot of child porn and similar stuff comes out of Denmark and Sweden, but they don't have anything that compares to our production or distribution. I don't know of anybody that does.

Even in Japan and those areas where they're starting to increase their production, they're in the Dark Ages compared to America.

Navarro: Another issue is that the porno material that's being shipped out of Los Angeles is sent into communities all around the country. Many of these areas have determined that such material is not consistent with their community standards and so is illegal in terms of federal and state law.

But even though it's illegal in these areas, they don't have the manpower, money, or experience to prosecute it, or, because of the vague "community standard" yardstick set up by the Supreme Court, they are unsure of what their community's pornography standard is and therefore hesitate to prosecute material that might actually be clearly illegal in terms of its content.

The material may not be prosecuted here in L.A., but the distributors are still committing federal violations and are still breaking the law in other states by transporting their pornography into those areas.

"SEE, FIRST SIGN OF A DECLINING SOCIETY—NOBODY WANTS TO READ BOOKS ANY MORE."

Selle: To what extent does organized crime control the porn business these days?

Peters: Well, it controls it to a large degree. I don't think we have the control we had ten or fifteen years ago. At that time, we had control so direct that people were actually coming into L.A. and strong-arming and so forth. But we still have control; we have organized-crime people owning porn-related corporations.

We are well aware of the fact that they control product distribution to their outlets. Let's say we have a company here in California that wants to hit a string of six or seven hundred different stores throughout the country. Their product has to go through one of these organized-crime distribution centers.

So in order to hit that market, they have to be associated with—and therefore to a certain extent controlled by—organized crime. I think we're seeing more money coming from hidden ar-

130

eas of organized crime in the industry. Whereas crooks like that used to be the owners or the people up front, now we're seeing more and more "covert action," where they're not listed on any documents or actually shown as officers of a corporation. But we know they're the money behind a company, because we've seen people that were broke one year and all of a sudden they're running a $10 million corporation the next. . . .

Selle: Do you see any trends in the production and marketing of pornography?

Navarro: I think a big move is going to be in the direction of pay-per-view. We're reaching a point where people will be able to just plug in from their homes and rent a totally sexually explicit movie over the cable system. It's just a matter of time, and when that happens there will be no doubt in the world that children will be able to access these things with no effort at all.

An interesting aside to all this. As part of our work, we used to arrest the producers of porn videos as panderers under the pandering laws, because sex acts were being performed in the videos and because people were being hired to perform the acts.

We were prosecuting them on a state statute for pimping and pandering. After we did several cases, one of them reached the California Supreme Court and got reversed. The justices said we could no longer crack down on sexually explicit movies by enforcing the prostitution and pandering statutes. It's unfortunate, but that's the way it is.

When they make these movies nowadays, they take out filming permits and film in private homes, using them as a backdrop. They can do it anyplace at all. They're making so many of them now they're just saturating the market, and they're a dime a dozen. . . .

The Pornography Consumer

Selle: Here's a somewhat different question. Could you tell me something about the pornography consumer? What kind of person is he? Is there a typical profile?

Navarro: I deal with community groups that try to get feedback on the nature of "community standards," and there are a few organizations of an Alcoholics Anonymous type whose members try to help each other overcome their sexual addictions. Every one of those who are sexually addicted like this are involved heavily in pornography.

The feedback I've gotten is that the porno users are a good cross section of our society. They tend to be white, middle-class Americans. It seems that the higher the intelligence level, the more they get involved. But we're finding that now, with this material entering virtually every community over the past few years, we can't generalize quite like that anymore.

131

No one has to go very far to get hard-core pornography in their hands these days—only to the local video store.

Many people have testified as to their extreme addiction to the material in terms of having their whole lives consumed by it, sitting for hours masturbating to adult material and needing progressively stronger, heavier, harder material to give them a bigger kick.

Like an alcoholic or a drug addict, they're looking for that big kick, and they need more just to keep them at that level of feeling OK. And often their addiction will push its way into real-life acting out.

Peters: Ending up with something like [serial killer] Ted Bundy.

Navarro: That's very, very true. We've had a number of people testify that they would actually act out the movies, go out and duplicate the violence in the films.

Peters: We've got crime reports we've taken from rapists and perpetrators of other sex crimes saying the reason they did it was because they were stimulated by a movie or a magazine, and they wanted to see if it could be done. I think Ted Bundy's probably the most notable individual who attributed much of his criminal behavior to pornography.

America Must Speak Out

Why must we put up with pornography? The answer to that question is that we must not. I think Thomas Jefferson and the other framers of our Constitution would be disgusted to see that, in the name of freedom, America has elevated the business of objectifying and degrading human beings to an amazing $8 billion per year enterprise.

America must not allow pornography, one of the lowest forms of exploitation, to set its moral and social climate. It is time to speak vehemently *against* pornography, and not allow the pornography industry to censor its critics.

Nancy Clausen, *Standing Together*, Fall 1993.

Selle: How does the market for hard-core porn get built up? Would it be accurate to say that the soft-porn producers like Playboy *and* Penthouse *magazines and the videos they make serve to cultivate a market for the harder material?*

Navarro: Yes, definitely. No question about it.

That soft-core stuff is even more available, more acceptable throughout society. If you buy any one of those magazines, you'll notice it's packed with hundreds of ads for hard-core stuff, including phone sex, rubber goods, personal ads, and prostitution come-ons. The next step after consuming soft porn often is visiting prostitutes.

Peters: If the advertisers didn't think that soft porn was the stepping-stone to hard-core, they wouldn't be advertising in those publications.

Navarro: It's definitely a progressive thing. The person starts longing for harder material, until he's fully addicted. One psychologist said that what with the kind of pornography available out there and the way that attitudes are built up by viewing it, we're creating a whole bunch of Ted Bundys. It's very, very frightening.

And this fear is reinforced because the number of rapes has increased considerably from years ago, the deviancy acted out in sex crimes has gotten worse and worse, and such crimes much more frequent and commonplace. There probably are a number of serial killers out there you never heard of before.

I've listened and talked to people in the California Youth Authority [a correctional institution] who've done extensive studies with children and violent adolescent sex offenders, and just about every one of them started off using pornography. It progressed to the harder-core stuff, and then they began acting it out, at first exposing themselves in public, because they thought that would excite their victims, as it's portrayed as doing in the pornography.

In just about every porno video, you'll have a woman who looks out the window, sees a man, he somehow exposes himself, and she immediately becomes aroused, of course, and goes after him.

So, there's a road from pornography to sex crimes; the porno users end up raping and molesting children or siblings. Very commonplace. This is the conclusion of a study produced by the Youth Authority.

Exploiters Behind Pornography

Selle: One pornography creator described women as "dogs" whose only worth is as "pawns for my pleasure." Is that an extreme example of a perverse pornographer, or does it reflect the mainstream philosophy behind what pornographers do?

Peters: Basically, it's the mainstream. There are some of them out there that are a little less extreme than that, but that's basically it. Women are meat on a block to be used.

Navarro: They say there are no victims. But I've talked to model after model—or performer after performer, whatever you want to call them—and believe me, they are victimized. I don't care if they even realize it themselves. They are given extra money for double penetrations; they're all required to have gay sex—sex with other women—whether that's their inclination or not. They have to do that to be accepted into the industry.

And there's a tremendous amount of drug use in the industry, cocaine use, and enormous pressure to conform to that kind of life-style.

Peters: If you have any inhibitions, then they use that to break you down.

Easy Money

Navarro: Unfortunately, a lot of these performers really believe that they're getting involved in the movie industry and that this is the first step in a film career. They're not sophisticated young ladies, believe me. They've worked it out in their minds so that it's a business to them, but the majority of them are not very sophisticated and they do it because it's the easy way of making a buck.

Peters: It's easy money. It's hard to turn down three, four, five hundred dollars a day for work when you're a runaway and you're living on fifty cents. They easily get talked into this kind of stuff.

Navarro: There's a tremendous amount of guilt and regret after they're cajoled into doing these things by the industry. The producers might start out by saying, Hey, why don't you do a nude pose? And then the next "nude pose" turns out to be one with another person there, and the next might involve simulating sex, and suddenly there's still photography of actual sex acts, and then filming of full sex scenes. They get a prospective performer on a set and say, Oh, all you have to do is some nude scenes; you don't have to get involved in it. But pretty soon the script calls for her to have sex and she's over her head in it.

That's very commonplace.

Selle: With so much pornography around in the country, some people have said we're in an age of vulgarity. What do you think about that? Has vulgarity triumphed in America?

Navarro: It seems like it. And I think a lot of it has to do with attitudes toward sex, women, and children changing under the influence of pornography. Men have been coming more and more to regard women as just sex objects.

Even in music now you can see the vulgarity erupting. You have all the sexually explicit lyrics in rap songs, for example.

Pornography is ruining homes and families. A wife certainly can't perform or look like the models in these videos, so by comparison she becomes a lot less desirable to her husband.

And a great many children, as I said, are getting hold of porno material, and they're formulating their sexual concepts at a very early age based on what they see on these videos, which is not a normal or healthy view of sexuality.

Peters: And you've also got people who are apathetic; since pornography hasn't affected them, or it's not in their neighborhood, they ignore it.

Or they may be actually ignorant of it. Many people think that *Hustler* is as bad as pornography gets; they're not really aware of the deviant, graphic, violent stuff that's flooding the market out there in videos and special-interest magazines. But we find that when people are educated as to the reality of pornography, they become really upset.

I think we could turn the country around, but I think, like Bob said, we're seeing a real decay in America right now. We've got to do something about it. Otherwise we're going to be a society of degenerates. The apathy and the ignorance have to be corrected. We try to do that all the time. We go out speaking to civic groups all the time, and we tell them what law enforcement is facing and show them what is actually on the market today.

Some of these people go absolutely berserk after our presentations. They weren't aware the stuff was out there or that it's having the effect it's having. I think if we could get more people getting concerned about it like that we could start turning things around. If we don't, I don't see any end of it. Like Bob says, you're even seeing pop music starting to go that way, and people are so worried about First Amendment rights that they ignore the effect that the music or whatever is having on their kids or their community. Now that's stupid.

A Proper Legal Yardstick

Navarro: Canada's equivalent of our U.S. Supreme Court came down with a good ruling. They concluded that anything that's degrading to women is obscene. I really have to applaud that decision. It's very simple. If it degrades women in a sexual way then it would be obscene and viewing of it should not be allowed. That's simple. Not violating anybody's personal political rights or anything.

That's what they're using now as their legal yardstick. If it's sexual in nature, shows any kind of penetration, and is degrading to women, then it's obscene. If we had that type of standard in the United States, in the state of California, we'd really be able to keep this kind of material from further corrupting our society. I think we have that responsibility.

It's a moral issue. All our laws are based on moral issues. People say we can't legislate morality. But we do it every time we make a law. They're all moral.

"The chief harm from pornography comes not from its use but from attempts at its suppression."

Censoring Pornography Harms Society

Philip D. Harvey

Many Americans, regardless of whether they approve or disapprove of pornography, believe that government should not censor it. In the following viewpoint, Philip D. Harvey agrees and argues that censorship of pornography is an unconstitutional attack on freedom of speech and interferes in the private lives of Americans. Harvey contends that pornography causes no harm and has legitimate positive values, and that government has no business imposing its idea of morality on the public through censorship. Government so zealously censors sexual material it deems obscene, the author writes, that it has placed a "chill" on important public discussions of serious problems related to sex. Harvey is the founder and president of PHE, Inc., a mail-order company in Carrboro, North Carolina, that provides contraceptives, adult videos, and other products.

As you read, consider the following questions:

1. Why can there be no single definition of pornography, according to Harvey?
2. In Harvey's opinion, how can some sexually explicit material be educational?
3. Why does the author disagree that adult films degrade women?

Abridged from Philip D. Harvey, "Federal Censorship and the 'War on Pornography.'" Reproduced with permission from the *SIECUS Report*, February/March 1992, vol. 20, no. 3. Copyright Sex Information and Education Council of the U.S., Inc., 130 W. 42nd St., Suite 2500, New York, NY 10036. 212/819-9770, fax 212/819-9776.

Do adults have the right to use sexually explicit material in the privacy of their homes?

In the conservative community of Rocky Mount, North Carolina, that was exactly what a random selection of people was asked in a 1991 newspaper poll. The specific issue was whether adult videos should be available for rental in local stores. These are some of their responses:

"I don't approve of X-rated videos, yet if minors are not involved, I think they should be available."

"If the renters are over 21 and children are not involved, then I think people should have the right to rent cassettes like that."

"If that's what people choose to do, yes. It's a matter of personal choice."

"Personally, I'm against them. But people have the right to view what they want in their homes."

This small survey, taken right in the back yard of [antiobscenity crusader] Senator Jesse Helms, is no aberration. Whenever the issue is raised, Americans speak out strongly for their right to read, see, and think what they wish, whatever the subject—sex included—and for the right of others to do the same.

Freedom Under Attack

This fundamental respect for the right to privacy is, of course, one of our greatest national achievements. It has produced a freedom that has fueled the growth of our nation, won us the envy of most of the peoples of the world, and helped inspire by example the breakdown of Communism. Yet the crowning irony is that this freedom that Americans hold so dear, and which is on the rise elsewhere, is under attack today by government at all levels here at home. The government censors are out in force and sex is their target.

The assault began in earnest in 1986, when the report of the Meese Commission on Pornography, employing a brand of fear-mongering reminiscent of the McCarthyism of the 50s, claimed that pornography was rampant everywhere and was undermining our society. The campaign has gained considerable momentum ever since. The most publicized cases have involved the photography of Robert Mapplethorpe and the music of 2 Live Crew, but the chill of sexual censorship has been felt in many other places. . . .

The inescapable conclusion seems to be that government interference in sexual matters is at its highest peak in decades, perhaps since the turn of the last century.

Government Zealots

Spearheading and giving federal encouragement to this movement is a 13-lawyer obscenity unit in the U.S. Justice Department. A creation of the Meese Commission, this unit has undertaken a mission no less than the elimination of all sexually explicit material that it considers offensive, whether or not the material is protected by the First Amendment. This has included *Playboy* magazine and Alex Comfort's popular book, *The Joy of Sex*.

A 1991 study by the American Civil Liberties Union (ACLU) documented many of the obscenity unit's legally questionable tactics and led the ACLU to call for its abolition. Among other things, this study drew upon evidence uncovered in a lawsuit that PHE, Inc. brought against the Justice Department showing that the Federal Bureau of Investigation (F.B.I.) was so appalled by the obscenity unit's cavalier way of operating that it refused to cooperate with it. Various F.B.I. officials labeled the unit's leaders as zealots motivated mainly by religious beliefs. And the ugly truth is that these beliefs are now being imposed on everyone—with all the power and authority of the U.S. Department of Justice.

Censorship Endangers Social Change

Chipping away at the First Amendment is rarely a good idea, and especially dangerous for groups committed to radical social change. Censorship, as history teaches, is more likely to be used to silence leftists and feminists than pornographers.

Ruth Rosen, *Los Angeles Times*, February 9, 1994.

Government censorship and interference in sexual matters is harmful at any time, but it is particularly so in the present day. With HIV/AIDS, unwanted pregnancies, and so many other sexually related problems having become epidemic, there is a desperate need for honest, open, and responsible public discussion of sexuality. Yet the chill applied by government has put such discussion in desperately short supply and encouraged the flourishing of a fig-leaf mentality.

A major irony is that this represents a distinctly minority viewpoint that flies in the face of good old-fashioned American common sense. As I have stated, most Americans recognize the great danger in trying to regulate private behavior; they reject any suggestion that government has the right to tell them how to lead their lives, and they lack the fear of sexuality that seems to lie at the heart of the censorship effort. This is confirmed by a Roper Organization poll of June 1991, which found that, contrary to government policy, 81% of those questioned agreed it may take "pretty explicit sexual material" to teach teenagers about HIV/AIDS and 64% favored distributing condoms in senior high schools.

The Need to Speak Out

It is easy to over-dramatize where the government's activities may lead. Yet, it is also a fact of history in this century that when totalitarian governments have come to power, their first actions have included efforts to "improve morality." This tendency is alive today in places where religious fundamentalists have gained the ascendancy and where the establishment of "sexual correctness" has been accompanied by the imposition of political and religious values by the dominant group on all others—trampling tolerance, respect for diversity, and freedom in the process. Restricting a woman's right to dress as she chooses and to work outside the home is but one example of this kind of repression found in several Middle Eastern countries, for example. Moreover, there is an eerie parallel here in the United States, in the movement to coercively restrict a woman's right to choose for herself when it comes to abortion.

Thinking citizens *must* speak out against this growing infringement of their privacy and their rights and protest government efforts to label everything sexual that it does not approve of as "pornography," and therefore bad and even criminal.

Used indiscriminately, the very word pornography is a powerful weapon in the hands of those who would suppress any kind of sexually explicit material. It has so many negative connotations in the popular mind that it takes a strong person, indeed, to rise to the defense of anything called "pornographic." Yet unless such a defense is mounted, it seems likely that the "war against pornography" will spread to encompass more and more benign materials and activities.

Defining the Undefinable

When the Meese Commission first assembled, it declared that one of its goals would be to define pornography once and for all. Yet, when its work was over, the Commission had not supplied a definition. It had not done so for the very good reason that pornography is in the eye of the beholder. What constitutes pornography, and is perhaps unacceptable for one person, is perfectly acceptable and innocuous, even beneficial for another. There can be no one definition, because pornography is a matter that individuals define for themselves.

Yet, despite being unable to define what pornography is, the government has nonetheless declared that pornography is harmful and therefore deserves to be condemned, especially if it is "hard core." Just what constitutes "hard core" pornography is never made clear, but the current definition seems to be depictions involving visible sexual intromission, which would, of course, even include such material as *The Joy of Sex*. To base decisions about the legality of sexual material on their explicitness, rather than their usefulness, is, of course, an absurdity. And how ludicrous it is to imagine a handful of lawyers, most of whom share the same set of religiously and politically inspired beliefs, sitting down and deciding which sexual materials are fit for public consumption, and which are not and therefore must be prosecuted.

The most effective way to head off this campaign is to stress and highlight the facts of the issue, for when this is done, a persuasive case is made for allowing people to make their own decisions about sexually explicit material and wresting that authority from government. And it makes clear the fact that *the chief harm from pornography comes not from its use but from attempts at its suppression.*

Let me clarify that what I am talking about here is "adult" pornography—that which is used by adults, depicts cheerfully consenting adults, and does not involve either children or violence. This is also known as "mainstream" pornography, and it constitutes the vast majority of all such material in America, despite claims by officials who attempt to justify their censorship activity by stating that the harsher forms of pornography predominate.

The Facts of Pornography

When the facts about this kind of pornography are assembled, they support the following conclusions:

• Pornography causes no harm and is, in fact, socially and individually useful.

• Pornography does not undermine the social fabric. It is far less harmful than many other legal and acceptable things in our society.

• Pornography does not "exploit" members of our society.

• Pornography laws are counterproductive. They divert resources from combating actual criminal activity. They constitute a governmental attempt to legislate morality—a process that strikes at the heart of our freedoms.

A good way to begin to examine these points is to ask why, if a fellow citizen chooses to pursue her/his own happiness by reading a salacious book, we are justified in labeling that person or her/his bookseller a criminal.

Presumably, interference in the private lives of citizens is justified only when a compelling state interest is served. However, there is no compelling state interest achieved by the criminalization and suppression of pornography. First, unlike yelling "fire!"

in a crowded theater, pornography poses no threat to anyone's safety. Second, unlike slander or libel, pornography is not malicious; it threatens no one's reputation or career. And third, we now have a substantial body of social science evidence that clearly indicates that viewing nonviolent adult pornography does not lead to violent or antisocial acts.

The Violence Myth

When violence is introduced into pornography, research suggests that the attitudes of some viewers tend to harden in ways we may not like, but it is the *violence*, not the sex, that produces the negative results. Indeed, based on their review of all relevant research, the authors of the most authoritative book on this subject, *The Question of Pornography*, conclude that the R-rated "slasher" movies—seen by millions and often even shown on network TV—are probably the most harmful because they mix sexual themes with horrific acts of violence. In contrast, nonviolent pornography involving sexual activities between cheerfully consenting adults has consistently been found to be benign. Even the Meese Commission, albeit begrudgingly, conceded this fact, stating: "The fairest conclusion from the social science evidence is that there is no persuasive evidence to date supporting the connection between nonviolent and nondegrading materials and acts of sexual violence, and that there is some, but very limited evidence, indicating that the connection does not exist."

Censorship Hurts Women

We feminists who oppose censorship believe that such campaigns invariably exploit sexual fears and uncertainties. Moreover, these campaigns promote the false message that women are degraded by sex and that women's sexuality is dangerous and must be controlled. We refuse the offer of censorship in exchange for "protection" as a terrible bargain—and one that has, in any case, never worked. Again and again, such campaigns have led to attacks on sexually related art and literature, on education, on entertainment and on serious inquiry. Women's interests are invariably hurt, because—big surprise—it is the unpopular and disempowered who are most injured by censorship.

Leanne Katz, *In These Times*, March 7, 1994.

Further, such nonviolent pornography also serves useful purposes. Sex therapists routinely prescribe sexually explicit films for patients who do not understand certain sexual functions. These films are also often recommended to couples, as a way to promote improved sexual communication and thus a better sexual relationship.

If pornography causes no harm and indeed has legitimate positive values, the government's efforts to suppress it are revealed for what they really are—attempts to impose an *official* idea of morality on everyone. Not only are such efforts wrong and utterly at odds with principles of freedom, but they have never worked and probably never will.

The Use of Harmful Materials

Another way to view this subject is to examine the extent to which free societies permit, as an aspect of freedom, the use of substances and materials that actually do cause measurable harm. The following comparison of deaths [caused per year] in the United States is revealing: Cigarettes, 434,000; Alcohol, 105,000; Automobiles, 49,000; Handguns, 8,900; Lightning Strikes, 45; Pornography, 0.

Our society permits use of the first four items and even allows them to be advertised and promoted, yet criminalizes only the sixth item. If the American thirst for freedom is so great that we freely allow our citizens to destroy their lungs with smoke and their livers with alcohol, wreaking havoc not only on themselves, but on their families and others, and adding a great financial burden to society, how can we possibly justify outlawing sexual depictions that do not destroy life, but so often enhance it? Clearly, there is no acceptable answer.

The morally superior or the naively innocent say, however, that while pornography may not kill, it corrupts. They decry its effect on youth and fear that Main Street may soon become Times Square. Yet stripped of their emotional content, these concerns prove groundless, too. . . .

Respecting Privacy

Critics claim that pornography can pollute their communities and create a harmful environment, especially for the young. This hysterical leap of imagination totally ignores the ability of local governments to legitimately influence the character of their communities through zoning and other laws. Even more importantly, this fails to take into account the crucial distinction present in the law and in common sense between pornography that is used in private and other forms that may be thrust upon unwilling recipients. Thus, it is one thing for a community to mandate, for example, that posters for X-rated videos should not be displayed in store windows on public streets. Yet it is another thing altogether for government at any level to legislate what anyone can see or read in his or her own home, out of sight and sound of the general public.

Perhaps the newest argument used by the antipornography crusaders is one that has also been endorsed by some (but by no means all) feminists, namely, that pornography is especially harmful to women because it portrays them in a manner that reinforces sexist stereotypes. The argument was, in fact, one of the major points in the Meese Commission report—an amazing fact, really, when one considers that typical conservative supporters of the Commission, such as Phyllis Schlafly, had previously shown not the slightest scrap of sympathy for any feminist position.

Elliptical Reasoning

An important point here is to recognize that in the hundreds of new mainstream adult films produced each year women are almost always portrayed as active, enthusiastic, and equal participants in the sexual activity—as women who are, to use [sex educator] Marty Klein's phrase, "lusty without being bad." Yet, in the eyes of the would-be censors, this form of equality appears threatening and "wrong." Some even rationalize that such materials, while they may not *seem* degrading to women, still are, somehow. The mind is boggled by such elliptical reasoning (which pervades the Meese Commission report) and by the view it reflects, of women as innocent children who must be patronized and protected.

A thoughtful treatment of this issue was contained in a 1986 report by the ACLU entitled "Polluting the Censorship Debate," which critiqued the Meese Commission report. As the ACLU put it: "Individuals, mainly women, can indeed be hurt by the abusive production or use of pornography. Tragically, the Commission's final recommendations endorse virtually nothing which could make a real difference to the genuine victims of a still sexist culture. Where is the emphasis (or in most cases, even the mention) of strengthening sexual harassment laws . . . removing spousal immunity in sexual assault cases; providing meaningful law enforcement assistance to models abused in the production of sexual material? Where is the affirmation of the 1970 Commission's embrace of a serious sexuality education effort to empower the young to have a chance to develop a healthy and balanced view of sexuality in our culture?"

Instead of taking this approach, the Commission's report simply deplores and indiscriminately condemns all sexual material, virtually ignoring the evidence of its value and the supreme importance of letting individual Americans make their own decisions about such matters.

The Experience in Oregon

The censors have also ignored some real-life experience, especially that involving the state of Oregon. In 1986, the Supreme

Court of Oregon declared that its state constitution forbade the criminalization of any form of speech, including sexually explicit speech. In a single stroke, therefore, all pornography in Oregon except that involving children was made legal. To listen to the Meese moralists, one would have expected this action to have caused the earth to tremble, the sky to fall, and all decent behavior to vanish in the state. But what has happened? In actuality, no change whatsoever. The good citizens of Oregon have gone about their business behaving as honestly, ethically, and decently as ever before, and concern about the change in the law has been virtually nonexistent.

After the weakness in all the arguments used to defend anti-pornography laws has been exposed, what remains is the conclusion that these laws boil down to a governmental attempt to legislate morality—a process that strikes at the heart of the most fundamental principles governing a free and democratic society.

The writers of the Constitution, drawing on the ideas of John Locke, John Stuart Mill, and other leaders of the Enlightenment, recognized this. They agreed, as Mill had written, that "the only purpose for which power can be rightfully exercised over any member of a civilized community, against his will, is to prevent harm to others. His own good, either physical or moral, is not sufficient warrant." And they made this sentiment part and parcel of the letter and spirit of our Constitution.

Yet the crusade against sex, which runs directly counter to this wisdom, gains momentum, and threatens to steamroller other liberties that may get in its way. After the Meese Commission rendered its report, the press had a field day ridiculing it. One of the editorial cartoons that followed showed a man and woman in bed, probably husband and wife, with one saying, "Wait . . . I think we'd better have our lawyer present." It provided a good laugh, but if we're not careful and make known our opposition to the excesses of the government censors, we may well find that the last laugh is on us.

"For some men it is just pornography—and nothing else—which creates the predisposition to commit sexual abuse."

Pornography Causes Sexual Violence

Ray Wyre

Ray Wyre is a pioneer in the treatment of male sex offenders and is the director of the Gracewell Clinic, the first residential clinic for child sex abusers in the United Kingdom. In the following viewpoint, Wyre argues that a direct cause and effect relationship exists between pornography and sexual violence among some men. The author contends that pornography can cause men to sexually abuse women and children by breaking down their inhibitions to commit such acts and by fostering dangerous rape and sex fantasies. Wyre is the author of *Working with Sex Abuse* and coauthor of *Women, Men, and Rape*.

As you read, consider the following questions:

1. How does sexual arousal from pornography affect some men, in Wyre's opinion?
2. According to the author, how do sex offenders use pornography to overcome children's resistance?
3. In what context does Wyre believe that masturbation leads men to act out sexual fantasies?

©1992 by Ray Wyre. Reprinted from *The Case Against Pornography* (pp. 236-44, 246), edited by Catherine Itzin (1992), by permission of Oxford University Press.

I have worked with sex offenders in a number of different professional settings since the mid-1970s. In the course of my work I have developed a model which identifies the patterns that predictably operate in the cycle of sexual abuse. I have discovered that pornography can and does function at every stage in that cycle of abuse.

There are a number of characteristics that sex offenders have in common, and there are common factors to their sexual offences. Offenders always say it was a one-off. They always say it wasn't deliberate, it just happened. They always excuse, justify, explain, minimize. They always blame the victim for the experience, or they blame something or someone other than themselves. They always have fantasies as part of what they do, but they often in the early stages deny this. And they'll always reinterpret the behaviour of the victim. They will say the victim encouraged them, or seduced them, or asked for it, or wanted it, or enjoyed it. And if the victim survives the abuse they will interpret that to mean they were in no way harmed by it. They always objectify their victim, depersonalize them, see them as a type of woman, or a stereotype, representing something they can hate and hurt. They never see their victims as individuals or as human beings, and if something does happen to make them see their victims as human, they often cannot carry out their attack.

Pornography and Sexual Abuse

One reason why pornography is incredibly dangerous is because 97 per cent of all the rape stories in pornography end with the woman changing her mind and having orgasms and being represented as enjoying rape. Sex offenders use this kind of pornography to justify and legitimate what they do. It provides them with an excuse and a reason for doing what they do.

I'd like to explain how pornography relates to what I've discovered about sexual abuse. I initially took [family researcher] David Finkelhor's model of four preconditions for abuse: a predisposition, overcoming internal inhibitors, overcoming external inhibitors and overcoming victim resistance. I developed this into a fourteen-stage model. The stages of the cycle include: predisposition, fantasy, distorted thinking, internal inhibitors, external inhibitors, targeting, initiating, reinterpreting victim behaviour, arousal reinforcing and maintaining. When doing an assessment of a sex offender I want to explore all of these areas. It is impossible for the offender to abuse without going through the stages of this process. If you look at all the factors involved in what I call the cycle of behaviour of an offender, pornography plays a part in certain crucial points of that cycle.

The cycle of behaviour is maintained in lots of ways. The model may be useful in diagnosing men, for example, for sexually abusing a child. But it's no good just stopping there. You need to investigate all the needs that are associated with the abuser and why he does what he does. How are those needs met? You are challenging the behaviour and trying to reduce the risk of his doing it again. Group work is a way of interrupting that cycle, reducing the risk of men doing it again. At the same time you are trying to deal with the needs, and the justification and excuses he uses to go and do it. Pornography is important here.

Pornography does predispose some men to commit sexual abuse, and I have little doubt that the predisposition for some men can actually lie solely in the area of pornography. In other words, for some men it is just pornography—and nothing else—which creates the predisposition to commit sexual abuse. I have little doubt that there are men who in reading pornography, and particularly child pornography, will acquire ideas that they will put into practice. The ideas are initiated by pornography.

Sexual Arousal

Here there is, in fact, a direct cause and effect connection. I have little doubt there are some men whose attitudes and behaviour, how they see women and girls, and what they do to them, are determined by pornography. They are given ideas by getting caught up in the pornography. They then masturbate to the pornography, which creates orgasm that is directly connected to the distorted thinking of pornography. The orgasm legitimizes the distorted thinking and is also a reinforcer of the ideas and the behaviour. The actual sexual arousal and the orgasm are part of the reinforcing behaviour. Pornography makes the behaviour more acceptable and right because it reinforces the nice experience of sexual arousal and orgasm to something that is wrong. Pornography predisposes some men to act out that behaviour.

Look then at the next item, at fantasy. We don't know how many men are predisposed to abuse, but don't do it. Pornography may predispose men to rape and to have sex with children, who then don't do it. We don't know about that—yet. But we have discovered that for those men who do have a predisposition, their fantasy will always show you that they do, and pornography has a direct correlation with fantasy. Where there is fantasy, that fantasy is evidence of the predisposition. For example, if I am sitting in a restaurant with other male customers, each man in the room would know if he has a problem with children because his fantasy life would tell him that. If he has fantasies about having sex with children, then he has the problem and the potential for actually having sex with children. If he doesn't have those fantasies, then he won't have sex with children. The same is true of rape. So fantasy is very real and very important to behaviour and to predicting behaviour.

I think the feminist movement has made an important contribution to understanding rape and sexual abuse by identifying its basis in power relations. I have no doubt that this is true, but I think you miss something if you don't understand that within the power relations there are still sexual fantasy components. I have worked with the most outrageous, sadistic rapists whose whole motivation is anger, domination, putting down, controlling, but they still have a sexual fantasy element, connected to sexual thoughts during the rape. So even when they come into prison, even though their motive was anger and aggression, tied to all that is their own fantasy and thoughts and sexuality. Pornography obviously plays a very significant role in creating and reinforcing both sexual fantasy and power relations—including rape and child abuse fantasies.

A Stepdaughter's Abuse

Pornography destroys. Julie Schondel has lived to prove it.

Schondel was 5 years old when her stepfather began sexually abusing her. At the time, she didn't realize that most dads don't touch the private body parts of their daughters when tickling each other. She didn't know that most fathers don't get their children high on marijuana or drunk to make them more compliant with sexual acts. And she didn't understand that many of her father's actions were influenced by pornography.

"It had a major role in my abuse," Schondel, 27, now says of pornography. "My stepfather showed me porno movies when I was 9 years old. Had it not been for the pornography, I don't think I would have been abused to the extent that I was."

Sharon Hancock, *Focus on the Family Citizen*, September 20, 1993.

There is also a tendency for fantasy to escalate. It's a danger. And if you look at some of the cases I have worked with, even the material within the pornography wasn't enough to meet their fantasy needs: so that the man who raped a mother and daughter, for example, worked out and wrote down his own pornographic fantasies, influenced by the other pornography he had in his house, which included the rape of a mother and daughter which he then carried out for real.

There is then the distorted thinking. Pornography is incredibly powerful in creating and maintaining distorted thinking, the rape myths and the child abuse myths that exist in society. Any man may have the odd rape fantasy, but rapists have more. From pornography they get rape myths: women mean yes when they say no; women ask for it; women like force—all those sets of myths. Pornography reinforces those myths. They only have to look at pornography to acquire these myths. Not only does pornography reinforce rape at the level of idea, but, as I said earlier, in using pornography men learn to experience and to enjoy rape at a 'gut' level, through masturbation and orgasm to rape. And the majority of sex offenders of all types masturbate at least sometimes to images of rapes they have committed.

Child Sexual Abuse

I recently had referred to me a social worker who had told his supervisor that he was having sexual fantasies about children. He said he didn't know where they were coming from. But I discovered that he had a big stash of pornography, a whole suitcase full, which included a pornographic magazine with one story about father-daughter incest and another about a social worker having sex with all the girls in a girls' home. Needless to say, all the girls wanted it and were asking for it and enjoyed it. Furthermore this magazine was being sold legally in sex shops because the *photographs* were of women over the age of sixteen (made to look younger) and they had put a red dot over where the penis enters the vagina—that's how they get round the law.

But the message is that it is OK, it's good to have sex with under-age girls in your care as a social worker, that incest is good. This is the distorted thinking I refer to in my model. Pornography is amazingly powerful in maintaining that distorted thinking. So pornography certainly reinforces and can also create the predisposition to carry out abuse. It feeds the fantasy. And it creates distorted thinking.

Now we come to overcoming internal inhibitors. This is like conscience, really. It's whatever it is inside of people that stops them doing things that are wrong: our own internal set of values. Those values are never set in stone, they can be influenced, they can be changed, and I know pornography has a part to play in reducing inhibitions to rape and to child abuse. It does this by legitimizing the acts that are portrayed and by making it seem as if it is not that bad because other people do it. In pornography only 2 or 3 per cent of men who rape are portrayed as suffering any negative consequences. Whereas the opposite is happening to the women who are raped. They are all portrayed as becoming orgasmic and enjoying being raped. This distorted thinking will play a part in reducing internal inhibitions to rape. . . .

[Another] stage in the cycle of abuse is what Finkelhor called 'overcoming victim resistance' and what I call 'initiating'. Pornography is used in initiating sexual abuse in a variety of ways. It is used to show children that other children do it, as a way of getting children to talk about sex. Sex offenders use ordinary 'soft' pornography to trap children and get them interested in it. So one young man who had been sexually abused—and who was then caught sexually abusing—had been taken in by a teacher who was a paedophile. He'd been taken round the teacher's house and shown 'ordinary' heterosexual pornography. There were other boys around watching pornography and they were all involved in this naughty secret: watching pornography. Then gradually, unbeknown to them, the men involved started to suggest sexual play between them—you know, masturbate while they're watching. Of course, the boys don't know that they are the object and target of all this: they don't know that the men have designs on them. The boys just think they are watching heterosexual pornography, the stuff you buy at newsagents, you know, good twelve-year-old fun, that's all.

The men create an environment where they can have discussions and talks with the boys and make it appear harmless. The soft porn is used to soften the boys up, so the men can get access and abuse them. They introduce gay literature, they start talking about homosexuality, and say that boys go through this phase, don't they, it's just normal. Pornography is used in that way too. One man made child pornography with 200 girls. He would then play games: run a so-called soft porn video and wherever it stopped, they would act out the sexual bit that was on the screen. Pornography is often instrumental in initiating sexual abuse. In fact, it plays a part at every stage in the cycle of abuse.

Climate of Misogyny

I'm talking here about sex offenders. Many men see pornography and don't necessarily go out and abuse: though we are now discovering that the level of rape, sexual assault and child sexual abuse is much higher than we ever knew it to be. But the men who offend are 'ordinary' men from every walk of life. What pornography does is create a climate of thought and belief which influences attitudes towards women and children which is endemic in our society. So, although the vast majority of men will say, 'Well I don't go out and abuse because I watch pornography', what they're missing is that they're still taking on the myths those stories are portraying. That's the danger of it. It maintains that climate of misogyny. I believe that pornography influences the attitudes of all men regardless of the behaviour that takes place as a result.

If a man's wife is raped, for example, or his daughter is raped, and you look at that father or that husband's attitude or response to the rape, if he has been into pornography he will be saying things like 'What did you do to ask for it?' He will be affected by the pornography. It will be very hard for him to overcome the influence. I have known fathers [who] slap their daughters—beat them—after they have been raped, in the belief that they shouldn't have been so stupid, or they shouldn't have dressed like that, or been looking like that, and nice girls don't get raped. . . .

A Pedophile's Porn

Another example of the effects of pornography comes from Gary Bishop, convicted homosexual pedophile who murdered five young boys in Salt Lake City, Utah, in order to conceal his sexual abuse of them. He wrote in a letter after his conviction: "Pornography was a determining factor in my downfall. Somehow I became sexually attracted to young boys and I would fantasize about them naked. Certain bookstores offered sex education, photographic or art books which occasionally contained pictures of nude boys. I purchased such books and used them to enhance my masturbatory fantasies.

"But it wasn't enough. I desired more sexually arousing pictures so I enticed boys into letting me take pictures of them naked. From adult magazines, I also located addresses of foreign companies specializing in 'kiddie porn' and spent hundreds of dollars on these magazines and films. . . .

"Finding and procuring sexually arousing materials became an obsession. For me, seeing pornography was like lighting a fuse on a stick of dynamite; I became stimulated and had to gratify my urges or explode. All boys became mere sexual objects. My conscience was desensitized and my sexual appetite entirely controlled my actions."

Gary Bishop then continued to tell how he sexually abused and killed his boy victims.

Victor B. Kline, *Pornography's Effects on Adults and Children*, 1993.

I agree that pornography is one of the factors that contributes to rape. I do not agree with the arguments that fantasy is something that happens in your head and that behaviour is something else. In my experience fantasy and behaviour are directly connected. I am biased here. I work with men who have already put into practice some of their sexually violent fantasies. They have more fantasies that they haven't enacted, most of them, but all of them have put some of their fantasies into practice. So I know—because all of the men I have ever worked with have put into practice their fantasies of sexual abuse—that those fantasies do get put into practice. In my experience, therefore, there is a direct connection between fantasy and action. There is also a connection between an escalation in fantasy and more extreme forms of violent behaviour.

I don't know how many men actually have fantasies and don't put them into practice. But I don't care about that. What I do know is that the more they masturbate to pornography, the more likely they will be to put their fantasy into practice. Masturbating to fantasy is part of the trigger to act out the content of the fantasy. It is the masturbation itself which both reinforces and escalates the behaviour. It blurs and it disinhibits. If men have fantasies and they masturbate to those fantasies, it leads them further towards the acting out of the fantasies. The more bizarre the fantasies are, the less likely they will have a consenting partner to comply with what they want to do. Quite enough men do enact their fantasy to make me not too concerned about men who might not put their fantasy into practice yet. I know there are a lot of men who put their fantasy into practice and it is 'society's' responsibility to do what it can to reduce the likelihood that men will commit sexual crimes, to try to ensure that men don't do it.

Potential for Change

Men's fantasies are fuelled by pornography. It gives them ideas, and they act those ideas out. I know women have said this, and that when women say they have been raped and assaulted by men who have been influenced by pornography, they are discredited and dismissed and constantly trivialized. What women say is true. I know this because I hear it from the other side. I have met a whole range of men who have told me what they have done to women, acts which have come from the ideas they have accumulated from pornography. The ideas then go way beyond pornography. Pornography is a contributing factor to the development of what they do. When you get into the fantasy world of sex offenders you will find the bizarreness of it horrific. . . .

People can be influenced positively and negatively. People can change. This is where there is a very strong argument for legislation against pornography, because if pornography influences attitudes and behaviour, then, in its absence, people are not influenced and there is the potential for change. Not only that, we can have positive images of sex and sexuality: I am not against nakedness, not against sexuality and the portrayal of equality within relationships.

"One can study case after case of sex crimes and murder without finding . . . that pornography was present in the background."

Pornography Is Not the Cause of Sexual Violence

F.M. Christensen

F.M. Christensen is a philosophy professor at the University of Alberta in Edmonton, Canada, and author of the book *Pornography: The Other Side*, from which the following viewpoint is excerpted. Christensen maintains that there is no substantial evidence that the use of pornography causes crimes of sexual violence. Many factors besides pornography can trigger such acts of violence, he contends, and even statistics showing a connection between sexual crimes and exposure to pornography do not prove a causal relationship; indeed, sexually explicit material may reduce violence. Finally, he concludes, the social influences in a criminal's life include many other factors that are more likely than pornography to affect behavior.

As you read, consider the following questions:

1. Why is Christensen skeptical of rapists' claims that pornography caused them to rape?
2. In Christensen's opinion, how could pornography prevent acts of sexual violence?
3. According to the author, what statistics are needed to show a causal relationship between the viewing of pornography and rape?

Excerpted from *Pornography: The Other Side*, by F.M. Christensen (Praeger Publishers, an imprint of Greenwood Publishing Group, Inc., Westport, CT, 1990), pp. 126-32, 142, ©1990 by F.M. Christensen. Reprinted with permission.

The anecdotal variety of evidence is perhaps the most commonly abused in everyday thinking. . . . To put it schematically, merely finding instances of A accompanied by B is not legitimate evidence that A causes B. Such thinking has been especially common in regard to the charge that pornography elicits violence. We constantly hear claims about sex criminals found to own pornography—ignoring all those who do not, and all the noncriminals who do. Similar stories of rapists and murderers who were Bible readers can equally well be found, from Albert Fish to Leonard Lake.

Some of the most manipulative uses of this sort of reasoning are to be heard at those perennial governmental hearings on obscenity. Individuals presented as "victims of pornography" tell horror stories about physical and emotional violence they have suffered. It is even sometimes stated that if one does not believe pornography is to blame for the plight of these people, one does not have any compassion for them. Though their experiences are tragic, however, in most of the cases it is plain the sexual materials were present in only an incidental way in lives already disordered and violent for obvious sociological reasons. (In fact, sometimes those testifying merely assume pornography must have been present.) The same may be said of those cases where erotic materials were employed in the commission of an assault, say, where someone was forced to look at them or to participate in making them. They no more support the claim that pornography causes coercive tendencies than the existence of slavery and forced labor argues that labor in itself tends to produce coercive behavior. The fact that some are willing to use force to get what they want does not argue that what they want is itself evil or evil-inducing, be it sex or love or a baby or money or anything else. Yet that is the insane inference that is constantly being drawn.

Anything Can Incite Violence

Some of these stories turn out on closer inspection to involve serious distortions of fact, or even to be wholly fictional. From media reporters pandering to public fears to lawyers attempting to prove a client was not responsible for what he did, people are always susceptible to dishonesty. One must maintain an attitude of critical judgment in such matters. All the same, it is certain there have been instances of pornography triggering violent behavior. The reason is that virtually anything can incite such a response on the part of a psychotic or sociopathic personality. To mention just two infamous cases, the British murderer John George Haigh reported that he had been impelled to his acts of vampirism by an emotionally charging Anglican high mass. Then there was Nannie Doss, who poisoned four husbands in succession; when finally caught, she explained that none of them had measured up to the romantic males she read about in *True Romances*. Nevertheless, if we are to say meaningfully that some type of thing causes violence, singling it out from the multitudes of other elements in life that can incite the unstable, it must be involved in a more systematic way than is suggested by such incidents as these.

No Obscene Material

In most of the studies that demonstrate that exposure to sexual violence produces negative attitudes toward women, men have been shown films or have heard audio depictions of rape or other forms of violence against women that would under no circumstance be classified as "obscene."

The effects have been found using R-rated, commercially available films and using movies seen on network television.

Daniel Linz and Edward Donnerstein, *The Chronicle of Higher Education*, September 30, 1992.

One crude type of more systematic evidence are the reports of police and FBI agents who say they regularly find pornography in the possession of rapists. However, these tend to be subjective, nonquantitative impressions, and they are not shared by other police and agents. In fact, some of them are reminiscent of claims, made by certain officials in earlier years, that most civil rights workers were Communists; ideology exerts a powerful influence on what some people will report having found out. A few researchers have attempted to gather data on pornography and violent sex crimes in a more rigorous way by studying cases of rape reported to authorities. In general, these efforts have discovered no good reason to suspect a causal connection between the two. For example, the Williams Committee, which studied the pornography issue for the British government, reported it was unable to uncover any cases of a probable link between pornography and violent sex crime. Instead, the committee remarked, "One can study case after case of sex crimes and murder without finding any hint at all that pornography was present in the background." A similar conclusion was drawn earlier by researchers who surveyed juvenile criminal cases in the United States.

Interviews with violent sex criminals themselves have provided another type of evidence on this matter. One survey of a group of convicted rapists elicited reports from a large number of them that they had used sexual materials just before seeking out a victim. That certainly indicates a connection of some type, but the nature of the link is problematic. By itself, this information may be no more significant than the fact that rapists *think* about sex before raping. It is too obvious that a strong desire for sex could constitute a motive both for using pornography and for committing a sex crime; there is no reason to suppose it was the former that produced the latter. In fact, the researcher described many of the rapists as employing the materials to excite themselves in preparation for the act, so the intention was evidently there in advance. Without the pornography, they could just have stoked themselves up on their own fantasies, as rapists so often report doing.

As for the possibility that these rapists would have committed their crimes less often without the added stimulation, that encounters another question, . . . namely, how many would-be rapists have been deterred by the use of a sexual substitute. For all we know, they more often lose their cravings as a result of masturbating with sexual portrayals. To speak schematically again, the important question is not whether A ever causes B but whether it does so "on balance," that is, more frequently than it prevents it. In this same vein, stories are often told of rapists who were carrying sexual materials when caught. Doesn't *that* show a causal link? But by the account some rapists have given, pornography is used as a backup; they masturbate with it if they cannot easily find a victim. What they might do if they did not have a substitute to relieve their urges is a serious question. All these facts leave too many questions unanswered.

Rapists' Own Perception

What about criminals' own perception of what causes their behavior, then? In one questionnaire survey of convicted rapists, eleven out of sixty responded yes to the question of whether pornography had had "anything to do" with their being in prison or a psychiatric hospital. An even higher proportion, 39 percent, felt pornography had led them at some time to commit a "sexual crime." (Note that that vague phrase, given the laws in the area at the time, could have included noncoercive acts of oral and anal intercourse.) This is a worrisome result; but as various researchers have pointed out, it cannot be accepted at face value. For one thing, the indeterminateness of a questionnaire answer raises issues we have considered before. For example, perhaps the prisoners would have said pornography had something "to do" with their situation only in the same sense that any source of sexual knowledge of arousal might have done, such as seeing women in provocative dress. Questions concerning the latter sort of stimulus are conspicuously absent when rapists are asked about pornography these days.

A much more serious doubt hinges on the fact that violent criminals as a group tend to be very unaware of their own motivations (which may have a lot to do with their being violent in the first place) and highly prone to rationalization. They could simply have been falling back on an "explanation" they have often heard, one that would tend to relieve their own blame, at that. Statements of this type that we occasionally hear from rapists sound very like the politically correct "confessions" that turn up in other ideologically charged contexts (e.g., those old Chinese Communist "self-examination" sessions). Other excuses the rapists commonly give, such as "she led me on," are rightly regarded with skepticism and often clearly false. The notorious Ted Bundy [serial killer] case obviously could have involved such motives, including the desire for a last-minute stay of execution. (Sources close to Bundy have pointed to a broken home and other childhood factors to explain his murderous rage.) If we buy our psychological theories from a certified psychopath, he will be conning us even from the grave.

Pornography Can Prevent Violence

Quite apart from such doubts, however, there is positive evidence on the other side. For one thing, this survey result conflicts with those of others who have interviewed sex criminals extensively. From their questioning of convicted rapists and pedophiles, for example, Michael Goldstein and Harold Kant concluded that "few if any" had been appreciably influenced by pornography. Instead, they decided, real persons in the environment "are far more potent sexual stimuli" for the sex criminal. In fact, many psychiatrists who have worked with sexually disturbed patients believe that pornography often has the effect of preventing sexual violence. Many sex offenders themselves report that this is the case, moreover. According to Dr. John Money, persons requesting help in a sex-offender clinic "commonly disclose in the course of counseling therapy that pornography helps them contain their abnormal sexuality within imagination only, as a fantasy." In fact, in the questionnaire just discussed, 39 percent of the convicts also agreed that pornography "provides a safety valve for antisocial impulses." Overall, this type of evidence provides at least as much reason to believe sexually explicit materials prevent violence as that they incite it.

Correlations Are Needed

The attempt to solve the problems facing the foregoing kind of data has led researchers to statistical methods. Now, it would not help us to learn that a high percentage of rapists use pornography; after all, a very great proportion of them drink coffee!

What is needed instead is a correlation: that more pornography users than others commit rape (or, equivalently, that more rapists than nonrapists use pornography). Schematically, it is not whether or not most As are Bs that counts; it is whether a higher percentage of As than of non-As are Bs, even if both percentages are low. In such a case, provided the statistics are collected carefully enough to rule out biased data and coincidence, we have good evidence for a causal relationship of some sort between A and B. This relationship, however, could be different things, notably that A causes B, that B causes A, or that A and B are collateral effects of some common cause, C. As an illustration of the latter, consider the operation of a barometer. The falling of its fluid level does not cause a storm to come; instead, a decrease in air pressure tends to produce both a storm and a drop in the barometer level.

So merely finding a correlation does not reveal a cause. . . .

A Variety of Stimuli

Possibly pornography abets some sex crimes. But those disposed to them may also be inclined to consume pornography as an effect, not a cause, of their pre-existing criminal disposition. More important, if there is a disposition to sex crimes, an almost infinite variety of things may trigger the criminal action. A rapist does not need pornography. The sight of a woman, or even of an advertisement for lingerie, may be enough. There is no way to eliminate stimuli and no reason to believe that pornography is indispensable to sex crimes or sufficiently causative to justify controlling it.

Ernest van den Haag, *National Review*, November 1, 1993.

One important type of statistical survey brought to bear on this question attempts to compare the backgrounds of those who have and those who have not committed violent sex crimes, in order to see if they differ, on average, in their prior exposure to sexually explicit materials. For we would expect a correlation between such acts and some aspect of such exposure if the one tends to cause the other. Five studies of this type were performed at the request of the U.S. Commission on Obscenity and Pornography at the end of the 1960s. To the surprise of many, only one of them found a larger amount of exposure to pornography in the backgrounds of those who had committed serious sex crimes than among those who had not. In fact, three of them, like an earlier study by the Kinsey Institute, found a *smaller* amount of prior exposure among violent sex criminals than in a "control group" of persons not known to have committed sex crimes. . . .

Factors Affecting Pornography Use and Violence

There are a number of reasons for suspecting that sex offenders would use erotic materials more, some of which have already been hinted at. For example, these individuals often have an obsessive preoccupation with sex; this would tend to express itself *both* in acts of sexual coercion and in more frequent use of sex substitutes. A study of men who admitted having raped but had not been prosecuted found they had an appreciably greater felt need for sex than other men, which suggests the same causal influence. Secondly, rapists as a group are known to feel alienated from women; this could also be a partial cause of a greater use of such substitutes as well as of a greater likelihood of hostile interaction with women.

For another such reason, rapists are known in general to come from social and family backgrounds that are less sheltered and stable, less constrained by the prevailing standards of society (e.g., the families are more violent.) Such persons might well be less inhibited about seeking out socially disapproved things like pornography, as well as in regard to the use of anti-social violence. Conversely, those who receive stronger training against harming others are often, in this culture, taught that pornography is degrading to women; they would be less apt either to commit violent crimes, especially against women, *or* to use pornography a great deal. (By way of analogy, in a culture teaching that both theft and eating pork are evil, a correlation between those two things would not be surprising.) This might be especially true for religious groups, which were disproportionately represented in the one study of the five mentioned earlier that did find a correlation between sex crimes and prior exposure to pornography. A society in which sexual openness is considered offensive to women may well display an association between rape and consumption of sexual materials, even if the latter has no tendency whatever to cause the former.

Correlation Differs from Cause

This last comment is the main point of the foregoing discussion. In circumstances where a common cause for two phenomena is not only possible but known to exist, a correlation between them is by itself useless as evidence that the one causes the other. To appeal to another simile, there is a very strong correlation between lying down and dying, but this is hardly evidence that the former produces the latter. Indeed, one who supposed that it did so and tried to avoid death by always standing up would probably hasten his or her own demise considerably.

As this example reveals, a correlation between two factors is quite compatible with the one *preventing* the other. Even should it ultimately become clear that rapists and other sex offenders do use more pornography, we would have no grounds to believe that such use in any way causes their behavior unless all the other plausible explanations for the correlation could be ruled unlikely by the evidence. . . .

Positive Portrayals of Violence

In a very special category are portrayals that combine sexuality with violence (actually a very small proportion of pornography). In particular, there is the case where violence is represented as bringing about some good end. This not only associates it with something desirable but makes it appear that the violence—something which in itself is an evil—is justified by the end it achieves. The particular scenario that has been experimentally investigated in connection with sex is that of a rape in which the victim is shown as becoming sexually aroused and enjoying it. Since this type of scene is found sexually exciting by many of both sexes, it is sometimes found in pornography and romances. It is also symbolically played out in many a Hollywood and TV movie. A kiss is forced on the woman; at first she resists but then becomes aroused and passionately returns it. Once again, such portrayals are not meant to send any general message about what women or men really want. But the question here is, might that message not be received by some individuals? Or might the use of force be seen as less serious, if not completely justified, by the positive outcome?

There is some evidence, acquired from experiments on college students, for a small effect of this type. After being exposed to the kind of scene just described, male subjects have been found to aggress more strongly against females in the laboratory. The effect is very short-lived, however, and it has been found to occur only immediately after exposure to violent sex films, not later on. Moreover, the seeming triviality of other laboratory results that involve aggression counsels against putting much weight on these.

Attitude Changes

Nevertheless, another type of experimental result does warrant concern, one that has to do with attitudes. After viewing rape scenes with a "positive" ending, certain males are a little more apt to report a belief that women may enjoy being raped. They also show a somewhat reduced perception of the amount of trauma involved or similar attitude changes. Such results have been obtained repeatedly, in fact. Even these tests have yielded mixed results, however; some of them have been unable to replicate the others. In one of the latter, male subjects assigned *longer* prison terms to rapists after viewing rape scenes of the type in question. Furthermore, whether the seeming attitude changes go very deep, or would last very long, is still not at all clear. It seems unlikely that a few books or movies could have much effect on a person's thinking compared to all the other influences of a lifetime of socialization.

"Pornography is a great destroyer of persons, therefore of families, and so surely of Church and nation."

Pornography Will Destroy Christianity

Paul Marx

Paul Marx is a Roman Catholic priest and the chairman of Human Life International, a pro-life and -family educational and research organization in Gaithersburg, Maryland. In the following viewpoint, Marx blames pornography and a sex-obsessed Western culture for destroying Christianity, families, and society. Marx cites the example of Austria, where he argues that socialists are promoting pornography to destroy religion and "destroy the Christian perception of man." The author argues that pornography is responsible for Austria's high abortion rate and Austrians' rejection of religion. The harm to religion and society there, generated by pornography, Marx concludes, affects all of Western society.

As you read, consider the following questions:

1. Why does Marx believe that humans are essentially sexual beings?
2. How do some politicians use pornography as a tool, according to the author?
3. In Marx's opinion, what is lacking in people who abuse sex?

Paul Marx, "Nature and Function of Pornography," *The Eternal Call*, Winter 1991. Reprinted with permission.

Pornography is not easy to define. According to Webster's *New World Dictionary*, the word comes from the Greek *pornographos*, meaning "writing about prostitutes"; Webster defines it as "1. writings, pictures, etc., intended primarily to arouse sexual desire. 2. the production of such writings, pictures, etc."

An American judge once said that he could not define it but knows it when he sees it. The U.S. Supreme Court has described "obscenity" as "patently offensive representations or descriptions of intimate sexual acts . . . masturbation, excretory functions . . ."

Playing on Lust

Pornographers prostitute man's God-given sexuality, his creative potential to work with God in bringing forth new life, as a way to promote pervasive lust. Lust is one of the seven capital sins. To become obsessed with physical sex exploits man's powerful inclination to lust. Pornography strikes at the center of human personality, since we are sexual beings in our total function; personality, sexuality and spirituality are co-terminous, and since man functions as a unitary composite of body and soul, everything we do—every human relationship—is sexual in the broad sense. Perhaps worst of all, pornography distorts his moral sense and snuffs out all thirst for religion and spiritual values. Playing on lust, pornography abuses women, brutalizes men, corrupts children and degrades human sexuality.

It is wrong to think that pornography is merely the work of those who want to make money. Surely there is that factor, but more important, pornography is often used as a political or religious (e.g., humanism) weapon to destroy a society or nation one wishes to change radically. Thus, the founder of Russian Communism, V.I. Lenin, said that "if you wish to destroy a nation, destroy its morality and it will fall into your lap like a ripe apple from a tree.". . .

Pornography in Austria

In Austria, for example, the godless Socialists use pornography in a most effective political way to destroy the Christian perception of man, man's dignity and worth. The results are readily seen: Austria is a dying nation, with one of the lowest birthrates in the world. In upper Austria, for example, every seventh parish [a unit of area committed to one Roman Catholic priest] has already been deserted. An increasing number of priests care for three to four parishes. Vocations to the priesthood and the religious life have alarmingly declined. If things continue as they are, by 1995 there will be in Austria not even 40% of parishes with a pastor of their own. Meanwhile, the decay of values is increasing year by year. . . .

Austria is a country of about seven million inhabitants. The birthrate has sunk to 1.4 children per completed family size (2.2 is needed for reproduction). Greedy doctors kill [i.e., abort] some 100,000 children annually. There are more abortions than births. Meanwhile, the foreign workers are fast changing the grand Austria we once knew.

Pornography Violates God's Gift

Pornography is immoral and ultimately anti-social precisely because it is opposed to the truth about the human person, made in the image and likeness of God (cf. Gen. 1:26-27). By its very nature, pornography denies the genuine meaning of human sexuality as a God-given gift intended to open individuals to love and to sharing in the creative work of God through responsible procreation. By reducing the body to an instrument for the gratification of the senses, pornography frustrates authentic moral growth and undermines the development of mature and healthy relationships. It leads inexorably to the exploitation of individuals, especially those who are most vulnerable, as is so tragically evident in the case of child pornography.

John Paul II, *Origins*, February 13, 1992.

Year by year, about 16,000 marriages are being destroyed by divorce, and the main cause of divorce is adultery. How preoccupied the Austrians are with sex can be seen from the fact that there are 8,000 registered prostitutes. Of course, there are many more prostitutes not registered. In Austria, more people earn their living and make more money by far in the sex industries of prostitution and pornography than the workers in Austria's largest factory.

The cause of this development is, in part, the sexual permissivism promoted for decades. Right now, Vienna is dotted with bordellos and has at least two hundred sex shops, to say nothing of the pornographic larder in the street kiosks. The pornographic advertising in the streets in sophisticated Vienna tells the sad degradation in a land once Roman Catholic. Never forget, man is a rational animal with a destiny beyond this world. The animals obey God by following their instincts. But man, having reason, can exploit his animal instincts and thus live lower than the animals. That's where most of the dying Western world is today when it comes to sex.

Mass pornography, mass prostitution, mass abortion and mass destruction of children at schools with pernicious, pornographic sexual education are the means by which sexual permissivism is carried into the larger society. State-controlled media (radio and TV) reinforce the godless philosophy. Proposed new sex education of the socialist Austrian government includes films depicting all manner of sexual practices and perversions. The accompanying literature suggests that a room be made available so that young boys and girls can experiment with one another and implement what they learn in the classroom!

The enemies of God know very well that sexual permissivism is a radical and sure means to "wash" God out of man's brain. The propagators of pornography and perversion are masters at producing well-aimed, well-prepared and well-functioning brainwashing of the worst kind. . . .

We Are Sexual Beings

A sex-abusing person loses the ability to enter into personal commitments, becomes unfit for a stable and loving marriage, to say nothing of destroying the basis of constructive citizenship. We need to remember that the powerful sexual drive needs to be controlled from early on, that the virtue of chastity is essential to proper human, loving, social relations, and that pornography strikes at the whole psychosocial structure of human personality. The reason is worth repeating: We are sexual beings; personality, sexuality and spirituality are co-terminous. Sigmund Freud was right in saying that in the widest sense everything we do is sexual. In other words, man is sexual not only physically but also psychologically and spiritually in his unitary function in all he does.

If we remember what the Bible tells us about the nature of human beings, that we are "prone to evil from the very beginning," we will see all the more clearly how the pernicious and pervasive power of pornography strikes a facet of personality in which man is very weak. While there are Ten Commandments, not just one, the fact is, the sex-abusing man or woman cannot be a lovely and creative person, and surely not a happy one.

The West Is in Danger

What I am saying and describing about Austria is also true of the whole West. It is dying out because of low birthrates accompanied by enormous abuse of sex. Moderns speak of population explosion; they say virtually nothing about the copulation explosion which is destroying the family, the Church and society. Particularly in the West there is lots of sexual activity, little new life because of comparatively few births. And yet, babies are the only future any nation has. All of this, of course, escapes the attention of the TV-drunk, modern, new pagans and too many worldly clergymen. As [British author and Roman Catholic convert] G.K. Chesterton wrote, birth control means no birth and no control.

Pornography is a great destroyer of persons, therefore of families, and so surely of Church and nation. It is used by some godless politicians and secular propagandists to spread the religion of humanism; they wish to destroy the prevalent moral order in order to implement their own. As psychiatrist Melvin Anchell has written, "Ecology of human sexuality is as essential for survival as the ecology of the earth."

"*[Christianity's] teachings . . . support the humiliation and degradation of women that is the . . . foundation for pornography.*"

Christianity Provides a Foundation for Pornography

Mary Jo Weaver

Christianity's traditional view that women are inferior and subservient to men provides a foundation for pornography to thrive, Mary Jo Weaver argues in the following viewpoint. Weaver asserts that religious conservatives' belief that Christianity can save people from pornography is mistaken because Christianity has itself fostered "the pornographic imagination." The author blames Christian teachings for propagating the beliefs that God designed women for subservient roles and that women must be ruled by men. Weaver concludes that pornography grows as a further distortion of these already distorted views. Weaver is a professor of religious studies at Indiana University in Bloomington.

As you read, consider the following questions:

1. How do antipornography feminists and religious conservatives view pornography differently, according to Weaver?
2. In Weaver's opinion, how does Christianity equate women and sex with evil?
3. According to the author, how does Jimmy Swaggart's conduct with a prostitute reflect the distortion of Christianity?

Abridged from Mary Jo Weaver, "Pornography and the Religious Imagination," in *Adult Users Only*, Susan Gubar and Joan Hoff, eds. Bloomington: Indiana University Press, 1989. Copyright ©1989, Indiana University Press. Reprinted with permission.

One of the more perverse images in the current debate about pornography pictures anti-pornography feminists and right-wing evangelicals joining hands to defeat a common enemy. In this scenario Susan Griffin, say, or Andrea Dworkin forms a chorus with Jerry Falwell or Jimmy Swaggart to raise their voices against those entrepreneurs whose fortunes are built on the debasement and dismemberment of women. While this imaginal coalition has been criticized by [author] Beatrice Faust as politically dangerous, because "people who are conservative about porn are usually conservative about lesbianism, abortion, health education and rape crisis centers," it has not been analyzed for its religious incongruities.

An alliance between an anti-pornography feminist like Susan Griffin and a right-wing evangelical Christian like Jimmy Swaggart is unwise on the basis of irreconcilable theological assumptions. A pact between Andrea Dworkin and Jerry Falwell is impossible because of their profound disagreements about the nature of pornography itself. Although I will use Susan Griffin and Jimmy Swaggart to concentrate on some theological issues raised by the pornography debate, I want to note a crucial distinction between militant feminists and fundamentalists that touches upon the vexing question of defining pornography. . . .

Two Sides of Pornography

To Jerry Falwell, for example, pornography means dirty movies, whereas to Dworkin it means representations of sexually explicit violent attacks upon women by men. As Alexander Bloom has said, "trying to define pornography is like peeling an onion . . . [but] what is at issue for the Right is not what is at issue for the feminists. It is, in fact, more likely that their notions of what is and is not pornographic are widely divergent." In fact, because religious conservatives imagine God as a dominating sovereign who demands human submission, they fail to criticize what anti-pornography feminists perceive as the root of pornography, power used to render others sexually docile.

Both Griffin and Swaggart make connections between religion (or the lack thereof) and pornography that are predicated on traditional Christianity. On the one hand, according to Susan Griffin, Christianity is the foundation of the pornographic imagination because it legitimizes patterns of domination and submission, patterns that are hyperbolized in pornographic enactments. When she warns that "we cannot choose to have both eros and pornography," she means in part that we must choose between Christianity and eros, between the bondage and discipline of traditional Christianity and the biophilic [life-loving] freedom of erotic nature. Jimmy Swaggart, on the other hand, links pornography with the failure of Americans to follow fundamentalist Christian teachings. For him, a strong religious commitment is the only means of saving American culture from the "demons of pornography." When he warns, as he often does on his televised revivals, that we must choose between pornography and religion, he means that a return to that "old-time religion" is the only defense against the perverse panderings of the pornography industry. . . .

I will argue that the elective affinity between Christianity and pornography does not rest with Christian teachings about sex but with traditional Christian teaching about women as inherently inferior. Although such teaching is not peculiar to Christianity—it can be shown that the patterns of domination and submission found in Christianity are based on an ancient male fear of women found in virtually all religions—the Christian tradition appropriated ideas about female inferiority and combined them with a tendency to spiritualize erotic language in its mystical tradition.

Traditional Christianity and Pornography

To both anti-pornography feminists and anti-pornography religious conservatives, Christianity is an institutionalization of divine/human interaction based on a dualistic system in which the divine is understood to be transcendent, superior, and dominant, whereas humanity is considered immanent, inferior, and submissive. This revealed order of things, as found in the Bible and in the Christian tradition, is presumed to be replicated in human relations so that the male inherits the lordly qualities of God the Father, while the female is enjoined to be submissive to God's rule as it is enacted by the male (father, husband, brother, bishop). But if critics like Griffin and preachers like Swaggart both accept this traditional version of Christianity as normative, they disagree about how to interpret it.

Anti-pornography feminists condemn traditional Christianity because it provides a religious justification for the pornographic imagination. According to them, its teachings about the inferiority of the body and the identification of the body with the female support the humiliation and degradation of women that is the emotional and theoretical foundation for pornography. Feminist theologians like Rosemary Ruether and Mary Daly, as well as critics like Susan Griffin, condemn traditional Christianity both for its treatment of women and for its teachings about sex. From the very beginning, they say, Christianity has taught us how to debase women and hate sex. And, indeed, even a casual reading of the "Fathers" of the church shows that the Christian tradition is full of scorn for women, scorn that overflows into canon law and medieval theology. The notion of women as inherently lustful, an opinion of "the Fathers," is reflected in clerical attitudes toward women and in the witchcraft mania.

If the Gospel is "good news" about salvation, it is bad news about sex. Ancient warnings against the allurements of "the world, the flesh and the devil" were most easily imagined in terms of the flesh, and although one could easily make a case, as Rosemary Ruether has done, that the explicitness of patriarchal warnings against sexual expression constituted a way for agitated celibates to discharge some of their sexual energy, the fact remains that the teachings of traditional Christianity are built upon a hatred of women and a profound abhorrence of sex. Friedrich Nietzsche's chilling comment—"Christianity gave Eros poison to drink; he did not die of it, but degenerated into a vice"—seems no more than a commonsense interpretation of a flawed tradition. When Christian crimes against women are castigated, especially in the context of the witchcraft mania, Christian teaching about sex is often cited as bearing the burden of those crimes. R.E.L. Masters says simply, "Almost the entire blame for the hideous nightmare that was the witch mania, and the greatest part of the blame for poisoning the sex life of the West, rests squarely on the Roman Catholic church." To overcome pornography, therefore, it appears as if one must reject Christianity, with its dominating God and its double standard of sexual relations as substantiated in Christian sexual ethics. . . .

Christianity and Phallic Symbols

In its incipiency, Christianity was a phallic cult. Being a Jewish heresy, it embraced many concepts of the old Yahweh worship of the Hebrews, as well as innumerable pagan religions; hence the survival of various phallic observances, rites, and "emblems," or symbols such as the Trinity, the Triangle, and the Cross, to name but three which are still going strong today, although their original phallic significance has been forgotten by almost everyone.

The Christians "borrowed" the Trinity, known irreverently as "The Three Musketeers," from the pagans, and it will be recalled that Pope John Paul II, in his fifth encyclical, *Dominum et Vivificantem* (The Lord and Giver of Life), plugged it as the sole allowable concept of god. But the Trinity was originally the phallus and its appendages. Unconscious compulsions must have goaded "His Holiness" into expressing the desire that all Roman Catholics, bar none, worship this most obscene, ancient, and *universal* phallic symbol.

Soledad de Montalvo-Mielche, *American Atheist*, April 1987.

Ironically, I would suggest that Christian sexual ethics are bad for women not because of Christian teachings about the life of the body, but because of religious beliefs about the life of the soul. The Christian roots of the pornographic imagination, as described by Griffin and others, are to be found not in moral handbooks about sexual conduct, but in the textbooks of theology and the spiritual life, both ancient and modern. Theology, the study of God's nature and of the relationships between the divine and human realities, is based on a dualistic understanding of the spiritual and material worlds, a distinction upheld by the belief that God is a radically transcendent and dominating being. In Western Christian spirituality, especially in Roman Catholicism [according to Donald Weinstein and Rudolph Bell], virginity, as "an ideal that derived ultimately from pre-Christian sources in Hellenistic dualism, pervaded every segment of medieval society."

Christian Theology

Blaming Christian sexual teachings, themselves, for the pornographic imagination, therefore, is untenable; it will be more productive to look for the foundations of the pornographic imagination in the patterns of domination and submission that are found primarily in Christian beliefs about women as inferior creatures, and in the tendency of the Christian tradition to separate procreative sex from erotic pleasure, or in the teachings that place eroticism within a context of female submission.

Traditional Christian theology is based on a belief in the radical transcendence of God and a consequent division of all reality into higher and lower realms. In this system, everything is divided according to a pattern of heavenly (spiritual) existence and earthly (bodily) life. In the creation story in the Bible, for example, the maker is divided from the thing made in such a way that the creator is inherently superior to the created order and stands in a relationship of mastery over it. According to traditional Christology, the redeemer, though "truly man," has a divine nature and so is divided from those redeemed by virtue of his status as the preexistent son of God. In human relations, the "degrading idea that 'man is the beginning and end of woman' is reinforced by the parallel man: woman; God: creature," as Mary Daly reminded us. In religious life the spiritual realm is divided from earthly life on the assumption that bodily life is inherently inferior to the life of the soul. . . .

Men Rule, Women Serve

In traditional Roman Catholicism and conservative fundamentalism, women must be ruled by a father and then by a husband (or, in the case of nuns, by a bishop). The medieval adage—*aut maritus, aut murus*, either a husband or an enclosure wall—presented women with their only options. Furthermore, the doctrine of complementarity—a form of sex-role discrimination that relegates men and women to specific roles on the basis of their supposed divinely assigned natures—continues to tell Christian women that God designed them for subservient roles. Since this traditional vision operates on a model in which women are necessarily subservient, anti-pornography feminists rightly suggest that it must be rejected, and anti-pornography religious conservatives wrongly link the defeat of pornography to the Christian vision. It is not far-fetched to say that pornography is an intensification of the gender differences in traditional Christianity. "Good Christian businessmen" who spend their lunch hours in "adult" bookstores live not in two worlds but in one single universe in which men dominate women. Pornography, therefore, does not grow at the expense of traditional Christianity but as a further distortion of the already distorted social roles embodied in its own religious vision.

Defining Sex Narrowly

Jimmy Swaggart's fall from grace, resulting from his kinky sexual practices with a prostitute, underscores my point. It is revealing that Swaggart did not have sexual intercourse with the "fallen woman" he accompanied to motel rooms but "used her" for autoerotic stimulation and fellatio. In his tearful public confession he admitted to weakness and "shameful conduct" but was able to assure his congregation that he had not "committed adultery" with her, thereby ensuring that his own personal pillar of a good Christian society—the sanctity of his marriage and family—remained solid. Religious traditions that tend to be overly agitated about sexual misconduct often define legitimate sexual activity in narrow ways so that "proper" sexual expression is limited to "the missionary position." As long as a man does not assume this position, he has not had "sexual intercourse." Swaggart's conduct may not be typical, but his theological beliefs are shared by a majority of religious conservatives who inhabit a world where God dominates men and men dominate women. . . .

A Newly Imagined Religion

There can be no real relationship between Christianity and eros in a religious system that insists on subservience from women and is built upon the double standards derived from the God of mastery. Religion as defined by conservatives is not antithetical to pornography but supportive of it, and an appropriation of the "old-time religion"is an affirmation of the very framework upon which perverse extensions of dominating masculinity are constructed. The anti-pornographic views of religious conservatives that purport to be deeply religious, are, therefore, profoundly pornographic, whereas the anti-pornographic views of feminist critics that appear to be anti-religious are open to the designs of a new theological vision. . . . It is not possible to imagine traditional religion and eros, nor is it possible to argue that conservative religion can save the world from pornography. It is possible, however, to have a newly imagined religion that welcomes eros . . . [and] not only undermines pornography but also undermines the old, tyrannizing tradition of conservative Christianity.

Periodical Bibliography

The following articles have been selected to supplement the diverse views presented in this chapter.

Andrea Dworkin — "Pornography," *Crossroads*, March 1993.

Ronald Dworkin — "Women and Pornography," *The New York Review of Books*, October 21, 1993.

Stephanie Gutmann — "Waging War on Sex Crimes and Videotape," *Insight*, May 3, 1993. Available from 3600 New York Ave. NE, Washington, DC 20002.

John Irving — "Pornography and the New Puritans," *The New York Times Book Review*, March 29, 1992.

John Paul II — "Pornography and the Exploitation of Individuals," *Origins*, February 13, 1992. Available from the Catholic News Service, 3211 Fourth St. NE, Washington, DC 20017-1100.

Wendy Kaminer — "Feminists Against the First Amendment," *The Atlantic Monthly*, November 1992.

Leanne Katz — "Censors' Helpers," *The New York Times*, December 4, 1993.

John Leo — "Censors on the Left," *U.S. News & World Report*, October 4, 1993.

Daniel Linz and Edward Donnerstein — "Research Can Help Us Explain Violence and Pornography," *The Chronicle of Higher Education*, September 30, 1992.

Ms. — Special section on pornography, January/February 1994.

The Nation — "Porn Again," December 6, 1993.

William Safire — "The Porn Is Green," *The New York Times*, November 25, 1993.

John Tierney — "Porn, the Low-Slung Engine of Progress," *The New York Times*, January 9, 1994.

George Will — "MacKinnon Would Repeal Freedom of Speech," *Conservative Chronicle*, November 10, 1993. Available from PO Box 11297, Des Moines, IA 50340-1297.

What Sexual Values Should Children Learn?

Sexual
Values

Chapter Preface

No issue concerning public schools may be more divisive than teaching children about sex. Although such instruction has been a part of public education for years, newer topics and strategies have further polarized parents, teachers, and others. These include AIDS education and teaching tolerance toward gays and lesbians, as well as condom distribution programs—all under the rubric of comprehensive sex education.

Proponents of such education, including Planned Parenthood and the Sex Information and Education Council of the United States (SIECUS), believe that teaching children about AIDS, homosexuality, and condom use is vital to youths as sexually transmitted diseases (STDs) and homophobia proliferate, and as more and younger children become sexually active. According to Planned Parenthood, comprehensive sex education "recognizes that ignorance, fear, and shame cause people to make sexual decisions that may endanger their well being and their lives." Planned Parenthood and SIECUS argue that comprehensive sex education, beginning as early as kindergarten, is needed to dispel myths and stereotypes about pregnancy, sexual orientation, and STDs.

But critics argue that comprehensive sex education is far too explicit, particularly for younger children, and that it encourages youths to engage in sex. According to research scholar Dana Mack, "It seems that no age is too young, no act too depraved to be excluded from the zealous reach of the 'sexuality-education' experts . . . [who] make the 'choice' of sexual activity look far more acceptable than that of celibacy." Referring to AIDS education, author and former teacher Sally D. Reed asks, "How would you feel if your eight-year-old was versed in the art of anal sex by your local school? How else do you teach a child about 'safe sex' and *not* catching AIDS unless you first inform him just how you get it?" These and other critics propose that sex education focus instead on topics such as abstinence, love, and monogamy.

Comprehensive sex education and alternatives to it are examined by the authors of the following viewpoints as they debate what sexual values children should learn.

"America needs a national commitment to comprehensive . . . programs in grades K–12, in every school."

Children Should Receive Comprehensive Sex Education

Planned Parenthood Federation of America

Planned Parenthood is an organization that promotes voluntary family planning in the United States and abroad and provides education and health-related services to more than four million Americans annually. In the following viewpoint, Planned Parenthood asserts that many parents are unable to provide sufficient sex education for their children and that most parents want schools to offer comprehensive sex education. Such education, encompassing topics such as abstinence, contraception, homosexuality, and sexually transmitted diseases, among others, should be taught to children of all ages to help them confront the realities of sexual behavior, Planned Parenthood argues. The national headquarters of Planned Parenthood Federation of America is located in New York City.

As you read, consider the following questions:

1. Why does Planned Parenthood believe young children should be instructed about sex?
2. How should abstinence be taught as a part of sex education, according to Planned Parenthood?
3. In the author's opinion, what are the benefits of teaching about contraception?

Excerpted from *Sexuality Education: Issues and Answers for Parents, Educators, and Policy Makers*, published by Planned Parenthood® Federation of America, Inc. Reprinted with permission.

Shouldn't sexuality education be left up to parents?

Sexual issues and values are a family matter, and parents are their children's earliest and most important teachers about sexuality. When teenagers visit Planned Parenthood clinics, our counselors always encourage them to discuss important sexual and relationship issues with a parent or another trusted adult.

Unfortunately, many parents are uncomfortable talking about sex with their children, and may not know the answers to their kids' important questions. Most parents want schools to share the responsibility for helping their kids learn to make healthy choices that protect themselves and others. According to a 1985 Louis Harris poll, nine out of 10 parents say they want their children to receive sexuality education in school.

Schools Need Sexuality Education

Why should schools get involved in sexuality education?

While more families are talking openly about sexuality, most parents still avoid the issue—or unintentionally hand down harmful myths and fear. Keeping our children ignorant endangers their lives—especially for the millions of teens who have already begun having sex (61% of male high school students and 48% of female high school students). We can't expect children to become sexually responsible if the adults in their lives are uninformed about sex or uncomfortable talking about it.

Schools can give young people the facts and the relationship skills they need to become responsible adults—and can break the cycle of ignorance, denial, and shame that often passes from one generation to the next. Most parents say they want their children to receive sexuality education in school.

In countries like England, Wales, France, and the Netherlands, national policy encourages comprehensive, reality-based sexuality education in schools, and young people have confidential access to contraception. Yet their rates of teen sexual activity are no higher than America's, and their rates of teenage pregnancy, childbearing, and abortion are two to seven times lower.

If sexuality education is so useful, why are so many teens still having sex and getting pregnant?

Reality-based education has not failed—it hasn't even been put to the test. Evaluations of the effectiveness of sexuality education in this country are based on efforts that have only been half-hearted at best.

America needs a national commitment to comprehensive, reality-based, age-appropriate programs in grades K–12, in every school. But only a handful of school systems in this entire country have such programs. Widespread, comprehensive sexuality education remains a distant ideal.

In a national survey of 4,200 sexuality education teachers,

nearly all felt that their programs provide "too little, too late." For example, most teachers think topics like contraception, condom use, and abortion should be taught before the end of seventh grade—but only a third say their programs include those subjects. And while 97% of teachers think sex education classes should teach students where they can go to obtain contraception, less than half are in schools where this information is taught.

Sometimes the only sexuality education a child or teenager receives in school is a single, 45-minute class! You can teach the facts of anatomy and birth control in an hour . . . but it takes a lot longer to teach kids to respect themselves and others, make responsible decisions under pressure, and clarify their personal and family values.

Ignorance Is Not Bliss

Sexually active students who are ignorant about protection become victims of cruel and misguided censorship. A responsible protective program must stress abstinence first and foremost, but also must reach out to students who choose not to abstain to avoid sending the message of "I told you so!" to any who fall victim to AIDS, other sexually transmitted diseases or premature parenthood.

I ask those who oppose sex education: How could education ever be wrong? How could ignorance ever be right? What good is reading, writing and arithmetic to a student who will die of AIDS because he or she was denied education by our schools? There are many reasons why schools must educate students on life issues like protective sex education. Ignorance is not bliss.

Travis Lund Moon, *Los Angeles Times*, February 28, 1994.

Aren't schools required *to teach sexuality education?*

Very few states have passed mandates for comprehensive sexuality education in grades K–12. (DC, DE, FL, GA, IA, IL, KS, MD, NJ, NV, RI, SC, VT, and VA). Even in these states, there's often a very big difference between what the law requires and what is actually taught. The fact is, only a handful of school systems in this entire country give their students comprehensive, reality-based programs.

Risk of Sexual Involvement

Hasn't sexuality education caused more *teens to experiment with sex?*

On the contrary, reality-based education has been shown to encourage responsible behavior among teens—especially when young people receive education prior to initiating intercourse.

There is no evidence that the increase in sexual intercourse among young people over the past decade is attributable to the few reputable education programs that have been implemented. Rather, this increase has grown out of complex societal changes— including a huge increase in sexual imagery in popular media, increased influence of the media on young people, and a decline in the influence of traditional sources of authority.

One reality-based education program, "Reducing the Risk," has been shown to be highly effective with young people who had not already begun having sex. After taking the program, these teens were more likely to delay initiation of sexual intercourse, had higher levels of knowledge and parent-child communication, and, when they did initiate intercourse, decreased their levels of unprotected intercourse by 40%.

In another program, participants at high risk for early sexual activity who had not yet had sexual intercourse were five times less likely to become sexually involved in the eighth grade than similar students in a control group. By the end of the ninth grade, those who were in the program still were only two-thirds as likely as others to be sexually involved. . . .

Ultimately, the most effective deterrents to too-early intercourse are strong self-esteem, the ability to make informed choices, and meaningful life options that give young people futures worth protecting and healthy ways to express their identity. Reality-based sexuality education is an essential ingredient of this strategy.

Young Children Need the Truth

Does sexuality education stimulate an interest in sex?

No. Interest in, and learning about, sexuality begins at birth and continues throughout the life cycle. Beginning in kindergarten, schools can and should provide age-appropriate instruction about sexuality—beginning with simple concepts and progressing to more complex ideas as children approach adulthood.

Withholding the truth from young children leaves them vulnerable to myths and misinformation, the constant barrage of sexual imagery in the popular media, and peer pressure that intensifies as they grow older. Children who lack the knowledge, self-esteem, and decision-making skills taught in reality-based curricula are also far less equipped to fend off sexual abuse or to know what to do if they are abused. Ignorance does not guarantee innocence.

Does sexuality education teach too much, too soon?

No. Like all effective teaching methods, reality-based curricula are designed to be developmentally appropriate for the age being taught. When sexuality education is age-appropriate, it creates a safe setting in which to learn, and a cohesive structure in which each lesson builds on the ones that preceded it. Even in the event of developmentally inappropriate instruction, it is unlikely that students would learn "too much to handle" at any particular age; children generally "tune out" when presented with ideas that are too complex for them to absorb.

The sexuality education going on in America today is too little, too late—especially with so many teens sexually active. One-fourth of all girls and one-third of all boys have had intercourse by age 15; 75% of females and 86% of males by age 19.

Do reality-based programs condone homosexuality and masturbation?

Teaching that something exists is not the same as promoting it, and students understand the difference. Reality-based education recognizes that the range of human sexual expression is extremely broad . . . that masturbation is a healthy, normal, and safe mode of sexual expression, for adults as well as young people . . . that it is normal if you do, and normal if you do not.

Accurate curricula recognize that homosexuals are present in all cultures, and in most classrooms. Comprehensive programs acknowledge the diversity of our society, and teach respect for all families, whether the individuals in them are heterosexual or homosexual. Rather than imposing moralistic judgments about sexual behaviors, responsible education presents the facts, risks, benefits, and societal background involved in various forms of sexual expression—then helps young people clarify their own values and choose behavior consistent with those values.

So that means sexuality education is "value-free"?

Not at all. Responsible, reality-based education:

- validates commonly accepted social values—like honesty with oneself and others, respect for each person's dignity and well-being, and responsibility for one's actions;

- teaches that no form of sexual expression is acceptable when it physically or emotionally harms themselves or others;

- provides young people with the facts and social skills to make responsible decisions in the context of their own value system, which is usually determined by their family, cultural heritage, and religious background;

- neither promotes nor undermines any one set of religious or secular values—unlike fear- and shame-based curricula that withhold facts, demand abstinence, and devalue other people's beliefs and choices.

Teaching About Abstinence

What's wrong with teaching kids to abstain?

Nothing, as long as it isn't the only message. The bottom line is that the "Just Say No" message doesn't work. That message has been around for many years, in many cultures—and it has failed. Vows of abstinence break more often than condoms do—especially in today's atmosphere of growing peer pressure and sexual hype in the media. Millions of teens each year continue to make the choice to engage in sexual intercourse. Withholding information that can preserve their health and save their lives is cruel, counterproductive, and immoral.

While abstaining from intercourse is the most effective way to avoid pregnancy and disease, both teenagers and adults know that fewer than 50% of teens are abstinent. Curricula that ignore this reality, in the face of all evidence, only serve to undermine the credibility of adults, teachers, and other authority figures in teens' eyes.

When abstinence is presented as the only choice, students who have already rejected that choice are made to feel condemned, guilty, and sick. This stigmatization not only harms them emotionally—it makes them tune out to other educational messages. They become isolated, marginalized, and unreachable by adults who could help them. Teaching young people that there is only one acceptable choice does not help them develop critical thinking skills, clarify their own values, and achieve empowerment.

Good education isn't just for today—it's for life. Very, very few human beings will choose lifelong sexual abstinence. Young people need to acquire the information and decision-making skills that will guide them throughout their lives.

A Healthy Choice

What should *teens be taught about abstinence?*

Reality-based education teaches that abstinence is the only 100% effective way to protect against unintended pregnancy and sexually transmitted diseases, including AIDS. It also encourages young people to view abstinence as a healthy choice that people may make at different times in their lives.

Every Planned Parenthood program or curriculum includes abstinence as a healthy option; one of Planned Parenthood's most popular pamphlets is "Teensex? It's OK to Say No Way"—hundreds of thousands of copies have been distributed to young people over the past several years.

However, reality-based education recognizes that by age 15, one-fourth of all girls and one-third of all boys have had intercourse; by age 20, 77% of females and 86% of males have had intercourse. For the sake of their health and lives, these young people need and deserve straightforward information on sexuality—including (but not limited to) facts on how to reduce the risks that can accompany sexual activity.

Even for teens who choose to postpone sex, abstinence is not likely to be their lifelong choice. And while many parents hope their teens will abstain now, most also hope their children will have a satisfying sexual relationship later in life. Without appropriate knowledge and skills, young people cannot be expected to become sexually responsible and healthy adults.

A Balanced Message

Isn't it hypocritical to teach kids to abstain, then teach them about contraception?

No. Teaching facts is not the same as telling kids what to do, and teens know the difference. Teaching both the benefits of abstinence and the facts about contraception is not a mixed message—it's a balanced message, which teenagers are perfectly capable of understanding. They grow up learning many such messages, for example: "Drive safely so you can avoid accidents; and wear your seat belt just in case." "Candy tastes good, but eating a lot of it isn't good for you." "It's best to avoid too much sun exposure; but if you're going to be in the sun a lot, wear a sunscreen."

In all the above examples, there are two halves to the message— and censoring the second half would be both cruel and unwise.

But isn't it just like telling kids not to use drugs, then telling them where to get them? Or telling them not to rob banks, then supplying them with a getaway car? (The latter analogy is used in the fear- and shame-based "Teen Aid" curriculum.)

Sexual urges are healthy and normal for teens, and they need to learn how to handle those feelings in ways that are responsible and caring. Healthy sexual behavior should *never* be compared with substance abuse or criminal behavior. Such comparisons only further stigmatize sexually active teenagers, making them harder to reach with messages about responsibility and safety. Sexual intercourse is a behavior that most human beings practice at some time in their lives. When it is respectful, responsible and healthy, it can be a positive, life-enhancing experience. That is not the case with substance abuse or crime.

Won't teaching about contraception and making condoms available encourage kids to have sex?

No. Teaching young people to use condoms properly can only protect their health and lives. Research indicates that educated, correct use increases the effectiveness of condoms in preventing pregnancy and sexually transmitted disease.

Condoms and foam have been available to teenagers in pharmacies, supermarkets, and convenience stores for years. The National Research Council, in its 1986 report on teen pregnancy, found that "there is no available evidence to indicate that availability and access to contraceptive services influences adolescents' decisions to become sexually active, while it does significantly affect their capacity to avoid pregnancy if they are engaging in intercourse."

In a three-year study of school-based clinics that dispense contraception, the Center for Population Options concluded that making birth control available in schools "neither hastened the onset of sexual activity nor increased its frequency." In a 1992 national [Gallup] poll, 68% of American adults supported the availability of condoms in public schools.

As Jeannie Rosoff, president of the Alan Guttmacher Institute, has said, "Fire engines are present at the site of fires, but they do not cause them. They only limit their destructiveness to property and their harm to human beings. The causes of fires must be sought elsewhere."

Overwhelming Public Support

Does the American public support sexuality education in schools?

Yes. A 1988 Louis Harris poll found that 89% of American adults support sexuality education in schools, and 73% want schools to make contraceptives available to students. A 1991 Roper Organization poll found that 81% of Americans agree that "it may take some pretty explicit sexual material to fully inform teenagers" about the dangers of AIDS; and 64% support the availability of condoms in high schools; and 65% think sexuality education is "very effective" in helping people avoid AIDS. . . .

Who are the people who oppose reality-based sexuality education?

Among the religious right, conservative network, the following organizations have been particularly active: American Family Association, American Life League, Citizens for Excellence in Education, Concerned Women for America, Eagle Forum, Focus on the Family, and National Association for Abstinence Education. They are in the minority, but they are noisy and well-organized. They are the same people who use every means possible to try to invade family privacy, dictate personal decisions, and impose narrow religious doctrines on everyone.

Some extremists try to camouflage their opposition to contraception and sexuality education by claiming to be anti-abortion—even though education and prevention of pregnancy are the most effective means of *reducing the need* for abortion. Such extremists view all sexual activity outside of marriage as sinful, and think pregnancy or even fatal diseases are appropriate "punishments" for those who don't live by their narrow moral doctrine. Their true aim is to eliminate all options for women, and *all* people who disagree with them.

While they claim to act out of concern for families and children, these same extremists have refused to join pro-choice groups in fighting for better health care and social services for women and for children once they are born. Instead, they block access to health care facilities. They harass and threaten health care workers and their families. They subject clinic workers and patients to violent attacks, including firebombs, chemical warfare, and gunfire. They terrorize women and try to lure them into phoney "counseling centers," where they bombard them with false information and intimidation. And they promote dangerously inaccurate, religiously based programs for brainwashing schoolchildren.

Reproductive and Other Rights

What does sexuality education have to do with reproductive choice and other fundamental rights?

Truthful education is the cornerstone of choice. No individual can make healthy, responsible, self-empowering choices without accurate information about his or her sexual and reproductive life.

Many opponents of abortion rights also oppose contraception and sexuality education, which are the most effective means of *reducing the need* for abortion. Meanwhile, they censor life-saving information. And they refuse to support public policies that help women, children, and families. The covert aim of such extremists is to eliminate *all* options for women and girls.

Where efforts to suppress sexuality education have succeeded, extremists have sometimes also engaged in other forms of radical activity: oppression of sexual and racial minorities, book banning, censorship of the arts, and other violations of constitutional freedoms and fundamental American values.

What kind of sexuality education does Planned Parenthood provide?

With more than 900 community-based centers in 49 states, Planned Parenthood offers the services of more than 600 professional educators and trainers and 300 volunteers. Most often Planned Parenthood is invited into schools to do presentations on contraception, but educators also address a broad range of other topics in schools, churches, youth centers, and other settings. In 1991, we reached 1.7 million Americans, with educational and training programs that include:

- programs to help parents become more comfortable discussing sexuality, so they can help prepare their children to make healthy, responsible choices;

- parent-child workshops and programs for teenagers and their parents that encourage family communication;

- specialized programs for people who are emotionally, developmentally, and physically disabled, and for their families.

When teenagers visit our clinics, Planned Parenthood counselors always encourage them to discuss important sexual and relationship issues with a parent or another trusted adult.

Each year Planned Parenthood Federation of America leads a coalition for National Family Sexuality Education Month with 50 other national organizations to promote programs and publications that support parents as the primary educators of their children.

"Wherever comprehensive sex education programs exist, teenage promiscuity, pregnancy, abortion . . . and accompanying emotional problems increase."

Children Should Not Receive Comprehensive Sex Education

John Ankerberg and John Weldon

Many Americans believe that comprehensive sex education teaches the wrong message about sex and goes far beyond what adolescents or younger children should learn. In the following viewpoint, John Ankerberg and John Weldon agree, arguing that this approach to sex education fails to teach children necessary moral values and results in teenage promiscuity and its consequences: soaring rates of pregnancy and sexually transmitted diseases, as well as the emotional pains caused by illicit sex. Ankerberg is the host of the nationally televised *John Ankerberg Show*. Weldon is the author of books on cults and the occult. Ankerberg and Weldon are coauthors of many booklets on religion.

As you read, consider the following questions:

1. What are the common errors of comprehensive sex education and what are their effects, in the authors' opinion?
2. According to Ankerberg and Weldon, why is the "values-neutral" method of sex education wrong?
3. Why do the authors criticize Planned Parenthood?

Excerpted from John Ankerberg and John Weldon, *The Facts on Sex Education*. Eugene, OR: Harvest House, 1993. Copyright 1993 by The Ankerberg Theological Research Institute. Reprinted with permission.

What is comprehensive sex education (CSE)?

Some studies have suggested that 75 percent of all teenagers have now had "comprehensive sex education."

A Louis Harris poll on teenage sexuality commissioned by Planned Parenthood used six criteria to determine the definition of this term. If a course contained four or more of the six elements listed, it could be classified as comprehensive sex education: 1) biological facts about reproduction; 2) talking about coping with sexual development; 3) information about different kinds of birth control; 4) information about preventing sexual abuse; 5) facts about abortion; and 6) facts about where to get contraceptives. Today, we might also add a discussion of "sexual lifestyle options."

The Wrong Approach

Unfortunately, this approach to sex education is a biased one—and may be more sexually explicit than the above list suggests. CSE involves a philosophy of sexual instruction based on a number of false premises. It assumes that teenage sex is inevitable, so schools should openly discuss erotic behavior in explicit detail. It believes it is good for educators to take a neutral stand on morality while simultaneously teaching students about contraceptive methods and the particular techniques of so-called "safe sex," such as oral sex and other forms of petting.

Thus, the basic approach of CSE is to teach kids how to have sex "responsibly" and to help them feel at ease with naming the different parts of their body and the body of the opposite sex. It even teaches them different ways to have sex, perhaps including homosexuality and lesbianism. It teaches children to be accepting, rather than discriminating, about whatever sexual behavior they or someone else might choose to engage in.

Today, comprehensive sex education is administered under various names such as progressive sex education, contemporary sex education, modern sex education, contraceptive sex education, values-neutral sex education, family life education, various family life/planning programs, etc.

What is the major issue concerning modern sex education?

Ideally, sex education should be taught at home by parents who love their children. But since the government is convinced sex education should be taught in the schools, the major issue becomes the *kind* of sex education that is in the best interest of the children.

The government does have a case:

• Millions of Americans are now HIV positive—and teenagers apparently comprise the most rapidly growing segment of those infected.

• In 1993, Harvard University released *AIDS in the World*—

1992, a report estimating that by the year 2000, 38 to 110 million adults plus 10 million children will be HIV-infected worldwide.

• There are now some 60 sexually transmitted diseases (STDs) which every year affect millions of adults and teenagers.

• A million teenage girls get pregnant each year, and at least half have an abortion.

• Modern attitudes on sexuality have led to serious psychological problems in hundreds of thousands of teenagers.

• Even some children (preteens) are sexually abusing (and raping) other children.

• Millions of teenagers are alcohol abusers and suicide is growing so fast that authorities are at a loss to know how to stop it—these too are related to the climate of American sexual permissiveness.

Peter Steiner. Reprinted with permission.

Any government facing problems of this magnitude that didn't try to stem the tide would be considered negligent. As a result, the U.S. government has become the largest funder of sex education programs in America.

The problem is that current sex education programs usually emphasize a "values-neutral" approach, and thus are doing far more harm than good. For example, it can be demonstrated that wherever comprehensive sex education programs exist, teenage promiscuity, pregnancy, abortion, sexually transmitted diseases, and accompanying emotional problems increase. . . .

What are some common errors of comprehensive sex education?

CSE frequently involves a number of false assumptions, some of which we enumerate below.

• *Error One: Young people really can't control their sexual drives and are going to have sex no matter what adults say.*

Operating under this false assumption, CSE concludes that the best approach is to teach kids how to have sex "responsibly" and to help protect them from the consequences of pregnancy, AIDS, and other STDs.

Unfortunately, this view of sex education places the cart before the horse because what really determines premarital sexual behavior is the moral climate of society, not individual hormones. Kids are more sexually active today only because they are fulfilling the expectations of a sex-saturated society. And certainly, the fact that some individuals will always engage in unhealthy behavior is no reason for society to reject the promotion of moral order.

To say that it is impossible for children to control their sexual behavior is ludicrous. For most of human history most young adults have done just this and postponed sex until marriage. The vast majority do so *today* in China, Japan, and other countries—and even in the U.S., 40 to 50 percent of all teenagers continue to remain virgins.

Why do we send rapists and child molesters to jail if physical drives are really uncontrollable and people are victims of their individual biology? Why did we censure former presidential candidate Gary Hart for infidelity if we can't control our sex urge?

Control of Sex Drive

The famous Dr. Ruth Westheimer was speaking to 1500 students at a major university. She made the statement, "Young people, it is unrealistic to expect you to wait. Your libido, your sex drive, is too strong." What is she saying? That our children are like animals and can't wait. They *can't* control themselves.

But she's wrong. For example, if an 18-year-old guy comes to Dr. Ruth and says, "I want to have sex with my girlfriend, but she doesn't want to have sex with me. What should I do?" Dr. Ruth would say, "Then you should wait." But why? She just said it's unrealistic to expect young people to wait. Their "libido" is too strong. What she really means is this: If you are 18 and you want to have sex with your girlfriend and she is willing, go ahead. Your sex drive is too strong. You can't wait, and it's unrealistic to expect you to wait. But if she *doesn't* want to have sex, then *wait*. Your libido, your sex drive, is *not* too strong *now*. You can wait.

If young people can wait at any time, they can control their sex drive *all* the time. Certainly, they are not animals. They are our children. We are talking about *human* sexuality, where people clearly do have the capacity to make right moral decisions and abide by them.

Courts Say No to Condom Program

In a smashing victory for parents over arrogant public school administrators who are aiding and abetting promiscuity, on December 30, 1993, the New York state courts threw out the distribution of condoms to New York City students. . . .

The [state supreme] court took note of the fact that many believe that the condom distribution plan is "tantamount to condoning promiscuity and sexual permissiveness, and that the exposure to condoms and their ready availability may encourage sexual relations among adolescents at an earlier age and/or with more frequency, thereby weakening their moral and religious values."

Phyllis Schlafly, *The Washington Times*, January 5, 1994.

• *Error Two: It is improper to tell children that sex before marriage is morally wrong.*

Allegedly, a moral approach to teenage sexuality imposes an "old-fashioned" adult morality upon children when kids themselves should be free to choose their own sexual behavior. Further, according to CSE, marriage should not necessarily be emphasized as a personal goal, nor should a monogamous, heterosexual marriage necessarily be emphasized as the relationship that brings greatest fulfillment. Neither is it necessarily helpful to talk about absolute values such as virginity, honesty, and character because all values are relative to begin with.

But this is precisely the kind of reasoning that has produced the destructive sexual behaviors that have plagued our kids and our country. What our children do *not* need is absolute freedom in determining their sexual behavior and choices. What they *do* need is responsible guidance from adults. If we don't encourage such virtues as virginity, honesty, and character, is it surprising that our kids wind up ignoring these values?

• *Error Three: Supplying teenagers all the facts regarding sexual matters will enable them to make responsible choices.*

Unfortunately, it has been proven that teenagers do not make responsible choices sexually, even with sex education. Further, sex education characteristically presents only the positive side of sexual involvement, not the negative side. Important information such as the side effects of contraceptive drugs, contraceptive failure rates, the harm of abortion, the serious results of sexually transmitted diseases, etc., are downplayed or ignored.

Comprehensive sex educators have skewed their decision-making models by giving teens the impression that responsible choices equate with contraceptive usage rather than with abstinence. One tragic result of this approach is that sexually transmitted diseases and abortions are now epidemic among teenagers, with AIDS becoming a very serious concern.

Hurt by Sex

• *Error Four: It's okay to have sex as long as it doesn't hurt anyone.*

Modern sex education tells teenagers that they must be "responsible young people" in deciding when and with whom to have sex. Presumably, if both parties agree, and "safe sex" is practiced, children are free to have all the sex they want. No one will get hurt.

But how can anyone tell what having sex will do to someone, and whether sex is going to be harmful? Ask those teenagers who have engaged in sex if they were ever hurt by it and you'll discover that most were, especially girls. There are thousands of young people—and adults—for whom a single illicit sex act has brought great pain, distrust, bitterness, and sometimes ruined lives. For example, [according to the American Family Association] "Premature births, abortion, drug and alcohol abuse, suicide, venereal disease, juvenile delinquency, and the perpetuation of the poverty welfare cycle are but a few of the consequences of teenage pregnancy." Many sensitive children have even committed suicide because, through sex education, they were philosophically coerced into certain behaviors, the consequences of which they were unable to handle.

Unless sex is nurtured in a protective and loving marriage commitment, no one can know the final result of sexual behavior. . . .

What are some problems with a "values-neutral" approach to sex education?

Sex education today is usually taught under the premise of a "values-neutral" method. Other terms used to describe this approach are "morally neutral," "values clarification," "non-directive education," "decision-making education," "process education," "affective education," and "experiential education."

Despite the good intentions of many who stand behind these

191

programs, the end result is that such curricula work to under-mine the moral character of students. Why? Not surprisingly, because morality is rejected. Objective morality is denied and replaced with a subjective morality based on feelings, which is, in the end, no morality. Students are taught that moral values which lie outside themselves are unnecessary, old-fashioned, or unenlightened.

Supporters of values-neutral curricula argue that students should be free to decide their own sexual preferences based on what is "right for them." (Supposedly, this is being morally neu-tral.) They further allege that exposure to a variety of sexual lifestyles/techniques will help students make such a decision. Finally, they think that ideas regarding sex based on "repres-sive" religious or absolute moral standards are to be rejected from classroom teaching. Such things as parental values, tradi-tional society, absolute morality, and religious instruction are not believed to be in the student's best interest.

Those who promote this kind of thinking apparently feel they are acting in the children's best interests. But there are prob-lems. First, it is intellectually and philosophically impossible to be morally neutral. Everyone must advocate a morality of some kind—the only question is whether the morality advocated is a good one or bad one. Second, morality can never logically be ex-cluded from sexuality because sex is inherently moral. Sexual behavior is inextricably bound up with character and personal-ity, and therefore, cannot be values-neutral. . . .

Contraception and Promiscuity

Is providing students with contraceptive information and devices the answer?

Liberal sex educators have stressed the importance of provid-ing contraceptive information to young people. But is it really surprising that telling students exactly how to use the Pill, di-aphragms, condoms, and IUDs [intrauterine devices for birth control] would lead to greater promiscuity? Even [family plan-ning researcher] Alan Guttmacher confessed in 1963 that con-traceptive information for teens would bring about an increase in sexual promiscuity.

Dr. Robert Kistner of Harvard Medical School, one of the in-ventors of the birth control pill, said in 1977, "About ten years ago I declared that the Pill would not lead to promiscuity. Well, I was wrong."

Another scientist responsible for the development of the Pill, Dr. Min Chueh Chang, said in 1981, "I personally feel the Pill has rather spoiled young people. . . . It has made them more permissive."

The research of Dr. Jacqueline Kasun [Humboldt State (Calif.)

University] showed that "states that provide easy access to publicly funded birth control tend to have higher rates [of teenage pregnancy, abortions, and illegitimate births]."

In one survey of more than 400 randomly selected psychiatrists and family physicians, most agreed that availability of contraceptives had led to increased promiscuity among teenagers. And a study by Planned Parenthood concluded that "neither pregnancy nor contraceptive education exerts any significant effect on the risk of premarital pregnancy.". . .

Effects of Planned Parenthood

Is Planned Parenthood the answer?

Today, the Planned Parenthood Federation of America (PPFA) and related organizations are largely responsible for the kind of sex education students encounter in the public schools. PPFA materials are entrenched in sex education throughout the nation. These materials actively promote sexual freedom, claiming that a morally free approach will dramatically reduce teenage promiscuity, pregnancy/abortion, sexually transmitted diseases, etc. And they believe that those who reject their methods of teaching human sexuality—especially those of a religious persuasion—are ignorant, old-fashioned, or even dangerous to the welfare of children and society at large. Thus, PPFA emphasizes it must "be ready as educators and parents to help young people obtain sex satisfaction before marriage."

Critics argue that Planned Parenthood 1) sees parents, in its own words, as "disoriented, ignorant [and] irresponsible"; 2) denounces the religious community and opposes its influence; 3) views increased homosexuality as a population control measure; 4) promotes abortion; and 5) seeks to become the nation's clearinghouse for all sex education materials.

Undermining Parent/Child Relationships

Researcher Douglas R. Scott writes, "Despite their view that parents should be the primary sexuality educators, Planned Parenthood materials often undercut the parent/child relationship." As one of many examples, he quotes a Planned Parenthood advertisement printed in the *Dallas Observer*. The young people reading the advertisement are told: "Myth—I can't get birth control, I'm under 18. Fact—Wrong. If your parents are stupid enough to deny you access to birth control and you are under 18, you can get it on your own without parental consent. Call Planned Parenthood right now."

Thus, Scott concludes,

> Planned Parenthood publications attempt to place young people at odds with their parents. Planned Parenthood urges teenagers to question the teachings of their parents, and young

193

people who choose to adhere to such teachings are made to feel "behind the times." Most parents would surely be opposed to any organization that works to undermine their authority and teachings on sensitive matters, especially when those issues relate to morality and when the morality advocated by Planned Parenthood clearly endorses premarital sex.

We believe that Planned Parenthood is one of the most socially consequential influences in America today. Books such as George Grant's *Grand Illusion: The Legacy of Planned Parenthood*, Robert Marshall and Charles Donovan's *Blessed Are the Barren: The Social Policy of Planned Parenthood*, and Douglas R. Scott's *Inside Planned Parenthood* provide ample documentation of the chilling and even disastrous social effects of this organization and its policies. . . .

Good Sex Education

The problems of modern sex education will not be solved overnight. It will take a concerted effort by parents, teachers, politicians, and administrators to implement the changes that almost everyone knows are in the best interest of our children and our society.

Those who oppose implementing such programs should themselves be opposed and their errors exposed.

Good sex education will involve parents and teachers. It will promote true abstinence and include an honest discussion of the consequences of promiscuity. It will uphold absolute moral values and eliminate mixed messages. Finally, it will advocate personal responsibility and respect for authority. This is the kind of sex education that will be helpful to children who must grow up in an increasingly dangerous world.

*"[Abstinence] is the only surefire way to guard
against . . . AIDS, pregnancy, and venereal
diseases."*

Schools Should
Teach Abstinence

Rush H. Limbaugh III

Rush H. Limbaugh III is a popular conservative talk show host on
radio and television and the author of *The Way Things Ought to Be*,
from which the following viewpoint is excerpted. Limbaugh argues that abstinence must be stressed to youths as the only way
to protect them from the risks of sexual intercourse. Limbaugh asserts that distributing condoms to youths is wrong because it encourages sexual activity and because condoms are inadequate
protection against AIDS and venereal diseases.

As you read, consider the following questions:

1. Why does Limbaugh disapprove of condom distribution in
   schools and disagree with the notion that "kids are going to
   do it anyway"?
2. How have some people criticized abstinence education,
   according to Limbaugh?
3. Why does the author doubt the effectiveness of condoms
   against AIDS?

The logic and motivation behind this country's mad dash to distribute free condoms in our public schools is ridiculous and misguided. Worse, the message conveyed by mass condom distribution is a disservice and borders on being lethal. Condom distribution sanctions, even encourages, sexual activity, which in teen years tends to be promiscuous and relegates to secondary status the most important lesson to be taught: abstinence. An analysis of the entire condom distribution logic also provides a glimpse into just what is wrong with public education today.

A Wrong Assumption

First things first. Advocates of condom distribution say that kids are going to have sex, that try as we might we can't stop them. Therefore they need protection. Hence, condoms. Well, hold on a minute. Just whose notion is it that "kids are going to do it anyway, you can't stop them"? Why limit the application of that brilliant logic to sexual activity? Let's just admit that kids are going to do drugs and distribute safe, untainted drugs every morning in homeroom. Kids are going to smoke, too, we can't stop them, so let's provide packs of low-tar cigarettes to the students for their after-sex smoke. Kids are going to get guns and shoot them, you can't stop them, so let's make sure that teachers have bulletproof vests. I mean, come on! If we are really concerned about safe sex, why stop at condoms? Let's convert study halls to Safe Sex Centers where students can go to actually have sex on nice double beds with clean sheets under the watchful and approving eye of the school nurse, who will be on hand to demonstrate, along with the principal, just how to use a condom. Or even better: If kids are going to have sex, let's put disease-free hookers in these Safe Sex Centers. Hey, if safe sex is the objective, why compromise our standards?

Backward Policy

There is something else very disturbing about all this. Let's say that Johnny and Susie are on a date in Johnny's family sedan. Johnny pulls in to his town's designated Teen Parking Location hoping to score a little affection from Susie. They move to the backseat and it isn't long before Johnny, on the verge of bliss, whips out his trusty high school-distributed condom and urges Susie not to resist him. She is hesitant, being a nice girl and all, and says she doesn't think the time is right.

"Hey, everything is okay. Nothing will go wrong. Heck, the *school gave me this condom*, they know what they're doing. You'll be fine," coos the artful and suave Johnny.

Aside from what is obviously wrong here, there is something you probably haven't thought of which to me is profound. Not that long ago, school policy, including that on many college campuses, was designed to protect the girls from the natural and instinctive aggressive pursuit of young men. Chaperones, for example, were around to make sure the girls were not in any jeopardy. So much for that thinking now. The schools may just as well endorse and promote these backseat affairs. The kids are going to do it anyway.

Stayskal. Reprinted by permission: Tribune Media Services.

Well, here's what's wrong. There have always been consequences to having sex. Always. Now, however, some of these consequences are severe: debilitating venereal diseases and AIDS. You can now die from having sex. It is that simple. If you look, the vast majority of adults in America have made adjustments in their sexual behavior in order to protect themselves from some of the dire consequences floating around out there. For the most part, the sexual revolution of the sixties is over, a miserable failure. Free love and rampant one-night stands are tougher to come by because people are aware of the risks. In short, we have modified our behavior. Now, would someone tell me what is so difficult about sharing this knowledge and experience with kids? The same stakes are involved. Isn't that our responsibility, for crying out loud, to teach them what's best for them? If we adults aren't responding to these new dangers by having condom-protected sex anytime, anywhere, why should such folly be taught to our kids?

Sex and AIDS

Let me try the Magic Johnson example for you who remain unconvinced. Imagine that you are in the Los Angeles Lakers locker room after a game and you and Magic are getting ready to go hit the town. Outside the locker room are a bunch of young women, as there always are, and as Magic had freely admitted there always were, and that you know that the woman Magic is going to pick up and take back to the hotel has AIDS. You approach Magic and say, "Hey, Magic! Hold on! That girl you're going to take back to the hotel with you has AIDS. Here, don't worry about it. Take these condoms, you'll be fine."

Do you think Magic would have sex with that woman? Ask yourself: Would you knowingly have sex with *anyone* who has AIDS with only a condom to protect you from getting the disease? It doesn't take Einstein to answer that question. So, why do you think it's okay to send kids out into the world to do just that? Who is to know who carries the HIV virus, and on the chance your kid runs into someone who does have it, are you confident that a condom will provide all the protection he or she needs?

Doesn't it make sense to be honest with kids and tell them the best thing they can do to avoid AIDS or any of the other undesirable consequences is to abstain from sexual intercourse? It is the best way—in fact, it is the only surefire way—to guard against sexual transmission of AIDS, pregnancy, and venereal diseases. What's so terrible about saying so?

Abstinence Opposition

Yet, there are those who steadfastly oppose the teaching of abstinence, and I think they should be removed from any position of authority where educating children is concerned. In New York, the City Board of Education *narrowly won* (4-3) the passage of a resolution requiring the inclusion of teaching abstinence in the AIDS education program in the spring of 1992. No one was trying to eliminate anything from the program, such as condom distribution or anal sex education (which does occur in New York public school sex education classes). [The schools chancellor proposed to allow parents to prevent their children from receiving condoms after a state appeals court ruled the program unconstitutional in December 1993.] All they wanted was that abstinence also be taught. Yet, the Schools Chancellor, Joseph Fernandez, vigorously fought the idea, saying it would do great damage to their existing program! Well, just how is that? The fact is that abstinence works every time it is tried. As [my] book went to press, the New York Civil Liberties Union was considering filing a lawsuit to stop this dangerous new addition to the curriculum. Now what in the name of God is going on here? This is tantamount to opposing a drug education program which instructs students not to use drugs because it would not be useful.

The Jacksonville, Florida, school board also decided that abstinence should be the centerpiece of their sexual education curriculum, and the liberals there were also outraged about this. What is so wrong with this? Whose agenda is being denied by teaching abstinence and just what is that agenda?

Jacksonville teachers are telling seventh-graders that "the only safe sex is no sex at all." Sex education classes provide some information about birth control and sexually transmitted diseases, but these areas are not the primary focus of the classes. Nancy Corwin, a member of the school board, admits the paradox when she says that the schools send a nonsensical message when they teach kids not to have sex but then give them condoms.

Contaminated Thinking

Instead of this twaddle, the Jacksonville school board has decided to teach real safe sex, which is abstinence. However, six families, along with Planned Parenthood and the ACLU [American Civil Liberties Union], are suing the schools over this program. This bunch of curious citizens says that teaching abstinence puts the children at a greater risk of catching AIDS or other sexually transmitted diseases. Greater risk? !£#$£@! How can that be? What kind of contaminated thinking is this? The suit alleges that the schools are providing a "fear-based program that gives children incomplete, inaccurate, biased, and sectarian information." You want more? Try this: Linda Lanier of Planned Parenthood says, "It's not right to try to trick our students." Trick the students? #£&@£!? If anyone is trying to trick students, it's Planned Parenthood and this band of hedonists who try to tell kids that a condom will protect them from any consequences of sex.

Folks, here you have perhaps the best example of the culture war being waged in our country today. To say that "teaching abstinence is a trick" is absurd. Is Ms. Lanier having sex every night of the week? What adjustments has she made in her sex life because of AIDS? Does she think that a little sheath of latex will be enough to protect her?

This is terribly wrong. The Jacksonville public school system is attempting to teach right from wrong, as opposed to teaching that sex does not have any consequences, which I believe is the selfish agenda these people hold dear. . . . There are many people who wish to go through life guilt-free and engage in behavior they know to be wrong and morally vacant. In order to as-

199

suage their guilt they attempt to construct and impose policies which not only allow them to engage in their chosen activities but encourage others to do so as well. There is, after all, strength in numbers.

Selfish Lifestyles

Promiscuous and self-gratifying, of-the-moment sex is but one of these chosen lifestyles. Abortions on demand and condom distribution are but two of the policies and programs which, as far as these people are concerned, ensure there are no consequences. As one disgusted member of the Jacksonville school board said, "Every yahoo out there has a social program that they want to run through the school system. We are here for academic reasons and we cannot cure the social evils of the world."

The worst of all of this is the lie that condoms really protect against AIDS. The condom failure rate can be as high as 20 percent. Would you get on a plane—or put your children on a plane—if one in five passengers would be killed on the flight? Well, the statistic holds for condoms, folks.

"The so-called 'chastity' and 'abstinence' programs are even more dangerous to young people than the usual rot."

Schools Should Not Teach Any Sex Education

Randy Engel, interviewed by John F. McManus

Randy Engel is a longtime opponent of school sex education and the author of *Sex Education: The Final Plague.* In the following viewpoint, Engel criticizes classroom sex education, including that which stresses abstinence or chastity, for violating the intimate sphere—"the secret self"—of children. Engel argues that abstinence and chastity programs create much internal conflict within children by simultaneously exposing them to sexually stimulating information and teaching chastity. She maintains that this "chastity industry" insults parents, the natural and competent instructors of children, by portraying them as sexually ignorant. Engel is the founder of the U.S. Coalition for Life, a coalition of pro-life organizations based in Export, Pennsylvania. John F. McManus is the publisher of the *New American,* a biweekly conservative magazine.

As you read, consider the following questions:

1. In Engel's opinion, how do classrooms contribute to the brainwashing effects of sex education?
2. How are abstinence- and chastity-based programs similar to Planned Parenthood-type programs, according to Engel?
3. Why does the author believe it is wrong for all such programs to emphasize self-esteem?

Randy Engel, interviewed by John McManus, "What's Wrong with 'Abstinence Ed'?" *The New American,* January 27, 1992. Reprinted with permission.

McManus: How do you define "sex education"?

Engel: So-called "sex education" is the systematic instruction of children in explicit sexual matters in an open and public classroom setting at the elementary and secondary school level. It may be given either as a separate course or integrated into a legitimate course of study. A more precise term for what is being done in the schools would be "sex initiation" or "sexual conditioning."

Why are you opposed to organized sex education?

Group sex education amounts to a perversion of nature. It makes public and open that which is naturally private and intimate. Any teaching about sex in a public setting violates privacy and intimacy. Sex education in the classroom is an insidious and unnatural invitation to sexual activity; it is erotic seduction; and it is even a form of child molestation, violating the natural latency and post-latency periods of child development, periods which are crucial for normal development of the whole person.

Why do you consider sex education courses an invitation to sexual activity?

By systematically attacking what should be called "holy bashfulness," and by eroding the common sense of shame present in everyone, these programs clear the way for all forms of sexual activity.

Mass Indoctrination

Why was the classroom chosen to be the major vehicle for these sex initiation courses?

The classroom provides the ideal setting for mass indoctrination. It even includes some features that the mass media and other fountains of indoctrination do not have. The typical classroom has an audience of immature and impressionable young people, held captive for long periods of time, under the influence of an authority figure, and in the state of "parentectomy," when children are separated from their parents, the proper source of their religious and moral influence.

You are now combating a new form of sex education in the schools. What is it?

Many Americans have become aware of both the Planned Parenthood-type programs and the modified programs containing a smattering of "God-language.". . . The new kid on the sex-education block is being marketed under the label of "Chastity Education" in parochial schools and "Abstinence Education" in public schools.

What is wrong with "Chastity Education" and "Abstinence Education"?

These alternative sex education programs have been produced through the efforts of individuals who accept the fiction that youngsters in elementary and secondary schools must be given some form of sexual education.

In a certain sense, the so-called "chastity" and "abstinence" programs are even more dangerous to young people than the usual rot. In these programs, a child is deliberately exposed to information that stimulates sexually while at the same time being told to be chaste, i.e., pure in thought, word, and deed. This causes an unnatural psychological, moral, and spiritual conflict in the young.

A Daughter's Insecurities

Today, all my [eleven-year-old] daughter has to do to find out [about sex] is ask an anonymous question of a "totally honest" teacher. The only thing she has left to wonder about is when and with whom her first time will take place; she knows what will happen and what can happen in more detail than she needs.

I have been told by grade school teachers that I can accept sex education or be prepared for my daughters to get lessons from the school of the playground; I worry more about how my daughter must have felt when her teacher approached her class with the assumption that the students need to know about sex because either the students were or soon would be having sex. What sort of insecurities must have crept into her mind when she was confronted by the fact that, while she is not physically or emotionally ready for sex, the school thinks she ought to be prepared to deal with it. She must wonder if she is the slow one in the class.

Michael E. Gress, *Conservative Review*, December 1992.

Though there are some distinct differences, these programs actually have a great deal in common with Planned Parenthood-type programs. They employ values clarification techniques that are designed to effect in the young the dual conditioning processes of desensitization and desacralization in matters of sexuality. This is the hallmark of all forms of classroom sex education. To appreciate what I have just said, one must realize that the fundamental objection to classroom sex education courses is not to be found in their specific content, however horrible that content might be, or in the specific disposition of the instructor, no matter what his or her attitude might be.

The Secret Self

What is the fundamental objection?

It is that such programs make open and public what is and should remain a very private and intimate sphere of the human person—called "the secret self" by the brilliant philosopher and

203

crusader for purity Dietrich von Hildebrand. This consequence is unavoidable no matter how good and noble the intentions of the instructors or the type of program employed.

Even a program conducted by a good person will be harmful?

Oh, yes. In fact, one should keep in mind that, as a rule, the more innocent appearing and charming the instructor and the instruction, the more harmful is the desensitization and conditioning process. Thus, an instructor like the overtly obnoxious Sol Gordon, the king of kiddie porn and the Pied Piper of the sleazy, is not as effective in the conditioning process as Pat Miller, the attractive and charming host of the *In God's Image* series produced by the Franciscans. This is because Pat Miller's type of presentation lowers the child's natural defenses against the invasion of privacy. The child's resistance to what he or she may initially perceive as a violation of "the secret self" will be diminished.

What kind of instructions are teachers of these courses given?

Like their counterparts who use the Planned Parenthood-type programs, abstinence-based and chastity instructors are trained to speak openly and candidly to their students about sex so that the students may become "more comfortable" with their sexuality. Since, initially at least, some students will sense a deep-seated anxiety due to the inappropriateness of discussing sexual matters in an open setting, the sex education instructor is urged to act quickly to assure the child that "sex is perfectly natural," or that "there is no need for embarrassment." Toward this end, various values clarification techniques are employed, including role playing, open-ended dilemmas, and the keeping of personal diaries.

Devaluing Parents

Are there other areas where these programs are similar to the Planned Parenthood-type programs?

Yes. One is that they separate the child from his or her parent. The new "chastity industry" pays lip service to parents as the natural and competent instructors of their children in matters of sexuality. But if you read through the manuals produced to accompany these courses, you get the distinct impression that parents as a whole represent a rather sexually ignorant class and are themselves in need of professional help. That professional help, of course, would likely be a sexual facilitator who would assist them in clarifying their values and relieving them of their sexual "hangups." As these courses proliferate, we can expect the introduction of seminars and courses designed to explain the facts of life to parents—as if the individuals who have produced children don't know what they're doing.

Another almost unbelievable problem with these programs is their position regarding "self-esteem." The entire thrust here is that everyone should put self first. Not God, not neighbor, not parents, not anyone but self. It is no surprise that Planned Parenthood has chosen to promote "self-esteem" because it conveys the notion that everyone should do what he or she wants to do, rather than what he or she ought to do according to the nature implanted in each one of us by God.

Mixed Messages

What can you tell us about the actual content of one of these "alternative" sex education programs?

Second Thoughts, a video designed in soap opera format for the "Sex Respect" course, comes in two versions, one for Christian schools and the other for public schools. Except for a few references to God in the former, they are virtually the same. The producers claim, "Without being moralistic, *Second Thoughts* presents teenagers believable and compelling reasons for abstinence until marriage." Yet, in the discussion guide accompanying the video, there are exercises for open-ended group discussions involving sexual intercourse, options for an unplanned pregnancy, and the consequences of lost virginity. The video itself contains a negative bias toward marriage in the case of a teenage, out-of-wedlock pregnancy, and abortion is listed as an option.

If someone wants more information about the threat posed by these so-called "chastity" programs, where can it be obtained?

The best source is the National Coalition of Clergy and Laity, 1929 Tilghman Street, Suite B, Allentown, PA 18104 (Tel. 215-435-4190). Among other items, my article, *The Chastity Industry Revisited*, is available through the NCCL.

"Teens need condoms, information, and support now."

Teenagers Should Learn How to Have Safe Sex

Anne-Elizabeth Murdy and Carol Hayse

Carol Hayse has been an activist in Chicago for nearly thirty years, working for reproductive rights and lesbian visibility and, in recent years, fighting the spread of AIDS. She and Anne-Elizabeth Murdy are cofounders of the Coalition for Positive Sexuality (CPS), a Chicago organization that promotes safe sex among high school students. In the following viewpoint, Murdy and Hayse contend that teenagers need to learn how to practice safe sex to protect them from unwanted pregnancies and sexually transmitted diseases. The authors argue that because parents and schools fail to educate teens adequately about sex, activists need to spread crucial information about birth control, abortion, homosexuality, and other issues so that teens learn the healthy, positive aspects of sex.

As you read, consider the following questions:

1. How has CPS targeted its message to teens, according to Murdy and Hayse?
2. How do the authors respond to parents' objections to the *Just Say Yes* booklet?
3. Why do Murdy and Hayse believe that sex education is failing in Chicago public schools?

Abridged from Carol Hayse and Anne-Elizabeth Murdy, "Just Say Yes: The Coalition for Positive Sexuality." This article is reprinted with permission from the RESIST newsletter (vol. 2, no. 7, September 1993). RESIST is a national foundation funding grassroots social change projects since 1967. For more information, write RESIST, One Summer St., Somerville, MA 02143, or call (617) 623-5110.

"Hey! Look at this! Turn to page 12!" "Saran Wrap? What's that for?" "What are they doing!" It's 7:30 A.M., and about 12 members of the Coalition for Positive Sexuality (CPS) are standing in front of a Chicago public high school, handing out astrobrite green booklets titled *Just Say Yes*. The front cover pictures two couples kissing—very "industrial," very hip, very gender indeterminate. As we hand out the booklets, along with condoms, we say, "Safe sex and birth control information?" "Would you like a condom with that?" Most students take the book without much interest, even grudgingly; it is a little later, when they're hanging out with other students on the steps or at the curb, that they begin to respond and share it with their friends. A slow buzz can be heard as the crunch of students at the school door grows larger. Once word gets around, students shyly, or sometimes boldly, come up to us and ask for a copy. Some people request condoms in their favorite color. Some gather around trying to get a feel for who we are and what brought us here; and some even ask us questions.

Most mornings, a school administrator will appear at the door of the high school. She or he will exhibit behaviors ranging from equanimity, to threats, to near apoplexy. One principal waved his arms wildly and tore his hair. Another called the cops to harass us.

Positive Sexuality

Just Say Yes is a sexuality education booklet dealing with issues of self-respect and respect for others, sexual consent, birth control, safe sex practices, abortion, STDs and HIV, and sexual violence. It is unapologetically pro-sex, pro-lesbian and -gay, pro-woman, and pro-choice. We wrote *Just Say Yes* in teen-oriented language—some of it perhaps a little raw—which clearly positions its readers as thinking persons who are confronting important choices about sex and sexuality, and who deserve information and support with which to make those decisions. At the back we compiled an extensive resource section giving phone numbers and addresses for information on rape and incest, AIDS and STDs, women's healthcare, and social service agencies for young people of color, lesbians, and gay men.

The Coalition for Positive Sexuality was created by people from ACT UP (AIDS Coalition to Unleash Power), ECDC (Emergency Clinic Defense Coalition, a pro-choice organization), Queer Nation (a group working for queer civil rights), No More Nice Girls (a feminist theater group), and some high school students. Our acronym, CPS, is a tongue-in-cheek pun on the abbreviation for the Chicago Public Schools, and an announcement about our pro-sex stance. We first came together in the Spring of 1992, believing that ACT UP–style activism could be applied to preven-

207

tion education among those subject to the next "great wave" of HIV infection, unwanted pregnancy, and STDs—that is, teens. We are a small group of about 20 people; we are high school students, PhD candidates, teachers, and white/pink collar workers from diverse social backgrounds. Our ages range from 17 to 48.

©Kirk Anderson. Reprinted with permission.

Most of us are lesbian and gay and several of us are people of color. In our first meetings we articulated two main purposes: to get meaningful, effective, peer-oriented information into the hands of teens; and to create public debate about the lack of meaningful sexuality education in the schools. We passed out our first booklets in November 1992. In January 1993, after getting feedback from high school students (we conducted four focus groups, in addition to listening to lots of informal responses), AIDS and women's health service providers, and other activists, we revised and augmented the entire book. We added an introductory page that explained all that "just say yes" means, step-by-step instructions for putting on a condom, specific information on abortion clinics and bogus clinics, and much, much more. Finally, in April 1993, we starting handing out the new *Just Say Yes* at a different high school every week. From the booklet:

> Just Say Yes means having a positive attitude about sexuality—gay, straight, or bi. It means saying "yes" to sex you do want, and "no" to sex you don't. It means there's nothing

wrong with you if you decide to have sex, and nothing wrong with you if you decide not to. You have the right to make your own choices, and to have people respect them. Sex is enjoyable when everyone involved is into it, and when everyone has the information they need to take care of themselves and each other.

Just Say Yes maintains this frank, friendly, and uncompromising tone throughout the sections on sex, respect, safe sex practices, birth control, AIDS/HIV, HIV testing, STDs, pregnancy, and abortion. A few samples from the different sections:

Pro-Sex: Most messages we get tell us that sex is something dirty that we shouldn't talk about or an act of violence. Most of us learn that our bodies, and our sex, are things to be ashamed of. Most of us learn that sex means a man on top of a woman, and that the only other choice is abstinence. But sex can be lots of things. Women have sex with women, men have sex with men, women have sex with men—and sometimes the best sex is with yourself!

Our descriptions of the contraptions that safe sex can involve are upbeat, honest, and blunt.

Birth Control: Condom/Rubber: Looks like a rubber sock for a guy's dick. Use with spermicide. Using a lubricant during sex can prevent the condom from breaking and help prevent vaginal soreness.

(Our ten-step "how to put on a condom" guide has a page to itself.)

Diaphragm: Looks like a small rubber frisbee you put in your vagina. Use with spermicide. . . . Always use a condom in addition to other forms of birth control.

Real Teen Communication

Just Say Yes is consciously woman-oriented, both acknowledging young women's sexuality and providing information which has been denied them because men have controlled definitions of our sexuality:

The CLIT (CLITORIS) is the main sexual pleasure spot for women. To find your clitoris, feel inside the top of your crotch for a button-like thing. Rubbing or licking the clit gives women pleasure, and makes the clit hard. In fact it is the way most women cum. . . . Remember women: THE CLIT IS IT!

But *Just Say Yes* is and probably will always be work-in-progress; we are coming up with more revisions. Some of the feedback we get in the mail and on our voicemail reflects our own ongoing discussions: the "language debate," for example. How do we use language that represents real teen communication but doesn't come across as condescending, and doesn't play into homophobia, misogyny, and so on? Penis or dick? Lesbian, gay, queer, homosexual? We've decided to interchange penis and dick, since dick is not commonly used pejoratively. We decided not to use queer, dyke, or fag because, while we ourselves have appropriated these words and reconfigured their meanings, in high schools they are almost always the terms of vicious homophobia. Related to the language debate is a fundamental decision that this booklet is primarily about sexual behavior, not labels or categories. Thus the pro-sex section (the booklet's most controversial page) uses gender-neutral words like "you," "your partner."

The Realities of Teen Sex

We have earned considerable media attention (all the local TV news, The Jerry Springer Show, *The Windy City Times*, *Chicago Tribune*, *Chicago Defender*, *The Reader*, *The Advocate*, *Young Sisters and Brothers*, and smaller publications have run stories), which assists us in our effort to stir up public debate about the lack of decent sexuality education in the public schools. Some of the media attention is pure sensationalism, some of it pure gay-baiting. Generally the schools and some parents express indignation that their control over teenagers is being circumvented.

While there are plenty of attacks launched against our booklet, our tactics, and our very existence—there is very little that either the media or our opponents can say about the realities that motivated us to do this work in the first place.

Our actions have been called "offensive" and "shocking." The truth is, what ought to be deeply offensive and shocking to all of us is the litany of health problems besetting young people in Chicago and all over the United States. One fifth of all newly diagnosed people with AIDS are in their 20's, which means they probably contracted HIV in their teens. In Chicago, in 1992 50% of new cases of people with AIDS were African Americans and 16% were Latinos. In 1991 the number of women with AIDS had doubled over the year before. Nationally, one in six sexually active teens is infected with an STD every year—that's 2.5 million teenagers. The United States has the highest teen pregnancy rate of any industrialized country, over 1 million teenage women per year, Chicago itself has the fourth highest rate in the country. One in four girls and one in six boys in this country are sexually assaulted by age 18.

Ignorance Is Not Bliss

Given this context, it is difficult to understand how schools and parents can continue to hide the information that may save children's lives. Many parents insist that we should have asked their permission before distributing *Just Say Yes*. Our response is that 75% of women and 86% of men are sexually active by age 20, without asking or even informing their parents, and it is important that they know how to take care of themselves. We believe that ignorance is not bliss, but rather information is (a component of) power; that adult hypocrisy is intolerable to teens; that teens have a right to make their own choices, and they should be informed so that those choices are healthful and respectful; that the numbers of teens who have unwanted pregnancies, HIV, or STDs demonstrates pretty clearly that "just say no" or scare tactics or whatever other anti-sex methods schools and many parents employ simply aren't working.

We urge parents to educate their teens, and we urge the schools to do so; but we know that as long as rape and HIV and unwanted pregnancy are a part of young people's lives, their parents and schools are failing them. And we refuse to wait—teens need condoms, information, and support *now*. One student, carrying her baby, refused a copy of *Just Say Yes*, saying we should have come to her school a year ago.

We offer *Just Say Yes* as an example of comprehensive and practical information. It's OK for people to disagree with the contents or the tactics; at least they are discussing safe sex. One parent told us that her daughter left the booklet on the coffee table and it prompted a long overdue discussion of their respective morals and sexual awareness. We are encouraged by that.

The educational potential of *Just Say Yes* lies not in the actual booklet, as arduous as our editorial meetings were, but in the ripple effect of conversations and arguments that *Just Say Yes* initiates. Teens are our most powerful resource for educating teens.

Concern for Minorities

Sexuality education in the Chicago public schools ranges from nonexistent to barely-there-and-ineffective. The "Family Life Curriculum" contains misinformation about AIDS, fails to answer the students' real questions, and attempts to discourage students from having sex. An optional unit on birth control, homosexuality, and abortion is rarely used, according to our School Board sources. . . .

In a city where 82% of the high school students are people of color, many of the recipients of *Just Say Yes* are Black teens. Within CPS we are addressing the concerns of some African Americans by working to increase our own membership both in numbers and diversity, and by talking with Black teens who support the project and have comments on the book itself. We're also developing a Spanish translation, working with Mexicans, Puerto Ricans, and a South American from various Latino organizations to ensure that *Just Say Yes* will meet the needs of teens from these groups.

The fact that the right wing is (sometimes successfully) linking race and sexuality to create a wedge between potential progressive allies in community struggles gives greater urgency to the efforts of lesbians, gays, sexuality educators, parents, students, and other activists to clearly put forth our message. It is crucial that we draw the connections between our own work and struggles for economic justice, racial equality, and other anti-discrimination efforts.

Collective Action

As AIDS, reproductive rights, and queer activists, we have tremendous political wisdom and experience to offer. We know that an adequate response to AIDS is not just based on individual choices and a "just say no" mentality, but on collective community action. We know that the right to abortion is an aspect of healthcare, and that healthcare is a fundamental human right. We know that gay rights organizing is a powerful weapon against the right wing. And in our own group, we see the benefits and strengths of intergenerational organizing; our different perspectives on sexuality and effective education and activism have made CPS a diverse group in unusual and productive ways. . . .

We will continue to pass out *Just Say Yes* until we have visited all 77 Chicago public high schools. We will continue to put pressure on the Chicago Department of Health for condom distribution and massive public education about safe sex, and we will work especially hard to build coalitions with other organizations for health, with lesbians and gay men, and with people of color—both here in Chicago and nationally. But our dilemma remains how to share our wisdom in ways which effectively project our message: how to ally with folks who share our vision of economic and social justice but may have an emotional response to the topic of sexuality; how to speak frankly to teens, but also maintain our ability to speak to their parents; and how to express our commitment to the health of African American and all young people, and to anti-racism, at the same time as we break the life-threatening traditions of silence around topics of sexuality.

Authors' note: The use of the term "safe sex" rather than "safer sex" reflects consensus reached within CPS. The group believes "safer sex" implies that no sexual practices are truly safe and that abstinence is the only way to be really safe. CPS, however, wants to challenge the notion that "sex" is limited to a few restrictive possibilities by putting out examples of many kinds of sexual practices that really are safe—*i.e.* they want to expand the notion of what "sex" can be.

"I'm going to scream the next time someone tells me—worse yet, my children—that promiscuous sex can be safe."

Teenagers Should Not Learn How to Have Safe Sex

Kristine Napier

Kristine Napier is a health and science writer and president of the board of directors of the Responsible Social Values Program, an abstinence-based sex education program for middle school students. In the following viewpoint, Napier maintains that the "safe sex" message is untruthful advice, and dangerous for teenagers who heed it. She argues that, while teenagers ignore the safe sex directives, hearing the message encourages them to engage in sexual activity. Thus, she contends, this type of sex education leads to increases in pregnancies and sexually transmitted diseases among teenagers. A successful alternative, the author asserts, is one that stresses abstinence only.

As you read, consider the following questions:

1. According to Napier, what are some consequences of sexually transmitted diseases? What other consequences of teenage sex does she discuss?
2. What does abstinence education teach about love and affection, in the author's opinion?
3. Why does Napier believe it is wrong to teach abstinence and safe sex together?

Abridged from Kristine Napier, "The Fallacy of Safe Sex," *Priorities*, Summer 1993, ©1993 The American Council on Science and Health, New York, NY. Reprinted with permission.

I'm going to scream the next time someone tells me—worse yet, my children—that promiscuous sex can be safe.

As a parent and a public health professional, I have taken a very close look at the evolution of sex education in this country. I have reached the conclusion that we may do more harm than good in introducing our kids to sexually explicit material and teaching them the mechanics of how to be sexually active.

Parents have naively acquiesced to the concept of "safe sex," driven first by an acceptance of the widespread belief that "all kids are going to become sexually active" and then by an intense fear of sexually transmitted HIV.

But, as parents, we don't have to accept the world we suddenly find ourselves in: a world that has forgotten the merits of teaching kids the tried and true concept of abstinence. We no longer have to put our children's health in jeopardy—as I believe we do when we accept the fallacious concept of "safe sex."

Threats from STDs

There are frightening statistics to verify that "safe sex" is threatening our kids' health and lives. According to *Testing Positive*, a study from the Alan Guttmacher Institute, over 25 percent of Americans are infected with at least one of the twenty sexually transmitted diseases (STDs) now identified.

While we all know that the consequences of HIV are no less than death, we seldom appreciate the consequences of much more common STDs such as gonorrhea, chlamydia and human papilloma virus (HPV). At least one million women suffer pelvic inflammatory disease (PID) yearly as a result of having had a sexually transmitted disease. In turn, 150,000 face life-long infertility, which plagues at least one in five couples. Forty-five thousand suffer tubal pregnancies, which can be life-threatening.

But HPV is rarely discussed. Although we as public health professionals would be irresponsible not to discuss the possibility of HIV transmission in heterosexual relationships, HPV is a far more urgent concern. The human papilloma virus, transmitted by sexual contact to infect one million new people each year, is thought to be associated with cervical cancer, which claims approximately 4,500 lives yearly. Cervical cancer rates, in fact, are skyrocketing among young girls who become sexually active early and have multiple sexual partners.

How "Safe Sex" Originated

Today's trend of accepting the idea that "everybody's doing it" originated with the 1960s sexual revolution. Extramarital sex became the norm, and the age of consent steadily decreased. The electronic media took their cue, creating movies, sitcoms and mini-series sizzling with sex. That is, sex that had no consequences nor responsibilities. Soon, teens simply had to turn on the tube to confirm their mistaken conception that "everybody's doing it."

The swelling incidence of teen pregnancy and sexually transmitted diseases soon caught the public's attention. People began to say that we should do something to prevent pregnancy and disease among our teens, defining the problem not as one of teen sexual activity, but as one of trying to prevent the consequences of becoming sexually active. Thus emerged the concept of "safe sex." It is to this response that we can trace the roots of promiscuous teen and even pre-teen sexual activity.

Teen Sex Is Not Inevitable

If we could turn the clock back, perhaps we wouldn't have accepted the foregone conclusion that teens are going to be sexually active and, worse yet, given them instructions on how to proceed. Perhaps we wouldn't have asked: "What can we do to prevent pregnancy and disease?" Instead, we might have asked: "What can we do to prevent teen sexual activity?" If we as parents, public health professionals and teen behavior experts had done that, perhaps we wouldn't see sexually active sixth, seventh and eighth graders or 11- and 12-year-old mothers.

Research conducted by the Centers for Disease Control and Prevention confirms that not all kids are doing "it." While CDC statistics reveal that an alarming 54 percent of all high school students are sexually active, that means nearly half are not. I, as a parent, find solace in that.

The Consequences of "Safe Sex"

Contraceptive-based sex education, the official guise under which "safe sex" is taught, operates under the philosophy that if kids receive comprehensive sex education beginning in kindergarten, they will be comfortable with issues of sexuality. A big part of that message is that if kids decide to become sexually active, they need to understand how to protect themselves. "Safe sex" is equated with protecting yourself against pregnancy and sexually transmitted diseases.

Let's consider the actual outcome of "safe sex." According to the Alan Guttmacher Institute, 36 percent of women in their early 20s will get pregnant within one year while relying on male condom use. Eighteen percent of teenage girls will get pregnant during their first year using oral contraceptives. Each year, more than 1.1 million teenage girls become pregnant. Every day, 29 girls under the age of 15 give birth.

The effectiveness of contraceptive-based education in convincing kids to use contraceptives is an even more significant issue. According to a Harris Poll commissioned by Planned Parenthood, kids who receive contraceptive-based sex education are 53 percent more likely to become sexually active than are kids who do not. And frighteningly, while these kids are choosing to become sexually active, the majority are not using the contraceptives they've learned about.

A congressional study revealed that just half of teens use condoms on first intercourse, and use drops off considerably after that. Worse yet, *Science* magazine reported that condoms are used by only 17 percent of respondents with multiple sexual partners and 13 percent of those with a high-risk sexual partner. Alan Guttmacher's statistics confirm this trend. They found that teens with multiple sexual partners are less likely to use condoms than are teens with a single partner. An alarming 58 percent of teenage women say they have two or more sexual partners and 19 percent of all teens admit to having four or more partners.

Wrong Attitudes

Pediatrics magazine reported that at least $3 billion has been spent in this country on so-called "safe sex" programs. There is no evidence that such programs have lowered the incidence of teen pregnancy or sexually transmitted diseases.

Although those who push contraceptives believe that kids use them, it is not so. The laws of nature combined with the teenage attitude of invulnerability and immortality create potentially deadly unintended consequences. Sexually active kids soon realize that sex is more pleasurable and less of a hassle, as well as more spontaneous, without condoms. They live according to their belief that pregnancy and disease simply won't happen to them.

Another consequence of imparting explicit information about sex and the attitude that "everyone's doing it" is the Posse of Southern California. A group of high school athletes, looked up to by their peers, had a contest to see how many girls they could have sex with. One boy commented that they were just doing what society already thought they were doing. Even more startling was the parental attitude that "boys will be boys." Similar activities are happening in such obscure, isolated towns as Green Bay, Wisconsin, where senior high school boys are challenging each other to score with freshman girls.

Abstinence Education: A Success

It is unfortunate that a successful alternative to the "safe sex" message, abstinence-based sex education, has basically been censored by the media. It's as if they believe that parents don't have the right to help their kids realize the benefits of abstinence. It is also discouraging that abstinence programs are being slandered by their contraceptive counterpart. A Planned

Parenthood publication, Reality-Based Learning and Education for Life, calls abstinence-based sex education "fear- and shame-based curricula . . . that promote only abstinence in a context of scare tactics and misinformation . . . that distort facts [and] hide the truth."

Abstinence education not only provides the only 100 percent effective method of preventing pregnancy, STDs and HIV transmission (and their life-threatening and life-long consequences), it also teaches teens to understand their raging hormones and that their pubescent and adolescent search for love and affection is distinct from sexual intercourse.

The Condom Lie

While I'm reluctant to put myself on a pedestal, I will take a stand for Christ. I'm proud to say that I am a virgin, and I don't hide the strength God has given me.

You may be wondering how my message reconciles with that of a former teammate of mine, Magic Johnson. I think the media and society are more willing to accept Magic's message—that kids are going to have sex anyway, and the best approach is to equip them with condoms to lessen the risk of disease.

My message is different. For openers, the facts show that condoms aren't as successful as many would have you believe. And for teens, the failure rate is even worse! It's a lie to say that putting a condom on makes you as secure as Fort Knox. I cringe when I hear that stuff. Condoms have a hard enough time just stopping a woman from getting pregnant, let alone blocking an HIV virus, which is 450 times smaller than sperm itself. It's like water going through a net.

A.C. Green, *Focus on the Family,* June 1993.

Abstinence education also helps teens realize that sexual intercourse involves more than just the sexual organs. They learn that because sexual intercourse involves the heart and mind, after engaging in intercourse they may attach more significance to a relationship than actually exists. In turn, this can lead to tremendous disappointment and heartbreak. By remaining abstinent, teens learn, they are not only protecting their physical health, but they are also avoiding the emotional upheaval produced by feelings of guilt, doubt and disappointment.

Abstinence education is meant to empower kids to resist peer pressure to become sexually active. Ultimately, they are also empowered to achieve higher life goals. Just 50 percent of teenage girls who become pregnant, in point of fact, ever graduate from high school, most with a General Education Degree (which even the army doesn't accept anymore!).

There is overwhelming evidence that abstinence education works to help kids resist the pressure to become sexually active. Teen Aid, one abstinence program, found that pregnancy rates fell in participating schools in San Marcos, California, and Spur, Texas. Another such program, Sex Respect, reported a significant drop in teen pregnancies in the Jessup, Georgia, school system after they presented the abstinence message. Low-income teens in Atlanta who were taught the value of delaying sexual intercourse were 15 times more likely to remain abstinent than their peers who did not receive this education.

Reinforcing Willpower

But what about the people who decide to cover all bases? They tell their kids to remain abstinent, but add, "If you don't, here's a little something to carry in your back pocket."

Consider a couple of analogies. How many of us tell our kids not to lie, steal or cheat, but if you do, don't get caught? How many of us tell our kids not to drink, but if you do, don't drive over the speed limit? How many of us tell our kids not to use drugs, but if you do, here's a clean needle?

Giving kids the abstinence message together with "safe sex" instruction isn't "waking up to the real world" as many people would like us to believe. It is a double message that leaves kids confused. Kids need all of the willpower they can muster to resist that for which their changing bodies and raging hormones scream. Giving them any indication that we expect them to become sexually active, as "safe sex" instruction does, may be all it takes to break down their willpower.

As parents, we should also consider that telling them: "Don't, but if you do, here's how . . ." is essentially telling them that we doubt their strength of character and their ability to control themselves. We are telling them at the outset that we think they will fail. I can't think of too many parents who tell their kids they are going to fail at academics, sports or other pursuits. Why can't we hold the same high standard for a matter of such consequence?

A Mother's Anger

I am angry that I had to tell my 9-year-old daughter what a condom was and answer the plethora of questions that followed because she heard about them on television. I never invited the "safe sex" message into my home and I am tired of hearing it.

I am angry that over $160 million of our tax dollars yearly go to teaching our kids a lie. At the same time, funding is denied for abstinence education.

It's time for parents to be courageous, to stand on the rooftops and proclaim the proponents of "safe sex" the charlatans they are. It's time for parents to demand that school impart one clear, strong message: that abstinence is an achievable goal— essential for students' good health and future lives. Parents then need to reinforce this message at home.

Abstinence is not simply a moral issue. It can mean the difference between life and death.

Periodical Bibliography

The following articles have been selected to supplement the diverse views presented in this chapter.

Joyce Brothers — "How to Talk to Kids About Sex," *Reader's Digest*, November 1992.

Midge Decter — "Homosexuality and the Schools," *Commentary*, March 1993.

Edwin J. Delattre — "Condoms and Coercion," *Vital Speeches of the Day*, April 15, 1992.

Hal Donofrio — "Abstinence Is the Answer," *The World & I*, July 1993.

Nancy Gibbs — "How Should We Teach Our Children About Sex?" *Time*, May 24, 1993.

Jane Gross — "Sex Educators for Young See New Virtue in Chastity," *The New York Times*, January 16, 1994.

Karen Houppert and Esther Kaplan — "Condom Nation," *The Village Voice*, January 25, 1994.

Douglas Kirby — "Sexuality Education: It Can Reduce Unprotected Intercourse," *SIECUS Report*, December 1992/January 1993. Available from 130 W. 42nd St., Suite 2500, New York, NY 10036.

Dana Mack — "What the Sex Educators Teach," *Commentary*, August 1993.

Anne Nordhaus-Bike and David Reich — "Fighting the Far Right on Sexuality Education," *World*, January/February 1994. Available from the Unitarian Universalist Association, 25 Beacon St., Boston, MA 02108-2803.

Anna Quindlen — "A Pyrrhic Victory," *The New York Times*, January 8, 1994.

Jane Rinzler — "Teens and Sex: What Every Parent Must Know," *McCall's*, July 1993.

Joseph P. Shapiro — "Teenage Sex: Just Say 'Wait,'" *U.S. News & World Report*, July 26, 1993.

Sharon Sheehan — "Why Sex Ed Is Failing Our Kids," *Christianity Today*, October 5, 1992.

SIECUS Report — "The Truth About Latex Condoms," October/November 1993.

Is Sexual Behavior Changing in America?

Sexual Values

Chapter Preface

In the 1960s, the sexual attitudes and behavior of millions of Americans were radically transformed by the Sexual Revolution. An entire generation that came of age in that decade had far fewer inhibitions about having sex or living together as unmarried couples than had its predecessors. But when the danger of AIDS surfaced in the 1980s, sex became to many a potential life-or-death issue.

As much as the Sexual Revolution fostered more liberal attitudes toward sex, the deadliness of AIDS has forced Americans to reevaluate their sexual behavior and mores. Since the outbreak of AIDS, many people have altered their behavior by avoiding promiscuous sex, postponing sex with a new partner, or relying on condoms. Such changes derive from both common sense and increased public awareness of AIDS and other sexually transmitted diseases (STDs). Indeed, slogans sounding the warning of AIDS and STDs are common even to youngsters: "The safest sex is no sex" and "If you have sex, use a condom."

In the minds of many Americans, AIDS awareness and safe-sex messages have ushered in a new era of monogamy and safer sex. However, such messages too often go unheeded. Many men, women, and teens—those who have one constant partner or few partners and feel they are not at risk of STDs—adopt the attitude of "It can't happen to me." Knowledge about AIDS and STDs has increased. However, the percentage of heterosexually transmitted AIDS has also increased, from 1 percent in 1983 to 9 percent in 1993, while the incidence of syphilis reached a forty-year high in 1990, according to the U.S. Centers for Disease Control.

Have AIDS and STDs then reversed the Sexual Revolution? Not necessarily, insists Michael Gross, who writes in *New York* magazine, "Even with AIDS, sex isn't dead in the nineties. In fact, there's a new revolution. It's sex as backlash—against social despair, the gloom of disease. Safety's an issue but it hasn't cooled hormones." Leslie Wolfe, director of the Center for Women Policy Studies, is more pessimistic: "Unfortunately, there really isn't such a thing as safe sex any longer."

The viewpoints in this chapter analyze how or whether sexual attitudes and behavior are changing in response to the threat of AIDS and other STDs.

"Casual sex is less acceptable . . . , [but] to declare that chastity or virginity are actually fashionable is nonsense."

Casual Sex Persists Among Young Adults

Simon Sebag Montefiore

Members of the media have created "a completely mythical, modern world of sexless twentysomethings," writes Simon Sebag Montefiore in the following viewpoint. Montefiore reports that even amidst the AIDS epidemic, many adults in this age-group are engaging in casual sex—one-night stands or brief affairs—often without condoms. He contends that members of this generation are lying to each other about their sexual exploits and their failure to use condoms, thus perpetuating their false image as a group that has rejected casual, risky sex. Montefiore is a special correspondent for the bimonthly magazine *Psychology Today*.

As you read, consider the following questions:

1. Which groups of people are most fearful of AIDS, in Montefiore's opinion?
2. What criteria do people use to decide whether to use a condom, according to Montefiore?
3. In the author's opinion, why do men and women lie about the number of their past sex partners?

From Simon Sebag Montefiore, "Love, Lies, and Fear in the Plague Years," *Psychology Today*, September/October 1992. Reprinted with permission from *Psychology Today* magazine. Copyright ©1992 (Sussex Publishers, Inc.).

Sex in the '90s is like war: Our leaders keep telling us that it is extinct, yet it is constantly breaking out all around us. The illusion of peace is called the New World Order; the illusion of safe sex is called the Post-AIDS Era. In both cases, our teachers are completely out of touch with the real world.

In the world of sex, the editors and feature writers have created—out of wishful thinking perhaps, as well as out of readership surveys and the ignorance that comes from splendid isolation—a completely mythical, modern world of sexless twenty-somethings.

Why are they so out of touch? The first reason is generational: Serious subjects in the media are assigned to experienced writers, older than the kids in question. The editors of prestigious magazines are often aging "youth experts," doubtless the very thrusting loins of the '70s hip, liberal, swinging, sexual revolutionary "scene." But that was two decades ago. They publish reminiscences of promiscuity and ponderous judgments about the sexual habits of the "younger generation."

I have nothing against anyone of any age. What I do object to is that, in one of the most important debates of our time—the AIDS epidemic and sex—a generation of dinosaurian hipsters sporting Armani suits, cowboy boots, and graying pony tails keeps telling me what *my* generation is doing wrong.

Casual Sex Is Thriving

I am a 26-year-old heterosexual male. I do not presume to write about the sexual habits of teenagers or 35-year-olds. I have read many stories telling me about the sexual habits of my generation that were not representative, so I conducted a sounding—not a poll—of guys and girls in their twenties. This is what I discovered.

Is sex still happening? Yes, no doubt, couples are still having sex. Second, are more people getting involved in serious relationships because they cannot have casual sex anymore? Perhaps, but of all the people I talked to, I could not find a single example of anyone forming a relationship for that reason. Third—and this is the big question mark—are people still being promiscuous? Are they picking up people and going home with them?

A column in the *New York Times* reads: "Chastity gains ground as a social virtue whereby one prefers one's friends to be virgins." The article uses "a random, totally unscientific poll of [the author's] own generation—educated, supposedly liberal people who had some direct experience with the sexual revolution"—to declare that casual sex is not acceptable anymore. On the other hand, an article in *New York* magazine announced: "Sex in the '90s—there's more going on, straight and gay, than you think."

Frankly, you do not have to venture through the hellish nocturnal odyssey of the club scene to find casual sex. While I agree that casual sex is less acceptable than it was in the Seventies or Eighties, to declare that chastity or virginity are actually fashionable is nonsense.

Truth is the first casualty not only in war, but also in sexual behavior. Here is a true story that neatly sums up the new regime, where lust, lies, and fear are strange companions.

A circle of friends is gathered in a Boston pub. They are young, fresh out of school, but they are not brash; brashness died last year. None of them knows anyone who has died of AIDS, but they are afraid of it. They all know someone who has been fired and they are afraid of that, too: AIDS and the recession dominate the conversation.

Unwanted Sexual Encounters

While men spend a great deal of energy looking for sex, it turns out that success doesn't always make them happy. One of the most startling studies, done at Texas A&M University in College Station, revealed that more men than women polled had engaged in sex that they didn't really want: Ninety-four percent of the men said they had engaged in unwanted kissing, petting or sexual intercourse; two-thirds had engaged in unwanted intercourse. Less than half the women had been involved in unwanted intercourse, but they logged in at about the same figure as the men for kissing.

The men cited peer pressure, drinking, inexperience, or the wish to make a woman feel attractive as the reasons for the encounters. "A man often feels like he's got to perform, because the image is that he's supposed to be ready for sex anytime, with anybody," says Stephen Cook, a co-author (with Charlene Muelhenhard, Ph.D.) of the Texas A&M study. "When he's in a potentially sexual situation, and he thinks the woman may want him to do something, he can't really say, 'I'm not that kind of guy.' He's afraid she might think he's not attracted to her, or that he's gay. He goes ahead, whether he really wants to or not."

Kevin Krajick, *Mademoiselle*, January 1989.

Pamela is an ambitious, raven-haired 24-year-old advertising executive from Philadelphia, a feminist who prides herself on being attractive. She dresses in business-as-usual corporate battle suits. Her demeanor says "I don't," and her friends believe her. But that is The Era speaking.

John, a Brooklyn dentist's son, is the same age, educated at Columbia, working miserably hard in a management consultancy firm. He is one of those men who other men ignore because he is frail, blond, and a loner; but women always notice him.

John and Pam have never met before. When the Seventies hyper-disco plays loud, they dance. She runs her hand through his hair; he tries to kiss her, but she pushes him away. Later, she agrees to a drink at his apartment. They kiss again, and this time it leads to the bedroom. Acting on the spur of the moment, neither has time for condoms or mutual inquiries.

But they have known each other for only a few hours, and in "this day and age" (the favorite euphemism for the AIDS era), people do not act this way. Everyone who knows Pam would agree, especially the girls who were at Penn [University of Pennsylvania] with her: In four years, you get to know someone. She, of all people, never does that sort of thing. Never. But they are all wrong.

The Circle of Lies

More than likely they would not necessarily *want* the truth. They would want to be reassured that the new natural order has been respected. Pam would probably lie and tell them that nothing happened, and her friends would be relieved.

The next day John tells all his friends about his "conquest." They ask if he used a condom. "Oh, yes," he lies. "Think I'm crazy?" And with that the circle of lies and fear, pleasure, and propriety that is the single greatest distortion caused by the AIDS epidemic is complete. This is sex in the age of death. Of course casual sex is alive and well. Naturally this generation thinks twice or perhaps thrice before they do it, but they still do it. The biggest difference is that they say they are *not* doing it. This is more than anything a matter of phraseology: A man may say he had great sex with a girl for "a couple of weeks"; the girl may say that she had a "relationship and went out with a guy for a month." But the events described were the same. And many people are still happy to risk it.

Harold is a 27-year-old black cab driver who hails from Las Vegas. A part-time model, he once posed naked for *Playgirl*. He tells me that women, white and black, proposition him all the time.

Harold: "Sure I do it, man. Why not? Yeah, I always wear a condom, but I do all the ones I can."

Me: "Every cab driver claims that."

Harold (laughing): "You don't believe me? You don't believe that even with AIDS they still want it? Well, look at this." He pulls down the window visor and throws a wad of paper scraps into my lap.

Each has a feminine scrawl on it, with a name and phone number. "And that was only last week," he laughs.

Are we afraid of catching AIDS? Of course we are. No gathering of twentysomethings is complete without an AIDS discussion, and without members telling each other that, while they know the risks, they themselves are not in danger.

The subject is dominated by wishful thinking. The prime rule about the fear of AIDS is: the less likely a person is to catch the virus, the more he or she is paranoid about it. Married couples are often inexplicably more afraid than swinging singles. And, recently, men were jubilant to read that, providing they were not gay or intravenous drug users, according to published reports, the *woman* was far more likely to catch the disease in any case. They were safe, and condoms were unnecessary; the woman bore the risk.

At a cheap Sunday brunch in New York's Greenwich Village, Jim, 25, a lawyer at a middle-size firm, is sitting with Brad, 28, an unemployed architect.

Jim: "The basic point is that we can't catch it, unless we're really unlucky, 'cause girls don't sleep with gay guys, right? And anyway, it's almost impossible to catch it from a girl. It's in the *Playboy* article."

Brad: "Sure, the whole thing is a myth. The only straight AIDS victims are drug addicts, or people who get infected blood. It's all a matter of statistics."

But where I live, the "statistics" totter the streets: pale spectres of death, leaning on walking sticks, with faces made of aged parchment stretched thinly over brittle bones.

Condoms, Class, and Looks

To use a condom is the Death of Love; not to use one is Love of Death. But safe sex is the big question: Is everyone using them all the time? No. Is everyone saying they use them? *Yes.*

The condom is now a fact of life (as is evident in the springing up of drive-thru "Condom Hut" shops—sort of like Fotomats for the sexually active guy and gal on the go), but most women still have no idea how much men hate them, and how they will often do anything—including taking a risk—rather than use one. Many of the guys I spoke to believed the best idea was to sleep with younger girls: less experienced, less risky. The trouble is that teenage cherubs can often have the morals of alley cats.

Greg, a 24-year-old fashion executive, has come up with a different solution: "If I decide that I need to wear a condom to have sex with a girl, I usually won't sleep with her at all. What's the attraction in having sex with a woman who may be carrying a fatal disease?"

Safe sex has given rise to a new set of double standards: Many women, for example, carry condoms in their purses, although the discovery of this treasure trove is enough to terrify any man into thinking his new partner is wildly promiscuous. I myself carry two condoms in my wallet at all times, and the usual reaction from girls when I pull them out is not to commend me for my safety, but to suggest that I obviously frequent "unsafe sluts."

Second and Third Meetings

Perhaps it's true that there generally is a decrease in the *number* of sexual partners any given person will take. And it may also be true that larger numbers of women and men than in the seventies don't fall into bed on first meeting. But this says nothing about what happens on second and third meetings, often with very little more information than people used to have on the first one. More important, how people choose their partners tells us nothing at all about the *content* of sexual behavior or about the *meaning* people attribute to it. Surely this is at least as significant in assessing the life or death of the sexual revolution as the number of partners people take.

Lillian B. Rubin, *Erotic Wars*, 1990.

So how do twentysomethings make the safe-sex decision to use a condom? The unpalatable truth is that the decision is often based on class and appearance. Guys and girls often feel the need to use a condom with partners of a "lower class." Why? Because they believe—quite wrongly—that people in lower classes are more promiscuous than those of their own status. (This is ridiculous. You don't have to read Jackie Collins to know that the richer the class, the more debauched its habitués.)

Two Examples

As an example, my friend Paddy, 23, who is from New Hampshire and works as a salesman, was with me one evening in a dance club. A girl he didn't know danced very close to him, and finally they gathered their things and came up to say goodbye. Paddy's face was triumphant, because he was taking her home, and apologetic, because he was abandoning your miserable reporter alone at the bar.

Me: "You'd better use a condom."

Paddy (leaning over and whispering in my ear): "No way. She was at [the University of California at] Berkeley. She knows Lisa."

The second unfortunate criterion for condoms is looks. Men will generally decide whether they will wear a condom simply by *looking* at the girl. If she is very good-looking, he will not wear one, choosing to believe that such a gorgeous girl could not possibly have AIDS because she looks so pure and clean.

On the other hand, men often go to bed with girls they know, or at least hope, they will never see again.

Women are sometimes just as absurd on this subject as men.

Hope, 29, a married secretary at a stockbroking firm, lives in Brooklyn with her husband, kids, and mother. At the office party, she had sex in the filing room with the firm's very straight, very married legal counselor, 34. When she tells me the story with great pride, I ask the condom question.

Hope: "Come on! He's an attorney from one of the best schools and he's not gonna have AIDS. He's not the ticket."

Of course Hope has no idea what school Mr. Legal Counsel went to.

A New Language

A whole new language of the AIDS culture has grown up in the last few years: an argot of personal mythology, reassurance, and lies. My generation does not mind discussing AIDS in the abstract (Magic Johnson, Rock Hudson, etc.), but can barely bring themselves to utter the word AIDS in referring to their own personal risks.

For example, no one says "I must be careful because, if I'm not, I might catch AIDS." Instead, it has become universal to say, "In this Day and Age, I must be careful."

Also, among twentysomethings, there are two sovereign phrases of the AIDS regime: "I've never done this before," (which implies "While we are indeed indulging in a so-called high-risk act and not using a condom even though we have only just met, be assured, I am quite safe. Believe me. Oh, believe me."); and "I haven't had sex in six months," which is believable only the first time one hears it. By the fifth, it is clear that either everyone stopped having sex on a specific day exactly six months ago or, mystically, Six Celibate Months (like Twelve Good Men or Seven Deadly Sins) are the symbol of a sexually safe girl in a time of plague.

Even men, who traditionally flourish on the implication that they have had sex with far more partners than they really have, are now halving the numbers which they claim on their score-cards. . . .

Girls know that men will never tell them their real number of bed partners for two reasons: one is that they have likely lost count; the other is that, in the age of AIDS, the number may sound alarmingly large. (Oddly, women seem to get asked this question more than men. Yet if indeed it is easier for a female to contract AIDS, they should get asking fast.) As it is, men are more likely to apologetically ask: "By the way, just how many men have you slept with?"

Women have always reduced the number, but never as much as they do now when both death and social morality dictate it.

Katherine, a 29-year-old journalist from San Francisco, reports: "Every girl *knows* the number, but we can't tell the truth. Even if we're not exactly sleazes, by the time we're my age, we've probably slept with, say, fifteen guys. No, probably more, but we can't admit to more than seven. So the female rule is, think of the real number and then halve it! But make darned sure it's below ten!". . .

Sex: The Gamble

So whoever keeps telling us that the twentysomethings have given up sex are wrong We're still having sex, but we're afraid of it, too. We are talking about it differently—confessing our pasts but lying about our presents. No more one-night stands, we say. Condoms are the only way to go, we say. Less casual sex, sure, but we have by no means stopped. Instead, the underground of sexual adventure has become a dangerous sex casino where love, lies, and fear are a perpetual threesome in the bedrooms of America.

"Many heterosexuals are placing themselves at risk for HIV and other STDs."

Many Heterosexuals Risk Contracting Sexually Transmitted Diseases

M. Margaret Dolcini et al.

M. Margaret Dolcini is an assistant research psychologist at the University of California at San Francisco Center for AIDS Prevention Studies. In 1990-91, Dolcini and several colleagues at the center conducted the National AIDS Behavioral Surveys (NABS), the largest survey of HIV risk factors among Americans. The authors discovered that a substantial number (almost half) of heterosexuals with multiple sex partners reported never using condoms—placing themselves and their partners at risk for HIV and other sexually transmitted diseases (STDs). The authors point out that while such individuals are not necessarily at high risk for HIV, the percentage of heterosexual AIDS cases is increasing and they may be at high risk of infection from other STDs.

As you read, consider the following questions:

1. Which survey respondents were more likely to report having multiple sex partners, according to the authors?
2. In the authors' opinion, how should STD prevention messages be tailored?
3. What are sexual networks and why are they important, according to the authors?

Reproduced with the permission of The Alan Guttmacher Institute from M. Margaret Dolcini, Joseph A. Catania, Thomas J. Coates, Ron Stall, Esther S. Hudes, John H. Gagnon, and Lance M. Pollack, "Demographic Characteristics of Heterosexuals with Multiple Partners: The National AIDS Behavioral Surveys," *Family Planning Perspectives*, vol. 25, no. 5 (1993).

The percentage of newly diagnosed cases of AIDS attributed to heterosexual contact increased from 1% in 1983 to more than 4% in 1988 and to approximately 6% in 1992. Other sexually transmitted diseases (STDs) also continue to be significant health problems. The incidence of primary and secondary syphilis has been increasing annually since 1986, reaching a 40-year high in 1990, and chlamydial infections are widespread. Moreover, although gonorrhea incidence rates have decreased during the last five years, rates of antibiotic-resistant gonorrhea increased from seven per 100,000 in 1986 to 23 per 100,000 in 1990.

Individuals who have more than one partner are at greater risk of contracting the human immunodeficiency virus (HIV) and other STDs than are those who have a single sexual partner, because the probability of encountering an infected partner increases with the number of partners. Even if individuals with multiple partners always use condoms during vaginal intercourse, condoms may break, slip off or be used incorrectly.

HIV Risk Factors

To curtail the spread of HIV and other STDs, we must identify groups of the population that engage in multiple sexual relationships and trace those relationships across social strata. However, there is a paucity of data on the sexual behaviors that place adult heterosexuals at risk of infection. . . .

We conducted the National AIDS Behavioral Surveys (NABS) to estimate the prevalence of HIV risk factors within the general heterosexual population across social strata defined by age, gender, race or ethnicity, social class and marital status, and to examine the psychosocial correlates of HIV risk behaviors and preventive actions. The NABS, currently the largest general population survey of HIV-relevant sexual behavior in the United States, surveyed approximately 14,000 U.S. adults aged 18-75 during a six-month period in 1990-1991.

Our initial examination of the NABS data indicated that a significant proportion of heterosexuals had had multiple partners during the limited period covered by the survey. . . .

Multiple Partners

Overall, 9% of heterosexuals in the national sample and 12% of those in the high-risk cities sample reported having had multiple partners during the previous 12 months. . . . Respondents who were male, younger or unmarried were far more likely to report having multiple partners than were respondents who were female, older or married.

Although we focused our analyses on the past year, we were also interested in a longer view. To estimate the proportion of respondents who were monogamous for longer periods of time, we examined the prevalence of multiple sexual relationships during the previous five years among those younger than 50 who had been monogamous in the year before the survey. Nationally, 24% had had more than one partner in the previous five years; in the high-risk cities, that figure was 31%. Thus, the proportion of young and middle-aged respondents who can be categorized as "monogamous" decreases substantially when the time period under consideration is lengthened. . . .

One in Five Infected

More than one in five of all Americans, or 56 million people, are infected with a viral sexually transmitted disease like herpes or hepatitis B, according to a study made public today. Such viral infections can be controlled but not cured, and often recur.

Moreover, the study by the Alan Guttmacher Institute estimated that even more Americans were likely to contract a sexually transmitted disease sometime in their life, and that these diseases would have the greatest effect on women and people under the age of 25.

In reaching these conclusions, the report noted that 12 million new sexually transmitted infections occur each year, two-thirds of them to people under 25, and one-quarter to teen-agers. The most common are bacterial infections like gonorrhea or the lesser-known chlamydia.

Felicity Barringer, *The New York Times*, April 1, 1993.

Consistent condom use (100%) was low among men and women with multiple partners (17% in the high-risk cities sample and 11% in the national sample). We performed separate analyses of condom use with primary and secondary sexual partners among respondents who had had multiple partners in the year before the survey. We used only the high-risk cities sample for these analyses because it was larger than the national sample and therefore provided more stable estimates. The proportion of respondents who consistently used condoms with secondary partners was higher than the proportion who did so with their primary partner (29% vs. 19%). However, substantial proportions of individuals with two or more partners reported never using condoms—51% never used them with their primary partner and 40% never did so with secondary partners.

The proportion of men who always used condoms showed no consistent pattern as the number of partners increased. The proportion of men who always used condoms with their primary partner changed little, regardless of the number of partners, and the proportion who always used condoms with secondary partners decreased among those who had more than three partners.

The proportion of women who always used condoms was higher than the proportion of men who did so. Although 26% of those with two partners said they always used condoms with their primary partner, almost 42% said they always used condoms with their secondary partner. Patterns of use among women with more than two partners were inconsistent, probably because of small sample sizes.

Risking Diseases

Nine percent of heterosexual respondents nationally and 12% of those in cities with a high prevalence of AIDS cases reported having had two or more sexual partners in the past year. Substantially fewer respondents reported a pattern of strict monogamy over a five-year period. These data, together with evidence of low condom use among those with multiple partners, indicate that many heterosexuals are placing themselves at risk for HIV and other STDs. Given the long incubation period of HIV, men and women should consider long-term, as well as current, sexual behavior patterns in making decisions about the need for protective action. . . .

Gender differences in multiple relationships are influenced by culture and marital status, creating a situation in which men and women are at risk for different reasons. Men are more likely to be at risk of contracting HIV and other STDs because of their multiple sexual contacts, while many women are at risk because of their partner's behavior. Consequently, prevention messages directed at women may need to be tailored in slightly different ways than are messages intended for men. Some monogamous women may not understand that they are at risk because of their partner's sexual behavior with others. Prevention programs need to focus on the health risks of the couple, rather than exclusively on the risk behavior of individuals.

As many other investigators have noted, prevention messages need to be tailored to specific cultural subgroups. We might add that messages also need to be tailored to particular sexual subgroups. For instance, because extramarital sex may often be unplanned, the usefulness of messages urging condom use may be limited. Single men and women who are dating and people who might have extramarital sex present different challenges for prevention.

Sexual Networks and STDs

Surveys like the one described in this viewpoint provide important data on the demographic correlates of risk behavior, but we need to know more about people's sexual networks to understand how HIV and STDs spread or to predict more precisely where they will spread next. It is important to know whether people within particular social strata tend to select sexual partners within those strata or whether they mix freely with people in other social strata. We expect multiple sexual networks to exist within social strata in a given geographical area. We need data on the social diversity, size and geographic distribution of sexual networks. These are important elements in understanding how HIV and STDs spread. At present, we know that the densest networks of multiple partners are found among the young and the unmarried. However, we need information on the sexual networks of people over their entire life span to provide direction for prevention efforts.

Research is also needed on developmental influences on risk behavior. Although our study focused on sexual relationships in the year before the survey, the population of individuals who currently have multiple partners changes over time. According to our findings and those of others, people are most likely to have multiple partners when they are aged 15-30. However, we must be aware that people of all ages move in and out of situations that put them at risk of HIV and other STDs. As our findings suggest, the number of partners fluctuates with changes in marital status, which can occur at any point in the adult life span.

Defining people with multiple partners as being at risk for HIV should not be understood to mean that they are necessarily at *high* risk for HIV, although they may be at high risk of infection with other STDs that are much more prevalent in the general population. The evidence to date suggests that rates of HIV infection, although increasing somewhat over time, remain relatively low in the general heterosexual population. Still, given the rapid spread of HIV among heterosexuals in many other countries, it would be unwise to dismiss the level of risk in the general heterosexual population as inconsequential. We have identified segments of the population in which multiple sexual relationships are common and for which prevention programs are essential.

235

"Every year, more teenagers are having more sex . . . with increasing frequency, and they are starting at younger ages."

Teen Sexual Activity Is Increasing

Douglas J. Besharov

Teenagers are having sex at earlier ages and with more partners than ever before, Douglas J. Besharov reports in the following viewpoint. Besharov maintains that these facts and teens' failure to use contraceptives are responsible for the consequences of unprotected sex: abortion, out-of-wedlock births, welfare dependency, and sexually transmitted diseases (STDs). Public policy, Besharov contends, should simultaneously focus on lowering the rate of teen sexual activity and raising their level of contraceptive use. Besharov is a resident scholar at the American Enterprise Institute, a Washington, D.C., conservative research and education organization.

As you read, consider the following questions:

1. Why does Besharov disagree that availability of contraceptives would reduce teen pregnancies and STDs?
2. How do methods of contraception change among teens, according to Besharov?
3. What evidence does the author provide that condom usage is low?

Abridged from Douglas J. Besharov, "Teen Sex," *The American Enterprise*, January/February 1993. Copyright ©1993 by *The American Enterprise*. Distributed by The New York Times/Special Features. Reprinted with permission.

Ten million teenagers will engage in about 126 million acts of sexual intercourse this year. As a result, there will be about one million pregnancies, resulting in 406,000 abortions, 134,000 miscarriages, and 490,000 live births. Of the births, about 313,000, or 64 percent, will be out of wedlock. And about three million teenagers will suffer from a sexually transmitted disease such as chlamydia, syphilis, gonorrhea, pelvic inflammatory disease, and even AIDS. This epidemic of teen pregnancy and infection has set off firestorms of debate in school systems from Boston to San Francisco. In May 1992, Washington, D.C. Mayor Sharon Pratt Kelly announced that health officials would distribute condoms to high school and junior high school students. Parents immediately protested, taking to the streets with placards and angry shouts. And the New York City Board of Education was virtually paralyzed for weeks by the controversy surrounding its plans for condom distribution. Both sides have rallied around the issue of condom distribution as if it were a referendum on teen sexuality. Proponents argue that teenagers will have sex whether contraceptives are available or not, so public policy should aim to reduce the risk of pregnancy and the spread of sexually transmitted diseases by making condoms easily available. Opponents claim that such policies implicitly endorse teen sex and will only worsen the problem. The causes of teen pregnancy and sexually transmitted diseases, however, run much deeper than the public rhetoric that either side suggests. Achieving real change in the sexual behavior of teenagers will require action on a broader front.

Thirty Years into the Sexual Revolution

Some things are not debatable: every year, more teenagers are having more sex, they are having it with increasing frequency, and they are starting at younger ages.

There are four principal sources of information about the sexual practices of teenagers: the National Survey of Family Growth (NSFG), a national in-person survey of women ages 15-44 conducted in 1982 and again in 1988; the National Survey of Adolescent Males (NSAM), a longitudinal survey of males ages 15-19 conducted in 1988 and 1991; the National Survey of Young Men (NSYM), a 1979 survey of 17- to 19-year-olds; and the Youth Risk Behavior Survey (YRBS), a 1990 questionnaire-based survey of 11,631 males and females in grades 9-12 conducted by the Centers for Disease Control (CDC). In addition, the Abortion Provider Survey, performed by the Alan Guttmacher Institute (AGI), collects information about abortions and those who provide them.

With minor variations caused by differences in methodology, each survey documents a sharp increase in the sexual activity of American teenagers. All these surveys, however, are based on the self-reports of young people and must be interpreted with care. For example, one should always take young males' reports about their sexual exploits with a grain of salt. In addition, the social acceptability of being a virgin may have decreased so much that this, more than any change in behavior, has led to the higher reported rates of sexual experience. The following statistics should therefore be viewed as indicative of trends rather than as precise and accurate measures of current behavior.

Sexual Experience & Birth Rates of Unwed Adolescents 15 to 19 — United States, 1970-1988

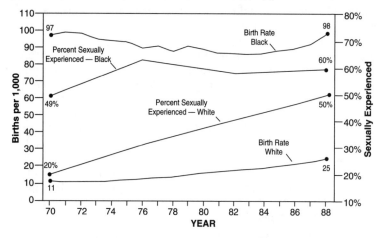

Source: National Center for Health Statistics, *Vital Statistics of the United States*, annual; *Advance Data from Vital and Health Statistics*, No. 107 and unpublished data; and Zelnik M. & J. Kantner, "Sexual and Contraceptive Experience of Young Unmarried Women in the United States, 1976 and 1971," *Family Planning Perspectives*, Vol. 9, No. 2, 1977.

The 1982 NSFG asked women ages 15-44 to recall their first premarital sexual experience. Teenagers in the early 1970s (that is, those born between 1953 and 1955) were twice as likely to have had sex as were teenagers in the early 1960s (that is, those born 1944 to 1946).

The trend of increased sexual activity that started in the 1960s continued well into the late 1980s. According to the 1988 NSFG, rates of sexual experience increased about 45 percent between 1970 and 1980 and increased another 20 percent in just three years, from 1985-1988, but rates have now apparently plateaued. Today, over half of all unmarried teenage girls report that they have engaged in sexual intercourse at least once.

These aggregate statistics for all teenagers obscure the second remarkable aspect of this 30-year trend: sexual activity is starting at ever-younger ages. The 1988 NSFG found that the percentage of 18-year-olds who reported being sexually active increased about 75 percent between 1970 and 1988, from about 40 percent to about 70 percent. Even more startling is that the percentage of sexually experienced 15-year-old females multiplied more than fivefold in the same period, from less than 5 percent to almost 27 percent.

Moreover, the increase in sexual activity among young teens continued beyond 1988. In 1990, 32 percent of ninth-grade females (girls ages 14 and 15) reported ever having had sex, as did 49 percent of the males in the same grade. At the same time, the proportion of twelfth-grade females (ages 17 and 18) who reported ever engaging in sex remained at 1988 levels.

Teenagers are not only having sex earlier, they are also having sex with more partners. According to the NSAM, the average number of partners reported by males in the 12 months preceding the survey increased from 2.0 in 1988 to 2.6 in 1991. Almost 7 percent of ninth-grade females told the YRBS that they had had intercourse with four or more different partners, while 19 percent of males the same age reported having done so. By the twelfth grade, 17 percent of girls and 38 percent of boys reported having four or more sexual partners.

A major component of these increases has been the rise in sexual activity among middle-class teenagers. Between 1982 and 1988, the proportion of sexually active females in families with incomes equal to or greater than 200 percent of the poverty line increased from 39 percent to 50 percent. At the same time, the proportion of females from poorer families who had ever had sex remained stable at 56 percent.

Comparing Blacks and Whites

Until recently, black teenagers had substantially higher rates of sexual activity than whites. Now, the differences between older teens of both races have narrowed. But once more, these aggregate figures obscure underlying age differentials. According to the 1988 NSAM, while 26 percent of white 15-year-old males reported engaging in sex compared to 67 percent of blacks, by age 18 the gap narrowed to 71 percent of whites and 83 percent of blacks. A similar trend appears among females. Twenty-four percent of white 15-year-old females have engaged in sex, compared to 33 percent of their black counterparts, reports the 1988 NSFG. By age 16, the proportions increase to 39 percent and 54 percent, respectively. Even by age 17, fewer white females have started having sex (56 percent) than have blacks (67 percent). On the other hand, white teen males reported having had almost twice as many acts of intercourse in the 12 months preceding the 1988 NSAM than did black teen males (27 versus 15). The white males, however, had fewer partners in the same period (2 versus 2.5). . . .

Use, Not Availability

Many people believe that there would be less teen pregnancy and sexually transmitted diseases if contraceptives were simply more available to teenagers, hence the call for sex education at younger ages, condoms in the schools, and expanded family planning programs in general. But an objective look at the data reveals that availability is not the prime factor determining contraceptive use.

Almost all young people have access to at least one form of contraception. In a national survey conducted in 1979 by Melvin Zelnik and Young Kim of the Johns Hopkins School of Hygiene and Public Health, over three-quarters of 15- to 19-year-olds reported having had a sex education course, and 75 percent of those who did remembered being told how to obtain contraception.

Condoms are freely distributed by family planning clinics and other public health services. They are often sitting in a basket in the waiting room. Edwin Delattre, acting dean of Boston University's School of Education and an opponent of condom distribution in public schools, found that free condoms were available at eight different locations within a 14-block radius of one urban high school.

And, of course, any boy or girl can walk into a drug store and purchase a condom, sponge, or spermicide. Price is not an inhibiting factor: condoms cost as little as 50¢. Although it might be a little embarrassing to purchase a condom—mumbling one's request to a pharmacist who invariably asks you to speak up used to be a rite of passage to adulthood—young people do not suffer the same stigma, scrutiny, or self-consciousness teenagers did 30 years ago.

Teenagers can also obtain contraceptives such as pills and diaphragms from family planning clinics free of charge or on a sliding fee scale. In 1992, over 4,000 federally funded clinics served 4.2 million women, some as young as 13. According to AGI, 60 percent of sexually active female teens use clinics to obtain contraceptive services, while only 20 percent of women over 30 do. In all states except Utah, teenagers can use clinic services without parental consent. To receive free services under the Medicaid program, however, a teenager must present the family's Medicaid card to prove eligibility.

In 1990, total public expenditures for family planning clinics amounted to $504 million. Adjusted for inflation, however, combined federal and state funding for clinics has declined by about one-third since 1980. But the impact of these cuts is unclear. On the one hand, the U.S. Department of Health and Human Services reports that the number of women using publicly funded clinics actually rose between 1980 and 1990, from 4.0 million to 4.2 million. When William Mosher of the National Center for Health Statistics analyzed the NSFG data, however, he found a slight decline between 1982 and 1988 in the proportion of respondents who had visited a clinic in the 12 months preceding the survey (37 percent versus 35 percent).

Whatever the effect of these cuts, the evidence suggests that as with condoms, teens know how to find a clinic when they want to. When they are younger, they do not feel the need to go to a clinic since condoms tend to be their initial form of contraception.

Susan Davis of Planned Parenthood explains, "The most common reason teenagers come is because they think they are pregnant. They get worried. Or they get vaginal infections. I had a whole slew of girls coming for their first pelvic exam and they all had chlamydia." The median time between a female teenager's first sexual experience and her first visit to a clinic is one year, according to a 1981 survey of 1,200 teenagers using 31 clinics in eight cities conducted by Laurie Zabin of the School of Hygiene and Public Health at the Johns Hopkins University in Baltimore.

The Conception Index

Two pieces of evidence further dispel the notion that lack of availability of contraception is the prime problem. First, reported contraceptive use has increased even more than rates of sexual activity. By 1988, the majority of sexually experienced female teens who were at risk to have an unintended pregnancy were using contraception: 79 percent. (This represents an increase from 71 percent in 1982.) When asked what method they use, 46 percent reported using the pill, 26 percent reported using condoms, and 2 percent reported using foam. In addition, the proportion of teen females who reported using a method of contraception at first intercourse increased from 48 percent in 1982 to 65 percent in 1988.

The second piece of evidence is that as they grow older, teenagers shift the forms of contraception they use. Younger teens tend to rely on condoms, whereas older teens use female-oriented methods, such as a sponge, spermicide, diaphragm, or the pill, reflecting the greater likelihood that an older female will be sexually active.

A major reason for this increase in contraceptive use is the growing number of middle-class youths who are sexually active. But it's more than this. Levels of unprotected first sex have decreased among all socioeconomic groups. Among teens from wealthier families, the proportion who reported using no method at first sex decreased between 1982 and 1988 from 43 percent to 27 percent. During the same period, non-use among teens from poorer families also declined, from 60 percent to 42 percent.

Unprotected first sex also decreased among racial groups. Between 1982 and 1988, the proportion of white females who reported using a method of contraception at first intercourse increased from 55 percent to 69 percent. Among blacks, the increase was from 36 percent to 54 percent.

How Teens View Sex

In every generation teens have had sex, and the latest studies show that these days teens are more sexually active than ever. Today in the United States, half of unmarried girls and 60 percent of unmarried boys, ages 15 to 19, have had sexual intercourse.

The reason for this upsurge in activity? While a sexually charged pop culture and peer pressure continue to influence teens, experts say today's teenagers view sex before marriage, and for that matter, promiscuity, as more socially acceptable now.

Jane Rinzler, *McCall's*, July 1993.

It's not just that teens are telling interviewers what they want to hear about contraception. Despite large increases in sexual activity, there has not been a corresponding increase in the number of conceptions. Between 1975 and 1988, when about 1.3 million more teen females reported engaging in sex (a 39 percent increase), the absolute number of pregnancies increased by less than 21 percent.

In fact, one could create a crude "teen conception index" to measure the changing rate of conception (composed of abortions, miscarriages, and births) among sexually active but unmarried teenagers. If we did so, the 1988 index would stand at .87, representing a decline of 13 percent from 1975 (down from 210 to 182 per 1,000 sexually active, unmarried teens). Most of this decline occurred between 1985 and 1988 as more middle-class teenagers had sex.

Effective Contraception

Although the conception index among teens is declining, the enormous increase in sexual activity has created a much larger base against which the rate is multiplied. Thus, there have been sharp increases in the rates of abortion, out-of-wedlock births, welfare dependency, and sexually transmitted diseases as measured within the whole teen population.

Teenage sexuality does not have to translate into pregnancy, abortion, out-of-wedlock births, or sexually transmitted diseases. Western Europe, with roughly equivalent rates of teen sexuality, has dramatically lower rates of unwanted pregnancy. According to a 1987 AGI study, the pregnancy rate among American teens (96 per 1,000 women) was twice as high as that in Canada (44), England and Wales (45), and France (43). It was almost three times higher than Sweden's (35) and more than six times higher than in the Netherlands (14). The answer, of course, is effective contraception.

The magnitude of the problem is illustrated by data about reported condom use. Between 1979 and 1988, the reported use of a condom at last intercourse for males ages 17-19 almost tripled, from 21 percent to 58 percent. A decade of heightened concern about AIDS and other sexually transmitted diseases probably explains this tripling. According to Freya Sonenstein and her colleagues at the Urban Institute, over 90 percent of males in their sample knew how AIDS could be transmitted. Eighty-two percent disagreed "a lot" with the statement, "Even though AIDS is a fatal disease, it is so uncommon that it's not a big worry."

As impressive as this progress was, 40 percent did not use a condom at last intercourse. In fact, the 1991 NSAM found that there has been no increase in condom use since 1988—even as the threat of AIDS has escalated.

The roots of too-early and too-often unprotected teen sex reach deeply into our society. Robin Williams reportedly asked a girlfriend, "You don't have anything I can take home to my wife, do you?" She said no, so he didn't use a condom. Now both Williams and the girlfriend have herpes, and she's suing him for infecting her. (She claims that he contracted herpes in high school.) When fabulously successful personalities behave this way, should we be surprised to hear about an inner-city youth who refuses his social worker's entreaties to wear a condom when having sex with his AIDS-infected girlfriend?

The Challenge to Change Behavior

This is the challenge before us: How to change the behavior of these young men as well as the one in five sexually active female teens who report using no method of contraception. First, all the programs in the world cannot deal with one vital aspect of the problem: many teenagers are simply not ready for sexual relationships. They do not have the requisite emotional and cognitive maturity. Adolescents who cannot remember to hang up their bath towels may be just as unlikely to remember to use contraceptives. Current policies and programs do not sufficiently recognize this fundamental truth.

At the same time, the clock cannot be turned all the way back to the innocent 1950s. Sexual mores have probably been permanently changed, especially for older teens—those who are out of high school, living on their own or off at college. For them, and ultimately all of us, the question is: How to limit the harm being done?

The challenge for public policy is to pursue two simultaneous goals: to lower the rate of sexual activity, especially among young teens, and to raise the level of contraceptive use. Other than abstinence, the best way to prevent pregnancy is to use a contraceptive, and the best way to prevent sexually transmitted diseases is to use a barrier form of contraception. Meeting this challenge will take moral clarity, social honesty, and political courage—three commodities in short supply these days.

"Each group of young men is behaving more dangerously than the one before."

Gay Teens Are Rejecting the Use of Condoms

Robert A. Jones

In the following viewpoint, Robert A. Jones highlights the toll that unprotected sex is having among gay teens: higher rates of HIV infection. Jones interviewed several gay teens who, in their own words, described why they never used condoms during sex. Most were fortunate enough to avoid becoming infected, but some were not so lucky and have tested HIV positive. Jones and the teens contend that their young age, their feelings of immortality, and their ignorance about condoms and HIV transmission are influences that can cause gay teens to reject using condoms. Jones is a *Los Angeles Times* newspaper columnist.

As you read, consider the following questions:

1. How has Gabe's home life differed from Jeff's and Alex's, according to Jones?
2. According to Jeff and Alex, what attitudes did older gay men have toward unprotected sex?
3. What influence did condoms have on Alex's sexual behavior?

Abridged from Robert A. Jones, "Dangerous Liaisons," *Los Angeles Times Magazine*, July 25, 1993. Copyright, 1993, Los Angeles Times. Reprinted with permission.

Gabe, at 18, represents a kind of mystery. Not that Gabe, if you met him, would seem particularly mysterious. He lives at home with his parents, makes medium grades in high school, earns gas money bagging groceries at Safeway. On the surface, Gabe appears almost too ordinary to contain any sort of mystery.

But the questions arise when Gabe describes his recent past. For two years, Gabe has slipped into his car on weekend nights, and some school nights, to escape his parents' suburban world. Still nothing unusual about that, except that Gabe happens to be gay. On his forays from home, he heads for bars, parks, coffee shops, anywhere he can meet older men. And have sex.

Finding Unsafe Sex

In fairness, Gabe sees himself as searching for something besides sex; love perhaps, or, as he puts it, "a relationship where people fall for each other and then stay together." But what he finds is sex. Gabe has had sex hundreds of times with dozens of men. Many dozens. And here's the mystery: During the two years in which Gabe has committed virtually every variety of sexual coupling with different men on different nights, he has never introduced the subject of safe sex with any of his older lovers. Nor, except on rare occasions, have they with him. In his search for love, Gabe can hardly remember stumbling across a condom.

Gabe knows about AIDS. He knew about it when he began his active sexual life at 16. He lives in a town on the San Francisco peninsula where AIDS is hardly kept a secret. Nor is Gabe mired in the kind of family that would create a kid bent on self-destruction. He views his life with good humor and often makes fine distinctions on points of personal behavior.

Yet he voluntarily and repeatedly engaged in unprotected sex with men whose chances of having HIV could be conservatively estimated at one in three. Gabe does not claim that his lovers forced him or even pressured him to forgo precautions. He just did it, willingly, and never thought about it afterward. In his words, "I didn't think about it." [He tested HIV positive in April 1992.]

What to make of Gabe? His behavior could be seen as an attempt at some subtle suicide, but Gabe does not believe it to be so. He enjoys life too much, he says. In truth, Gabe's behavior largely remains a puzzle.

For reasons that no one really understands, a generation of young gay men—not even men, really, but kids about to become men—seem to have turned away from the fundamentals of safe sex. They, like Gabe, appear to have abandoned caution, acting as if a decade of sexual education about AIDS had never taken place.

For several years, researchers have suspected that this rejection of safe sex was occurring. Then, a study by the San Francisco Department of Public Health in 1991 confirmed their fears. The study found that gay men between the ages of 17 and 25 consistently engaged in high-risk sex. And the younger the men, the riskier the behavior.

Among the men aged 23 to 25 in the survey, nearly 30% said they recently had unprotected anal intercourse. Among the men 17 to 19 years of age, the rate rose to roughly 43%. As for unprotected oral sex, about 82% of the older group said they had taken part, and the figure went up to a little more than 90% for the younger crowd.

A Second AIDS Wave

While the annual rate of new HIV-positive cases among homosexuals is decreasing, surveys in urban areas from Seattle to Mobile are finding signs of a relapse to pre-AIDS recklessness, marked by a resurgence of free wheeling gay night life. Even more worrisome, the evidence points to a growing generation gap in AIDS awareness: the importunate youth of the gay community apparently are practicing high-risk sex in significantly greater numbers than their elders. Studies say young gays are more likely to have had multiple partners and unprotected anal intercourse, the two leading risk factors for HIV infection, in the past 12 months. In the San Francisco area, where in 1992 the HIV-positive rolls grew by a thousand, a Department of Health survey indicates that a second wave of AIDS infections is taking shape, with the highest incidence among gay men between 17 and 25. Nationally, according to the Centers for Disease Control and Prevention, diagnosed cases of AIDS among homosexual men from 13 to 29 crept upward, in defiance of the overall trend downward.

David Gelman, *Newsweek*, January 11, 1993.

Finally, the study showed that the rejection of safe sex was taking its toll. In the 23-to-25 crowd, 10.4% turned up HIV positive. Among the 17- to 19-year-olds, the HIV rate jumped to 14.3%. In other words, the younger kids, who had less time to get infected, produced an HIV rate almost 40% higher than their older counterparts.

That study, which focused on young gay men in San Francisco, may reflect what's happening on the national front. In its final report, the National Commission on AIDS underscored the problem, stating that "while HIV transmission among older men who have sex with men is sharply reduced from the early '80s, transmission continues at high levels in younger gay men."

As of March 1993, a total of 978 AIDS cases have been reported to the U.S. Centers for Disease Control among men age 13 to 24 who have sex with men. While this may not be a number of epidemic proportions, officials are concerned that the number of cases will take off.

AIDS researchers have offered several explanations for the increase in unsafe sex. The young, they say, often see themselves as immortal and take terrible risks with their lives. And many have not developed the confidence or social skills to introduce the subject of safe sex with their partners.

While those theories offer some enlightenment, they assume that all generations of the young behave the same. But the San Francisco study has proven otherwise. It revealed that the youngest group of men are taking more risks than did the older groups when they were the same age. In other words, each group of young men is behaving more dangerously than the one before.

No answers have been offered by researchers for this acceleration. And so the mystery remains. In the following accounts, young gay men try to explain what the experts cannot. They represent a variety of backgrounds and experiences. Some have confronted the worst news about their lives; some have gotten lucky. Each tells his story in his own words.

Jeff

Jeff is 19 and lives in West Hollywood. He grew up in Los Angeles and, until recently, lived with his parents. He plans to enroll in college.

My parents found out I was gay a few months ago. I had just turned 19 and was living with my mother in Bel-Air. I guess you could say they reacted, like, hostilely. What they did was kick me out of the house.

My mother found out on her own. One day she read through my diary while I was gone and she found some stuff in there about the experiences that I had been having. So when I came home, she didn't waste any time. She said she knew I was gay and then she looked at me and said, "I didn't raise my son to be gay. I want you out of the house." She gave me some money and then said I had to leave.

It was like, just get out of my life, you know?

Up to that point I had gotten along with my parents fine. They are divorced and I lived six months with one and then six months with the other. That was the arrangement spelled out in their (dissolution) contract. My parents are both pretty high-powered people. They have married each other three times. (He laughs.)

They both work in the industry and I had always figured it would be OK with them about being gay because they are surrounded by homosexuals all the time. They're both producers and they work with these people constantly, so I didn't think they—at least I didn't think my mother—would have a problem with it. In fact, I met some of my first lovers through my parents. They didn't know it at the time, of course. (He laughs.)

I would meet men who came to the house or when they were invited to one of their parties. I would just be there, you know, because I was their kid and I would end up talking to these guys and sometimes we would have a relationship.

Anyway, it turned out not to be OK. I was totally surprised. When my mom told me she had read my diary and knew I was gay, I said, "Well, you're friends with gay men. You work with them all the time and that doesn't seem to be a problem." She just gave me a look and said, "This is different. You're my son."

I left the house that same night. She had given me a thousand dollars and pretty much said she never wanted to see me again. . . .

Never an Issue

During that whole time, I almost never practiced safe sex. I knew about AIDS. I remember Rock Hudson dying when I was about 12. That's the same year I had my first sexual experience. (He laughs.) I knew AIDS was scary and I knew people were dying. I think I just never connected it to me. It didn't seem to have anything to do with my life.

I remember there was this guy I met at (one of my parents' parties) that I really liked. I got to know this guy and pretty soon we had a relationship. I'm not the type of person who has sex on the first date but after a while we were doing everything. Everything that was unsafe.

Also I figured that this guy was older and he knew what was right. He never mentioned safe sex.

And that's how it always went. All through high school, AIDS was never an issue with me. In my junior year, I remember reading about AIDS in *Newsweek* and it described how bad it was. Even then I didn't change. I don't know why, really. I knew, and then I went out and did everything.

Discovering Safe Sex

Not so long ago, I finally changed my ways. I met this guy who taught me about safe sex. Actually, he called it "safer sex." I met him through my father. As usual. (He laughs.) He's 34 and works in Washington on health-care issues. Anyway, he changed everything. He was the first person who said, "Look, you gotta be real careful about this stuff." He showed me how safe sex works, and we tried it his way.

I know I've been lucky. I'm still healthy and don't have HIV. Almost all my friends have done the same thing—exactly the same—and some won't be so lucky. I think it's possible that my generation could be wiped out. So many of them are going to die in their 20s.

And I think it's mostly because we think, "Hey, I'm young and I'm safe. I don't sleep with every person in the world so there's nothing to worry about." And we think that if we have a relationship, there's no problem. We don't realize that the relationships won't last and that people don't always care about you. It's so stupid, but that's what kids are. Stupid.

I don't know what's going to happen with my parents. It's possible my mom's starting to adjust to the situation. We are talking a little bit on the phone. So that's going better, and maybe in the fall I will start college. I want to study film history and, yeah, eventually work in the industry. In fact, I'd like to be a producer. My father's a producer, you know.

Alex

Alex grew up in Azusa with his mother and a succession of her boyfriends. In his early years at school, he was regarded as a budding athlete and a bright student. But at home, life became intolerable and he ran away at age 11. In the years that followed, he alternated between return visits to his home and life on the streets of Hollywood. Alex is now 18 and lives on his own in Los Angeles. He has AIDS.

I met the man who gave me AIDS in front of the gay and lesbian center (in Hollywood). A lot of people don't know how they got AIDS, or at least they don't know exactly who gave it to them. I do. I was standing outside the front door of the center around 7 in the morning. I had been up for two days straight.

This guy walked up and started talking to me. He was older and sort of good-looking and I knew he wanted sex. After a while, he invited me up to his apartment and I said OK because I was so tired I didn't care. I figured I would go there, give him what he wanted and then get some sleep.

And that's how it worked out, except I ended up staying there and we became lovers. Wayne had a really easygoing way about him and he seemed sincere. We got along real well. I liked Wayne. No, I loved him.

He let me live my life the way I wanted, except now I can see that he only had one purpose for me. I was like this young thing that he kept around so he could have his fun. At night he would buy me something to drink so I would get loaded. My favorites were vodka and schnapps. He would go buy it and I would get so drunk I forgot my own name. And then I'd let him do anything he wanted. I never asked him to use a condom because I was nearly passed out from the liquor.

I'm not saying I didn't like the life we had. At the time, I thought it was great. I told myself, "Hey, this means I'm really grown up. I can make my own decisions, get drunk when I want, have sex, everything." I was 15 and I really wanted to feel like I wasn't a kid anymore.

This had been going on for a few months when one day I was hanging out and talking to some of his friends. And they said, "Don't you know Wayne is HIV positive?"

Testing Positive

Of course, he had never told me that. So I went out and got tested and the results came back positive. I mean, I knew before they told me. When I came in for my results, they told me I would be seeing a social worker rather than the doctor. And then I really knew.

After that, I made Wayne go get tested. It was stupid because he already knew and I knew he knew but I wanted to make sure. And he was positive.

I'm not in touch with Wayne anymore. (I turned him in and) got him charged for sodomizing a minor, contributing to the delinquency of a minor and statutory rape. I didn't even have to go to trial. He pled guilty. He did less than a year, and he's out now.

But even before Wayne, I never practiced safe sex. I didn't know condoms existed. I mean, I knew about condoms. I just didn't know what they were for. And even if I had known, it wouldn't have made any difference. I just thought, "I'm so cute, and I'm so good in bed, nothing will happen to me."

That's the way a 15-year-old thinks. They can't deal with a reality like AIDS. Death and dying is something that seems so far away, they can't connect it to themselves.

You would think the older gay men would let them know (about protecting themselves) but they don't. When I was 13 and 14, I was having sex with doctors and lawyers and stockbrokers, all these successful kinds of people in their 30s that I would meet in West Hollywood. And not once did any of them say anything about a condom. Maybe they think it can't happen to them, either, because they're successful and drive around in BMWs. But they're gonna be next.

251

"More students seem to be coming out, and they're coming out younger."

Teens Are Experimenting More with Homosexuality

David Gelman

More teenagers are experimenting with same-gender sex and openly declaring their homosexuality or bisexuality, writes David Gelman in the following viewpoint. Gelman describes this as a trend that is growing because of greater tolerance toward gays, influences of popular culture, and teens' desire to express their identity and be accepted. Gelman is a senior writer for *Newsweek* magazine.

As you read, consider the following questions:

1. According to Gelman, how have straight students reacted to gay youths?
2. Which celebrities have promoted homosexual experimentation, according to Gelman?
3. In the author's opinion, how can being identified as gay carry a stigma?

It was Coming-Out Day at Cambridge Rindge and Latin, an autumnal rite every bit as gala as graduation day at the elite Massachusetts high school. Triangular pink stickers were plastered everywhere, on Levi's, sweat shirts, high-top sneakers— even, prankishly, on the backs of unsuspecting football stars. For 16-year-old Khadijah Britton, perhaps the one student actually coming out, the stickers signaled acceptance, in spite of her uneasiness. She felt it her responsibility to tell other students that being "straight" wasn't the only possibility. Inevitably, Britton guessed, she would have to endure "weird looks" in the hallways. But later that day she announced before 250 classmates: "I've always known I was bisexual."

Things have come a distance at Rindge and Latin since it became the first public high school to join Boston's Gay Pride parade in 1991, with a delegation of just a couple of openly gay students. Now the contingent has grown big enough to carry the huge pink and black banner of Project 10 East, the school's formally recognized gay-straight alliance. Boston may be up front, but at high schools around the country, multiculturalism has begun to embrace multisexualism. With or without official blessing, student gay organizations have cropped up in Chicago, Berkeley, Miami, Minneapolis, New York. In Massachusetts alone, more than a hundred public and private schools have such groups, including George Bush's alma mater, Andover.

The schools tend to be upscale and memberships are small. But more students seem to be coming out, and they're coming out younger. A climate of greater tolerance is making it possible for teens to explore more openly what they've historically sampled in secret. "It's been going on for years and years, and now people have the courage to face it," says Meredith Grossman, a Ft. Lauderdale, Fla., high-school junior who conducted her own confirming survey of schools in her area and wrote an article about it for the local paper. The major shift, says Kevin Jennings, an openly gay teacher at Concord (Mass.) Academy, has been in the acceptance of gays by straight students. One 1993 survey of students by a task force set up by Massachusetts Gov. William Weld found that 64 percent of all students (78 percent of female students) condemned discrimination against homosexuals. Sixty percent favored gay support groups.

Becoming Chic

Some high schoolers are coming out homosexual, some bisexual. Others are admittedly confused. "It's very hard to figure out what you are in the core of your belly," says one Boston teenager who thought she was a lesbian until she found herself enjoying a relationship with a man. Teens' eagerness to experiment has made bisexuality almost "cool" in some schools. "From

Issues of Sexual Ambiguity

Ludwig, 20, is calling to talk about some homosexual experiences he had two years ago.

Dr. Drew Pinsky, better known simply as Dr. Drew, host of KROQ-FM's "Love Line" talk show [in Los Angeles], delves into Ludwig's past.

"Is this the first time . . . you had sex with a man?"

"Yeah."

"And then prior to that, no bisexual feelings or experiences?"

"No. I mean, not like strongly or anything. Maybe, like, minor. . . . That doesn't make me gay or anything, does it?"

"Perhaps this is sort of the beginning of your homosexual feelings, or maybe this was just experimentation, or maybe you're truly bisexual, I don't know."

"I mean, I don't really strongly feel that way, though."

"You sound kind of confused more than anything."

"Yeah, maybe."

The caller's question is much like others Pinsky has been getting recently. The South Pasadena internist, who fields queries on everything from dating to AIDS prevention, reports a recent increase in calls from young men and women grappling with issues of sexual ambiguity.

Some tell of getting drunk and having sex with someone of the same gender. They wonder if they're gay, or if they might have been infected with the AIDS virus. Others say their homosexual feelings clash with their desire to be straight. And some, like Ludwig, feel attracted to men *and* women and wonder what it means.

Jeannine Stein, *Los Angeles Times*, November 4, 1993.

---

where I sit, it's definitely becoming more chic," says George Hohagen, 20, a Midwestern market researcher not long out of high school himself. "It's trendy even to ask the question out loud: 'Do you think I am?'" At meetings of Boston Area Gay and Lesbian Youth, support-group leader Troix Bettencourt, 19, a public-health intern, has seen an increase in teenagers who identify themselves as bisexual. They don't want to be penned into one type of behavior, he says. "It [saying you're bisexual] just says you're not yet defined and gives you some freedom." It's also easier. "After all, you've still got the straight part," says

18-year-old Jessica Byers, a recent Rindge and Latin graduate who came out as a lesbian.

Pushing the Limit

Not surprisingly, a backlash has developed among parents. "The schools are just going overboard with this stuff," says Brian Camenker, a member of Newton (Mass.) Citizens for Public Education, formed to keep sexual issues out of the curriculum. Camenker, who has a daughter in second grade, fears that all the attention to homosexuality is influencing children. "They have gay assemblies, with speakers extolling the virtues of gayhood," he says. "The kids are sick of it." But some kids seem determined to push it even further. At Newton (Mass.) North high school, students say that one female couple is constantly "making out" in the hallways and the cafeteria. "I think they do it just to shock everybody," says senior Darlene Dottin. According to Dr. Frances Stott, a professor of child development at Chicago's Erikson Institute, some adolescents may experiment because of a biological predisposition, some because they think it's the thing to do. But they also have a deeper agenda, she says. "Teenagers are at that point in life where so many aspects of their identity are coming together. They're figuring out issues of sexual identity, occupational identity, role identity. They're really asking the question, 'Who am I?'"

They're also taking cues from the popular culture. Psychologists say the media fascination with sexual athleticism and androgynous pop icons like Elton John, Mick Jagger and Madonna help promote experimentation among teenagers. Kids today are willing to try "just about anything," says Carrie Miller, who operates Chicago's Generation Q, an informal rap group for young gays and bisexuals. "The truth is, they're open to everything."

Not that the lid is entirely off. There's still a high cost in stigma for coming out at all. In boys' locker rooms, "faggot" remains a favorite catchall epithet for anyone whose behavior is deemed even slightly out of the ordinary. The same Massachusetts task force that reported greater support for gays also found that 60 percent of students said they'd be "upset or afraid" if people thought they were gay or bisexual. "There's still an enormous amount of pain that these kids have to go through," says Frances Kunreuther, executive director of the Hetrick-Martin Institute in Manhattan, a gay and lesbian youth organization that serves more than 1,500 young people a year. "Young people are getting stronger," she adds. "They're more willing to come to us. But the fact is, gay-bashing is up." (Some say teenagers themselves are the worst bashers.)

Nationally, schools are growing more tolerant of gay students, but they're scarcely throwing their doors wide open to welcome them. No other state has followed the lead of Massachusetts, where the governor's task force has recommended that schools formulate specific policies to protect gay and lesbian students from harassment. The panel also urged special training for teachers and counselors, stocking school libraries with books and films for students who want to learn more about gay issues, and school-based support groups for gay students and straight students alike. Governor Weld backed the panel's recommendations, but declined to push for legislation, leaving communities to decide what, if any, changes to make.

Clearly, changes are in order. The task force was established after Weld saw a little-advertised 1989 Department of Health and Human Services report that said 30 percent of youth suicides occur among gays and lesbians. Sexually nonconforming students may feel bolder about stepping into the open these days, but they're finding it's still a cold world out there.

"Many young people say they are out to prove that not all teenagers are having sex."

Many Teens Are Affirming Their Virginity

DeNeen L. Brown

Many teenagers reject expectations to have sex and are proclaiming their virginity, DeNeen L. Brown maintains in the following viewpoint. Brown contends that these teens avoid peer pressure and are uniting with each other and their parents to take vows of chastity until after high school or marriage. Such teens, Brown writes, are determined to remain virgins because of such factors as AIDS, self-respect, and their lack of maturity. Brown is a staff writer for the *Washington Post* daily newspaper.

As you read, consider the following questions:

1. How can teen abstinence be a form of rebellion, according to Brown?
2. How are churches and community groups encouraging chastity, according to Brown?
3. According to the author, are boys or girls more likely to announce their virginity?

DeNeen L. Brown, "The New Age of Innocence?" *The Washington Post National Weekly Edition*, November 29–December 5, 1993, ©1993 The Washington Post. Reprinted with permission.

The hype about teenage sex doesn't faze her, and a boy with a pickup line is likely to get his feelings hurt. Yaminah Jackson, 17, a high school senior, says she is a virgin, and she intends to stay that way until she is married.

"Not too long ago when boys asked me, I was ashamed of it," says Yaminah, a member of a Washington, D.C., group that promotes sexual abstinence. "Now I don't see what is wrong with it. I'm not scared to tell them I'm a virgin. It's better to be a virgin because boys have more respect for you, and you don't have to worry about AIDS tests and pregnancy tests or anything.

"Sometimes boys say there are no more virgins in D.C. I don't want to be classified like everybody else. Not everybody is like the girls on the videos wearing that little skimpy stuff."

Yaminah is one voice in a growing chorus of teenagers calling themselves "vocal virgins" who have taken on chastity with a new attitude. In the age of AIDS and as teenage pregnancy rates increase, some teenagers have banded together—with the help of school counselors, community groups and churches—to maintain and even proclaim their sexual status.

Pure and Proud

They say they are pure and proud of it. Although studies still show that a majority of teenagers have had sex by the time they have graduated from high school and that the number of teenagers affected by sexually transmitted diseases is increasing, many young people say they are out to prove that not all teenagers are having sex.

Some adults who work with teenagers see abstinence as a form of rebellion against what seems to be an expectation that teenagers will have sex. It's become a counterculture. "Whatever is in vogue, you rebel the other way," says a counselor in Fairfax County, Va., schools.

Some young people are wearing T-shirts that say, "I'm a virgin and I'm proud." One D.C. community group, in an effort to counter a decision by school officials to pass out condoms, is planning to start virgin clubs at some high schools.

Some churches have had wedding-like ceremonies, in which parents exchange gold rings with their children. The children vow to their parents and God that they will not have sex until they are married. Other groups have required members to sign formal pledges that they will not have sex until high school graduation.

"It's a movement across the country. Virgin clubs are forming. People are no longer ashamed to say they are virgins," says Rita Kerrick, director of the office of adolescent pregnancy prevention for the Baltimore City Health Department.

"VIRGIN," in big red letters, is plastered on billboards in

Baltimore. In black letters underneath is the message, "Teach your kids it's not a dirty word."

The billboards are an example of a renewed push among educators and government officials to preach abstinence. Some officials acknowledge that many teenagers who say they are virgins may not be or may not remain so until marriage. But they consider the efforts to teach abstinence valuable in encouraging teenagers to wait until they are old enough to make a mature decision.

Okay to Say No

Andrea Massengile, a coordinator for Best Friends, a social and educational program for adolescent girls in the District of Columbia and Maryland, says a lot of teenagers don't want to have sex but need support from others telling them it's okay to say no. "We talk about values, and we talk about respecting each other and respecting yourself and not giving in to the crowd," Massengile says. "We tell them it's okay to say no. It's okay to just be a kid."

Helena Valentine, director of Teen Life Choices, a Southeast Washington pregnancy-prevention program, says the program teaches girls and boys about the consequences of having sex too early. They play roles. They get counseling. They have rap sessions.

A Sex-Out Campaign

The great American teen-age sex-out is gathering steam.

A campaign urging teens to postpone sex until marriage, started by the Southern Baptist Sunday School Board as an adjunct to a sex education program, has spread rapidly to other denominations and is well on its way to a goal of eliciting chastity vows from half a million teen-agers.

The "True Love Waits" campaign recently received its biggest boost to date when the nation's largest denomination, the 59 million-member Roman Catholic Church, came on board.

Associated Press, *The Washington Times*, January 1, 1994.

Some girls who had been sexually active have taken on a "second virginity," Valentine says. None of the girls who have been involved in the program has become pregnant, she says, and of those who once had been pregnant, none has become pregnant again.

The boys are taught the same thing, but during a recent meeting they would not say they were virgins. When asked, they hung their heads or looked away.

"If a boy says he's a virgin, they will laugh at him, tease him and jone on him," says Jamaal Daise, 15, a 10th-grader. "It's a peer-pressure, ego thing."

But during the meeting, they discuss the best way to say no. "It ain't cool for a dude to tell a girl no," says Quentin Galloway, 18, an 11th-grader.

"Why ain't it?" asks Rashaun Daise, 14, an eighth-grade student.

"You would tell a girl no?" asks Quentin incredulously.

"Yeah," says Rashaun, "because you might not be ready, and you don't want to take the responsibility. You might catch AIDS, STDs or pregnancy."

Sexual Experience

In a 1990 study, the Centers for Disease Control and Prevention in Atlanta found that three out of four teenagers said that by the time they graduated from high school, they had engaged in sex. And 40 percent said they were not virgins by the ninth grade.

Amy Sutnick Plotch, a spokeswoman for Girls Inc., a national organization to support girls, looks at the other side of those figures.

"At age 15, 27 percent of girls have had intercourse at least once," Plotch says. "That means 73 percent haven't. Seventy percent of 18-year-olds have had sex. That means 30 percent haven't.

"We try to give girls the message: Don't feel pressured into it. It is not true everyone is doing it."

Some teenagers say the fear of AIDS is the primary reason they do not want to have sex.

"Kids go to the nurses in schools, crying a day after the first experience, and they want to be tested for the disease," says Russell Henke, coordinator of health education for Montgomery County, Md., public schools. "The fear is they have done it, and now they are horrified. For some of them, that's enough. They say, 'I don't want to have that experience anymore.'"

Sandra Hill, a community health nurse for the Montgomery County Health Department who works at a local high school, says many girls have told her that keeping their virginity puts them in a position of control. "In fact, I had one girl tell me last week, 'It's a relief to me to be a virgin. I see some of my friends buying home pregnancy tests, and they are so worried and so distracted every month. I don't have to worry about that.'"

Pledging Virginity

Small groups of girls are pledging to each other not to have sex, Hill says. "All it takes is one supportive friend to say, 'I'm not going to do that.' And others will say, 'Well, I'm not going to do that either,'" she says. "My own daughter and five friends vowed to each other to remain virgins until high school graduation, and they all did it."

Joshua Wilson, 15, a ninth-grader, made a pledge of a different sort. He vowed to God during a church banquet that he wouldn't have sex until marriage.

Joshua made the pledge as part of a nationwide campaign sponsored by the Southern Baptist Convention to sign up virgins. The campaign, called True Love Waits, is set to culminate July 29, 1994, in Washington when self-proclaimed virgins from across the country are scheduled to descend on Washington and spread 500,000 pledge cards on the Mall.

Joshua says that whenever he is "tempted," he is reminded of the oath he took. "I consider it a sacred thing. Whenever I get in a situation where I'm tempted, I'm reminded," he says. "It's enough for me to keep me from going through with something I would probably regret."

Other pledges teenagers are taking are not based on religion. Danita Poole, 17, a member of Best Friends, says she took a pledge two years ago, promising she would maintain her virginity until at least high school graduation. She and 20 other teenage girls were part of a ceremony in which they signed a pledge and received diamond charms from the organization.

Danita, a senior, says that it hasn't been hard to wait. She usually hangs out with friends who have the same goals. "We just keep our mind off of it," she says.

Natalie Millar, 17, a senior, says many of her friends are proud of her, but she still gets teased. "The experienced people say, 'That's so immature. You're such a baby.' I say, 'I think I'm more mature for waiting than going ahead and sleeping with anybody.'"

Periodical Bibliography

The following articles have been selected to supplement the diverse views presented in this chapter.

Jerry Adler
"Sex in the Snoring '90s," *Newsweek*, April 26, 1993.

William F. Allman
"The Mating Game," *U.S. News & World Report*, July 19, 1993.

Felicity Barringer
"Report Finds One in Five Infected by Viruses Spread Sexually," *The New York Times*, April 1, 1993.

Patricia Bolen
"Abstinence Plan Grows Among Youth," *Moody*, January 1994. Available from Moody Bible Institute, 820 N. LaSalle Blvd., Chicago, IL 60610.

William F. Buckley
"How to Deal with Illegitimacy," *Conservative Chronicle*, May 5, 1993. Available from PO Box 11297, Des Moines, IA 50340-1297.

Mona Charen
"Being Gay Is the Rage Among Today's Teens," *The Human Life Review*, Fall 1993.

Sarah Crichton
"Sexual Correctness: Has It Gone Too Far?" *Newsweek*, October 25, 1993.

Amy Cunningham
"Sex in High School: What's Love Got to Do with It?" *Glamour*, September 1993.

Anke A. Ehrhardt
"Trends in Sexual Behavior and the HIV Pandemic," *American Journal of Public Health*, November 1992.

David Gelman
"The Young and the Reckless," *Newsweek*, January 11, 1993.

Mary Rogers Gillmore et al.
"Substance Abuse and Other Factors Associated with Risky Sexual Behavior Among Pregnant Adolescents," *Family Planning Perspectives*, November/December 1992. Available from The Alan Guttmacher Institute, 111 Fifth Ave., New York, NY 10003.

Gabrielle Glaser
"Swearing Off Sex: What About the New Chastity?" *Mademoiselle*, March 1994.

Sarah Glazer
"Preventing Teen Pregnancy," *The CQ Researcher*, May 14, 1993. Available from 1414 22nd St. NW, Washington, DC 20037.

Jesse Green

"Out and Organized," *The New York Times*, June 13, 1993.

Debra Kent

"Your Sexual Rights: What the Law Says About Birth Control, Pregnancy, and Sex," *Seventeen*, November 1993.

Alan J. Levine

"'Errorgenous' Zones? Kinsey's Sexual Ideology," *The World & I*, February 1994.

Stephanie Mansfield

"Gays on Campus," *Redbook*, May 1993.

Ruth Mayer

"Sex Plagues of the '90s," *Mademoiselle*, January 1994.

Amy Pagnozzi

"Virgins with Attitude," *Glamour*, April 1992.

Carin Rubenstein

"Generation Sex," *Mademoiselle*, June 1993.

'Teen

"STD's: What You Must Know," November 1993.

Jim Walsh

"The New Sexual Revolution," *Utne Reader*, July/August 1993.

For Further Discussion

Chapter 1

1. In their viewpoints, George Grant and Mark A. Horne as well as John Shelby Spong use quotes and stories from the Bible to debate whether homosexuality is immoral. What obstacles, if any, are there in choosing the Bible to condemn or defend homosexuality?

2. Francis Canavan argues that the Sexual Revolution began with growing social acceptance of the separation of intercourse from procreation, primarily because of contraception. How has contraception redefined the sexual act? Do you believe that contraception has benefited or harmed society in general? How has contraception affected you or people you know? Explain your answers.

3. Judith Levine disagrees with Francis Canavan about people's removing meaning from sex. She argues that separating sex from commitment would give women the same choices as men about what sex means in a relationship. What do you believe Levine means by this?

Chapter 2

1. Richard A. Posner, who argues against a military ban on homosexuals, remarks that police departments in some major cities have admitted homosexuals as officers without incident. Does this fact strengthen the case against a ban? Explain your answer. What are the similarities and differences between military and police duty?

2. According to Richard Schneider Jr., the "Religious Right" is exploiting fear of two types of gays and lesbians: "suburban couples" and "professional queens." What is meant by these terms and what are these fears? Do you believe that openly gay individuals are a threat to America's culture? Why or why not?

3. Melissa Wells-Petry maintains that the primary concern of soldiers toward gays in the military is their privacy. Would heterosexuals' privacy be affected by allowing gays and lesbians to serve in the military? Why or why not? Do you believe heterosexuals have legitimate concerns about sexual advances by gays and lesbians? Explain your reasoning.

Chapter 3

1. Bob Navarro and Bob Peters are police officers who investigate the pornography industry. Philip D. Harvey is president of a company that markets adult videos and adult-oriented products. How do you think their occupations influence their views toward pornography? What convincing points do the authors make about government control of pornography? What effect, if any, do you believe the availability of adult videos has on society? Explain your answers.

2. According to Ray Wyre, some of the factors that motivate the most violent rapists include anger, domination, controlling, and sexual fantasies. Do you believe that restricting the availability of pornography could help inhibit such thoughts? Why or why not? If so, which ones?

3. Ray Wyre and F.M. Christensen—both experts on the effects of pornography—disagree about whether pornography can cause rape. Compare their viewpoints. Is Wyre, who has extensively treated sexual offenders, more convincing than Christensen? Why or why not? How could his profession influence his opinion? Explain.

Chapter 4

1. In their viewpoint, Anne-Elizabeth Murdy and Carol Hayse defend the distribution of *Just Say Yes* booklets to teenagers, without parental consent. Do you agree with Murdy and Hayse that providing vital information to teens outweighs parental concerns? As a teenager, would you approve of the booklet's safe-sex message? As a parent? Why or why not?

2. Kristine Napier contends that past efforts should have focused on preventing teen sexual activity rather than preventing pregnancy and disease. Do you agree with Napier that sex education should be abstinence-based? Explain.

3. Randy Engel believes that schools should not teach children sex education in any form. After reading her viewpoint, rank the following school-based educational strategies according to what you believe is best for teenagers and, separately, for younger children: (a) abstinence only; (b) abstinence together with safe sex; (c) safe sex only; (d) no sex education.

Chapter 5

1. Simon Sebag Montefiore's viewpoint features interviewees' personal accounts to support his argument about casual sexual behavior. Compare this technique with that of M. Margaret Dolcini and her colleagues, who rely on statistics to describe

sexual behaviors. What are the strengths and weaknesses of their techniques in supporting their respective arguments? Explain your answers.

2. Douglas J. Besharov contends that although teens have access to contraceptives, their failure to use them properly contributes to teen pregnancy. Why, do you believe, are many teenagers failing to use contraceptives? List and describe various approaches that could encourage them to use contraceptives more diligently.

Organizations to Contact

The editors have compiled the following list of organizations concerned with the issues debated in this book. The descriptions are derived from materials provided by the organizations. All have publications or information available for interested readers. The list was compiled on the date of publication of the present volume; names, addresses, and phone numbers may change. Be aware that many organizations take several weeks or longer to respond to inquiries, so allow as much time as possible.

American Civil Liberties Union (ACLU)
132 W. 43rd St.
New York, NY 10036
(212) 944-9800
fax: (212) 354-5290

The ACLU, a national organization with many local chapters, champions human rights as guaranteed in the Declaration of Independence and the Constitution. It opposes censorship and supports civil rights for homosexuals. ACLU publications include the monthly *Civil Liberties Alert* and the quarterly newsletter *Civil Liberties* as well as handbooks and pamphlets.

Christian Coalition (CC)
1801 Sarah Dr., Suite L
Chesapeake, VA 23320
(804) 424-2630
fax: (804) 434-9068

Founded by evangelist Pat Robertson, Christian Coalition is a grassroots political organization of conservative traditionalists working to stop the moral decay of government. The coalition promotes the election of moral legislators and the passage of moral legislation and opposes extramarital sex and comprehensive sex education. Its publications include the monthly newsletter *The Religious Right Watch* and the monthly tabloid *Christian American*.

Coalition for Positive Sexuality (CPS)
3712 N. Broadway
Box 191
Chicago, IL 60613
(312) 604-1654

The Coalition for Positive Sexuality is a grassroots direct-action group formed in the spring of 1992 by high school students and activists. It is working to counteract the institutionalized misogyny, heterosexism, homophobia, racism, and ageism that students experience every day at school. It is dedicated to offering teens sexuality and safe sex education that is pro-woman, pro-lesbian/gay/bisexual, pro-safe sex, and pro-choice. Its motto is, "Have fun and be safe." For a copy of its booklet, *Just Say Yes*, write to CPS, 3712 N. Broadway, Box 191, Chicago, IL 60613; or call 312-604-1654. *Just Say Yes* costs $3 for adults; it is always free for teenagers.

Dignity/USA
1500 Massachusetts Ave. NW, Suite 11
Washington, DC 20005
(202) 861-0017
fax: (202) 429-9808

Dignity/USA is a Roman Catholic organization of gays, lesbians, and bisexuals and their families and friends. It believes that homosexuals and bisexuals can lead sexually active lives in a manner consonant with Christ's teachings. Through its national and local chapters, Dignity/USA provides educational materials, AIDS crisis assistance, and spiritual support groups for members. It publishes the monthly *Dignity Journal* and a book, *Theological/Pastoral Resources: A Collection of Articles on Homosexuality from a Catholic Perspective*.

Eagle Forum
PO Box 618
Alton, IL 62002
(618) 462-5415

Eagle Forum, founded by conservative Phyllis Schlafly, advocates traditional family values. It stresses chastity before marriage and fidelity afterward, opposes birth control and abortion, and warns teens and others about the dangers of pornography and sexually transmitted diseases. The forum publishes the monthly *Phyllis Schlafly Report* as well as various brochures.

Family Research Council (FRC)
700 13th St. NW, Suite 500
Washington, DC 20005
(202) 393-2100
fax: (202) 393-2134

The council is a research, resource, and education organization that promotes the traditional family, which the council defines as a group of people bound by marriage, blood, or adoption. It opposes schools' tolerance of homosexuality and condom distribution programs in schools. It also believes that pornography breaks up marriages and contributes to sexual violence. The council publishes numerous reports from a conservative perspective. These publications include the monthly newsletter *Washington Watch*, the bimonthly journal *Family Policy*, and *Free to Be Family*, a 1992 report that addresses issues such as pornography, sex education, sexually transmitted diseases, and teen sex.

Focus on the Family
420 N. Cascade Ave.
Colorado Springs, CO 80903
(719) 473-4020
fax: (719) 473-9751

Focus on the Family is an organization that promotes Christian values and strong family ties and that campaigns against pornography and homosexual rights laws. It publishes the monthly magazines *Focus on the*

Family and *Focus on the Family Citizen* for parents, children, and educators as well as the video *Sex, Lies, and . . . the Truth,* which encourages abstinence and criticizes safe-sex methods.

The Hetrick-Martin Institute (HMI)
Two Astor Pl.
New York, NY 10003
(212) 674-2400
fax: (212) 674-8650

The institute is an organization that offers a broad range of social services to gay and lesbian teenagers and their families. It also sponsors advocacy and education programs for gay and lesbian adolescents. HMI publishes the quarterly newsletter *HMI Report Card* and the comic book series *Tales of the Closet* and distributes articles, fact sheets, and pamphlets on homosexuality.

IntiNet Resource Center
PO Box 4322
San Rafael, CA 94913
(415) 507-1739

IntiNet advocates the "expanded family," a number of adults who are members of a group marriage, and who often share food, housing, and child rearing. Sexual relationships between the adults can be heterosexual or homosexual. IntiNet distributes information on the expanded family, which it believes will one day be the predominant lifestyle. Its publications include the book *Love Without Limits: Responsible Nonmonogamy and the Quest for Sustainable Intimate Relationships* and the quarterly newsletter *Floodtide.*

Love in Action
PO Box 2655
San Rafael, CA 94912
(415) 454-0960
fax: (415) 454-7826

Love in Action is a ministry that believes that homosexuality is learned behavior and that all homosexual conduct is wrong because it violates God's laws. It provides support to gays and lesbians to help them convert to heterosexuality. Love in Action publishes articles on the causes of homosexuality, homosexuality and sin, sexual abuse, and other topics; testimonies from homosexuals and parents of gays; the books *A Step Further* and *Helping People Step Out of Homosexuality*; and the monthly newsletter *Lifelines.*

National Coalition Against Censorship (NCAC)
275 Seventh Ave., 20th Floor
New York, NY 10001
(212) 807-6222
fax: (212) 807-6245

NCAC is an alliance of organizations committed to defending freedom of thought, inquiry, and expression by engaging in public education and advocacy on national and local levels. It believes censorship is dangerous because it represses intellectual and artistic freedom. NCAC maintains a library of information dealing with First Amendment issues and sponsors public meetings on these issues as well as special programs on countering censorship in public schools. It publishes the quarterly newsletter *Censorship News*.

National Coalition Against Pornography (N-CAP)
800 Compton Rd., Suite 9224
Cincinnati, OH 45231
(513) 521-6227

N-CAP works with civic, legal, and religious groups who seek to eliminate obscenity and adult and child pornography. It sponsors workshops and provides written, video, and audio materials about ways to campaign against pornography, sexual violence, and child victimization. Its publications include the bimonthly newsletter *Standing Together*.

National Gay and Lesbian Task Force (NGLTF)
1734 14th St. NW
Washington, DC 20009-4309
(202) 332-6483
fax: (202) 332-0207

NGLTF is a civil rights advocacy organization that lobbies Congress and the White House on a range of civil rights and AIDS issues and that works on the state level to abolish sodomy laws. The task force also works to eradicate prejudice, discrimination, and violence against gays and lesbians. It publishes numerous papers and pamphlets, including *Anti-Gay/Lesbian Violence Fact Sheet* and *Twenty Questions About Homosexuality*.

Parents and Friends of Lesbians and Gays (P-FLAG)
PO Box 27605
Washington, DC 20038-7605
(800) 432-6459

P-FLAG is a national organization that provides support and educational services for gays, lesbians, bisexuals, and their families and friends. It works to end prejudice and discrimination against homosexual and bisexual persons. It publishes and distributes booklets and papers, including *Why Is My Child Gay?*, *About Our Children*, and *Coming Out to My Parents*.

Planned Parenthood Federation of America (PPFA)
810 Seventh Ave.
New York, NY 10019
(212) 541-7800
fax: (212) 245-1845

Planned Parenthood supports people who make their own decisions about having children without governmental interference. It promotes comprehensive sex education and provides contraceptive counseling and services through clinics across the United States. Its publications include *R.E.A.L. Life: Reality-Based Education and Learning for Life* (a resource kit promoting sex education) and *LINK Line*, a bimonthly newsletter with annotated listings of pamphlets, booklets, instructional materials, and curricula of interest to sex educators. Also available are the brochures *Guide to Birth Control: Seven Accepted Methods of Contraception*, *Teensex? It's Okay to Say No Way*, *A Man's Guide to Sexuality*, and *About Childbirth*.

Respect, Inc.
PO Box 97
Golf, IL 60029-0039
(312) 729-3298

Project Respect is an organization that developed Sex Respect, a sex education curriculum that stresses abstinence among teens. The curriculum teaches youths that abstaining from premarital sex is their right, is in society's best interest, and is in the spirit of true sexual freedom. Sex Respect comprises separate guides for students, parents, and teachers and a one-hour teacher training or parent presentation video. A separate video, *Everyone Is Not Doing It*, promotes abstinence among high school students.

Sex Information and Education Council of the U.S. (SIECUS)
130 W. 42nd St., Suite 2500
New York, NY 10036-7901
(212) 819-9770
fax: (212) 819-9776

SIECUS is an organization of educators, physicians, social workers, and others who support the individual's right to acquire knowledge of sexuality and who encourage responsible sexual behavior. The council promotes comprehensive sex education for all children that includes AIDS education, teaching about homosexuality, and instruction about contraceptives and sexually transmitted diseases. Its publications include fact sheets, annotated bibliographies by topic, the booklet *Talk About Sex*, and the bimonthly *SIECUS Report*.

U.S. Public Health Service
200 Independence Ave. SW
Washington, DC 20201
(202) 619-0257

The Public Health Service's mission is to promote the protection and advancement of the public's physical and mental health. Agencies within the service, such as the Centers for Disease Control and Prevention (CDC), the Food and Drug Administration (FDA), and the National Institutes of Health (NIH), conduct research on contraceptives and sexually transmitted diseases. Their data is available in publications such as the CDC's *Morbidity and Mortality Weekly Report* and the *FDA Consumer*.

Women Against Pornography (WAP)
PO Box 845, Times Square Station
New York, NY 10036-0845
(212) 307-5055

WAP is a feminist organization that seeks to convince Americans that pornography is not socially acceptable or sexually liberating. It believes that pornography promotes the degradation, objectification, and brutalization of women. WAP publishes the periodic *Women Against Pornography—Newsreport*.

Bibliography of Books

John Ankerberg and John Weldon	*The Myth of Safe Sex*. Chicago: Moody Press, 1993.
Robert M. Baird and Stuart E. Rosenbaum, eds.	*Pornography: Private Right or Public Menace?* Buffalo: Prometheus Books, 1991.
Bruce Bawer	*A Place at the Table: The Gay Individual in American Society*. New York: Poseidon Press, 1993.
Betty Berzon, ed.	*Positively Gay: New Approaches to Gay and Lesbian Life*. Berkeley, CA: Celestial Arts, 1992.
Warren J. Blumenfeld, ed.	*Homophobia: How We All Pay the Price*. Boston: Beacon Press, 1992.
Emilie Buchwald, Pamela R. Fletcher, and Martha Roth, eds.	*Transforming a Rape Culture*. Minneapolis: Milkweed Editions, 1993.
Margaret Cruikshank	*The Gay and Lesbian Liberation Movement*. New York: Routledge, Chapman & Hall, 1992.
Peter M. Davies et al., eds.	*Sex, Gay Men, and AIDS*. New York: Falmer Press, 1993.
Randy Engel	*Sex Education: The Final Plague*. Gaithersburg, MD: Human Life International, 1989.
Family Research Council	*Free to Be Family: Helping Mothers and Fathers Meet the Needs of the Next Generation of American Children*. Washington, DC: Family Research Council, 1992.
Feminists Against Censorship (Gillian Rodgerson and Elizabeth Wilson, eds.)	*Pornography and Feminism: The Case Against Censorship*. London: Lawrence and Wishart, 1991.
Pamela Church Gibson and Roma Gibson, eds.	*Dirty Looks: Women, Pornography, Power*. London: BFI Publishing, 1993.
Judy Grahn	*Another Mother Tongue: Gay Words, Gay Worlds*. Boston: Beacon Press, 1984.
George Grant, ed.	*Gays in the Military: The Moral and Strategic Crisis*. Franklin, TN: Legacy, 1993.
Gilbert Herdt, ed.	*Gay Culture in America: Essays from the Field*. Boston: Beacon Press, 1992.

Nan D. Hunter, Sherryl E. Michaelson, and Thomas B. Stoddard	*The Rights of Lesbians and Gay Men: The Basic ACLU Guide to a Gay Person's Rights.* 3rd ed. Carbondale: Southern Illinois University Press, 1992.
Luce Irigaray	*An Ethics of Sexual Difference.* Ithaca, NY: Cornell University Press, 1993.
Catherine Itzin, ed.	*Pornography: Women, Violence, and Civil Liberties: A Radical View.* New York: Oxford University Press, 1992.
Samuel S. Janus and Cynthia L. Janus	*The Janus Report on Sexual Behavior.* New York: John Wiley & Sons, 1993.
E. Michael Jones	*Degenerate Moderns: Modernity as Rationalized Sexual Misbehavior.* San Francisco: Ignatius Press, 1993.
Marshall Kirk and Hunter Madsen	*After the Ball: How America Will Conquer Its Fear and Hatred of Gays in the '90s.* New York: Doubleday, 1989.
Susan Shurberg Klein, ed.	*Sex Equity and Sexuality in Education.* Albany: State University of New York Press, 1992.
Philip E. Lampe	*Adultery in the United States: Close Encounters of the Sixth (or Seventh) Kind.* Buffalo: Prometheus Books, 1987.
Daniel Linz	*Pornography.* Newbury Park, CA: Sage Publications, 1993.
Tony Marco	*Gay Rights: A Public Health Disaster and Civil Wrong.* Fort Lauderdale, FL: Coral Ridge Ministries, 1992.
Eric Marcus	*Is It a Choice?: Answers to Three Hundred of the Most Frequently Asked Questions About Gays and Lesbians.* New York: HarperCollins, 1993.
Robert G. Marshall and Charles A. Donavan	*Blessed Are the Barren.* San Francisco: Ignatius Press, 1991.
Connie Marshner	*Decent Exposure: How to Teach Your Children About Sex.* Franklin, TN: Legacy, 1993.
April Martin	*The Lesbian and Gay Parenting Handbook: Creating and Raising Our Families.* New York: HarperCollins, 1993.
Harry Maurer	*Sex: An Oral History.* New York: Viking Penguin, 1994.
Chuck McIlhenney and Donna McIlhenney with Frank York	*When the Wicked Seize a City.* Lafayette, LA: Huntington House Publishers, 1993.

Les Parrott III	*Helping the Struggling Adolescent: A Guide to Thirty Common Problems for Parents, Counselors, and Youth Workers.* Grand Rapids, MI: Zondervan, 1993.
Richard A. Posner	*Sex and Reason.* Cambridge: Harvard University Press, 1992.
John Preston, ed.	*Flesh and the Word: An Anthology of Erotic Writing.* New York: Dutton, 1992.
John Preston, ed.	*A Member of the Family: Gay Men Write About Their Families.* New York: Dutton, 1992.
Richard S. Randall	*Freedom and Taboo: Pornography and the Politics of a Self Divided.* Berkeley: University of California Press, 1989.
Judith A. Reisman	*"Soft Porn" Plays Hardball: Its Tragic Effects on Women, Children, and the Family.* Lafayette, LA: Huntington House Publishers, 1991.
Ira L. Reiss and Harriet M. Reiss	*An End to Shame: Shaping Our Next Sexual Revolution.* Buffalo: Prometheus Books, 1990.
Lillian B. Rubin	*Erotic Wars: What Happened to the Sexual Revolution?* New York: Farrar, Straus & Giroux, 1990.
Diana E.H. Russell, ed.	*Making Violence Sexy: Feminist Views on Pornography.* New York: Teachers College Press, 1993.
Lynne Segal and Mary McIntosh, eds.	*Sex Exposed: Sexuality and the Pornography Debate.* New Brunswick, NJ: Rutgers University Press, 1993.
Randy Shilts	*Conduct Unbecoming: Gays and Lesbians in the U.S. Military.* New York: St. Martin's Press, 1993.
Michelangelo Signorile	*Queer in America: Sex, the Media, and the Closets of Power.* New York: Random House, 1993.
Tom Smith	*Half Straight: My Secret Bisexual Life.* Buffalo: Prometheus Books, 1990.
Susan Sprecher and Kathleen McKinney	*Sexuality.* Newbury Park, CA: Sage Publications, 1993.
Tim Stafford	*Sexual Chaos: Charting a Course Through Turbulent Times.* Downers Grove, IL: InterVarsity Press, 1993.
Arlene Stein, ed.	*Sisters, Sexperts, Queers: Beyond the Lesbian Nation.* New York: Plume, 1993.
David Steinberg, ed.	*The Erotic Impulse: Honoring the Sensual Self.* New York: Putnam, 1992.

Robert J. Stoller   *Pornography: Myths for the Twentieth Century.* New Haven: Yale University Press, 1991.

Bonnie Nelson Trudell   *Doing Sex Education: Gender Politics and Schooling.* New York: Routledge, 1993.

Mariana Valverde   *Sex, Power, and Pleasure.* Philadelphia: New Society Publishers, 1987.

Linda Williams   *Hard Core: Power, Pleasure, and the "Frenzy of the Visible."* Berkeley: University of California Press, 1989.

Robert Williams   *Just As I Am: A Practical Guide to Being Out, Proud, and Christian.* New York: HarperCollins, 1993.

James D. Woods with   *The Corporate Closet: The Professional Lives of* Jay H. Lucas   *Gay Men in America.* New York: Free Press, 1993.

Frances Younger   *Five Hundred Questions Kids Ask About Sex and Some of the Answers: Sex Education for Parents, Teachers and Young People Themselves.* Springfield, IL: Charles C. Thomas, 1992.

Index

282

National Research Council, 183
National Survey of Adolescent Males
(NSAM), 237, 239, 240, 243
National Survey of Family Growth
(NSFG), 237, 238-39, 241
National Survey of Young Men
(NSYM), 237
Navarro, Bob, 128
Netherlands
  homosexuals in, 113, 114, 124
  sex education in, 178
  teen pregnancy rates in, 243
New Jersey
  homosexual discrimination laws, 97
New York
  homosexual discrimination laws,
  107
Nietzsche, Friedrich, 170
No More Nice Girls, 39, 207
North American Man-Boy Love
  Association (NAMBLA), 71, 105-106
Nugent, C. Robert, 51
Nussbaum, Martha, 63

Oregon
  homosexual discrimination laws,
  107
  pornography laws, 143-44
Ozick, Cynthia, 65-66

parents
  reactions to gay children, 248-49
  and sex education, 178, 185, 193
    should teach at home, 187, 204,
    211
  single
    in military, 119-20
pedophilia
  and homosexuals, 71, 105-106, 150,
  151
peer pressure, 38, 180, 182, 260
pelvic inflammatory disease (PID),
  214, 237
Peninsula, 86
Perkins, Robert S., 53
Peters, Bob, 128
Planned Parenthood Federation of
  America, 177
  against teaching abstinence, 199,
    216-17
    con, 181-83
  on contraceptive education, 183-84,
    193
  poll on sexually active teens, 215-16
  sex education programs, 178-85
    are destructive, 202-205
    undermines moral values, 193-94
Plato

on homosexuality, 63
Playboy, 18, 138, 227
police
  homosexuals in, 114
  vice officers' duties, 129
pornography
  around the world, 129, 163-65
  benefits of, 141-42
  on cable system, 131
  Canadian laws on, 135
  causes sexual violence, 132-33,
    145-52
    con, 141, 153-61
  censoring harms society, 136-44
  child, 129, 140, 144, 147, 163
  Christianity provides
    foundation for, 167-73
  and civil rights, 106
  community standards criteria, 129,
    131
  consumers of, 131-32
  definitions of, 135, 139-40, 163, 168
  degrades women, 133-34, 150, 159,
    169
  destroys morality, 163-66
  distribution of, 129-30
  and fantasy, 146, 147-49, 151-52,
    156
  harms society, 26, 128-35, 163
    con, 140-42
  kinds of
    hard-core, 132-33, 139-40
    mainstream, 140
    soft-core, 132-33
    violent, 135, 140
  and masturbation, 132, 147, 149,
    151, 152, 156
  and organized crime, 130-31
  as political tool, 163
  and pop music, 134-35
  and power, 168
  profits from, 132
  and prostitution, 133, 164
  and rape, 132-33, 146-49, 155-59
  ruins families, 134
  and sexual addictions, 131-33
  in the United States, 129
  will destroy Christianity, 162-66
  women in
    exploitation of, 133-34
      con, 140, 143
    and misogyny, 150
    positive portrayals, 143
Posner, Richard A., 109
Posse of Southern California, 216
Postrel, Virginia, 103
Prager, Dennis, 107
privacy